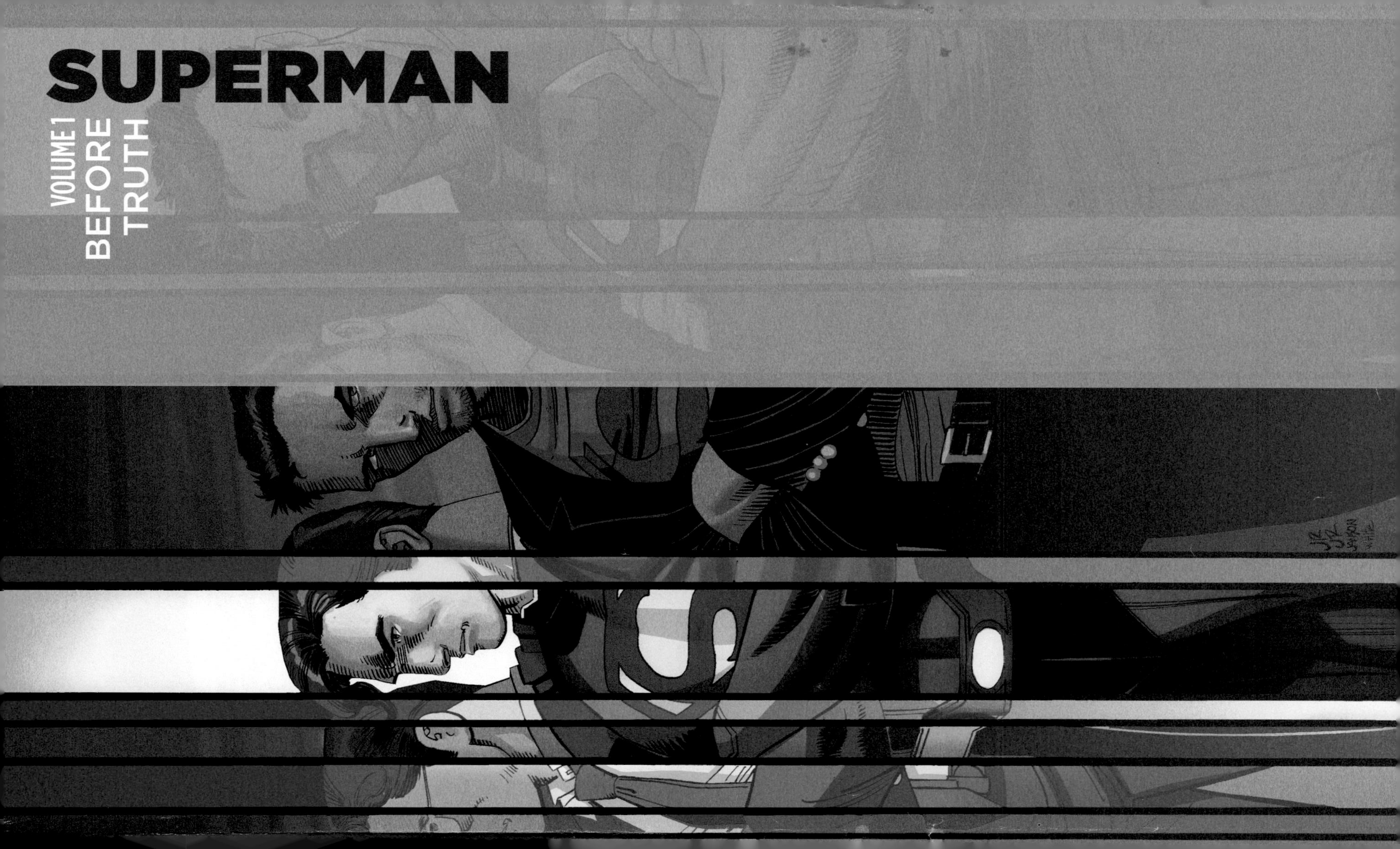
SUPERMAN
VOLUME 1
BEFORE
TRUTH

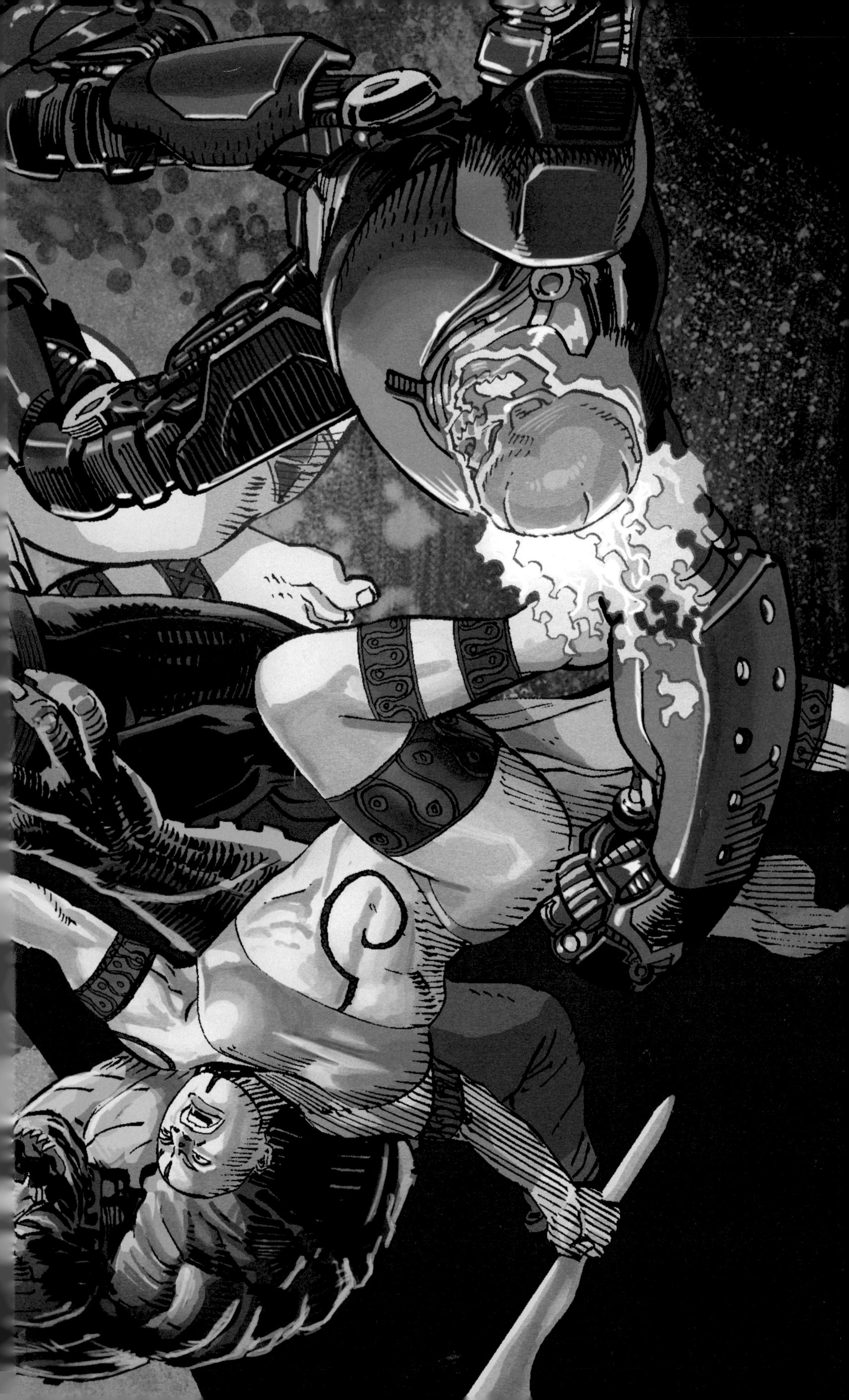

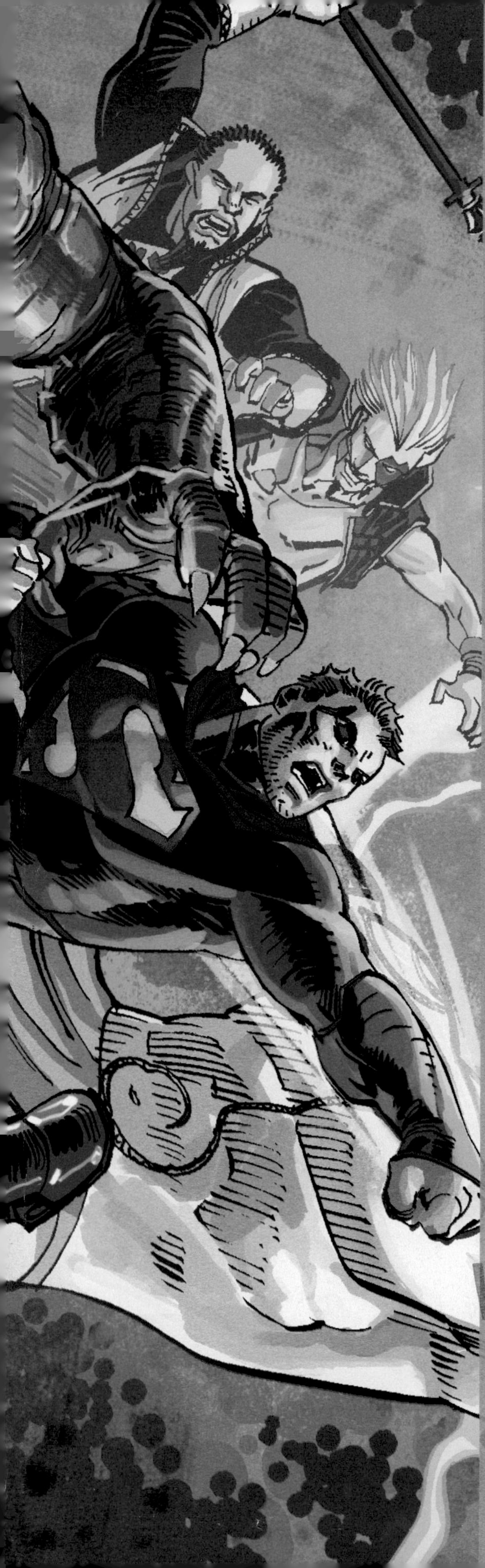

# SUPERMAN

VOLUME 1

## BEFORE TRUTH

WRITTEN BY
**GENE LUEN YANG**

ART BY
**JOHN ROMITA JR.**
**KLAUS JANSON**
**SCOTT HANNA**

COLOR BY
**DEAN WHITE**
**WIL QUINTANA**
**TOMEU MOREY**
**LEONARDO OLEA**
**BLOND**
**HI-FI**

LETTERS BY
**ROB LEIGH**
**TRAVIS LANHAM**

COLLECTION COVER ART BY
**JOHN ROMITA JR.**
**KLAUS JANSON**
**DEAN WHITE**

ORIGINAL SERIES COVERS
**KLAUS JANSON**
**AARON KUDER**
**DEAN WHITE**

SUPERMAN CREATED BY
**JERRY SIEGEL**
AND **JOE SHUSTER**
SUPERGIRL BASED ON
CHARACTERS CREATED BY
**JERRY SIEGEL**
AND **JOE SHUSTER**
BY SPECIAL ARRANGEMENT WITH
THE JERRY SIEGEL FAMILY.

EDDIE BERGANZA Editor - Original Series
RICKEY PURDIN Associate Editor - Original Series
ANDREW MARINO  JEREMY BENT Assistant Editors - Original Series
JEB WOODARD Group Editor - Collected Editions
SCOTT NYBAKKEN Editor - Collected Edition
STEVE COOK Design Director - Books
DAMIAN RYLAND Publication Design

SUPERMAN VOL. 1: BEFORE TRUTH

DC Comics 2900 West Alameda Ave, Burbank, CA 91505
Printed by RR Donnelley, Salem, VA, USA. 2/26/16. First Printing.
ISBN: 978-1-4012-5981-5

Library of Congress Cataloging-in-Publication Data

Names: Romita, John, author, illustrator. | Yang, Gene Luen, author. | Janson, Klaus, illustrator. | Hanna, Scott, illustrator. | White, Dean (Dean V.) illustrator. | Quintana, Wil, illustrator. | Morey, Tomeu, illustrator. | Olea, Leonardo, illustrator. | Blond, illustrator. | Leigh, Rob, illustrator. | Lanham, Travis, illustrator.
Title: Superman. Volume 1, Before truth / John Romita Jr., Gene Luen Yang, writers ; John Romita Jr., Klaus Janson, Scott Hanna, artists ; Dean White, Wil Quintana, Tomeu Morey, Leonardo Olea, Blond, colorists ; Rob Leigh, Travis Lanham, letterers ; John Romita Jr., Klaus Janson, Dean White, collection Cover Art.
Other titles: Before truth
Description: Burbank, CA : DC Comics, [2016]
Identifiers: LCCN 2015049454 | ISBN 9781401259815
Subjects: LCSH: Graphic novels. | Superhero comic books, strips, etc.
Classification: LCC PN6728.59 R66 2016 | DDC 741.5/973—dc23
LC record available at http://lccn.loc.gov/2015049454

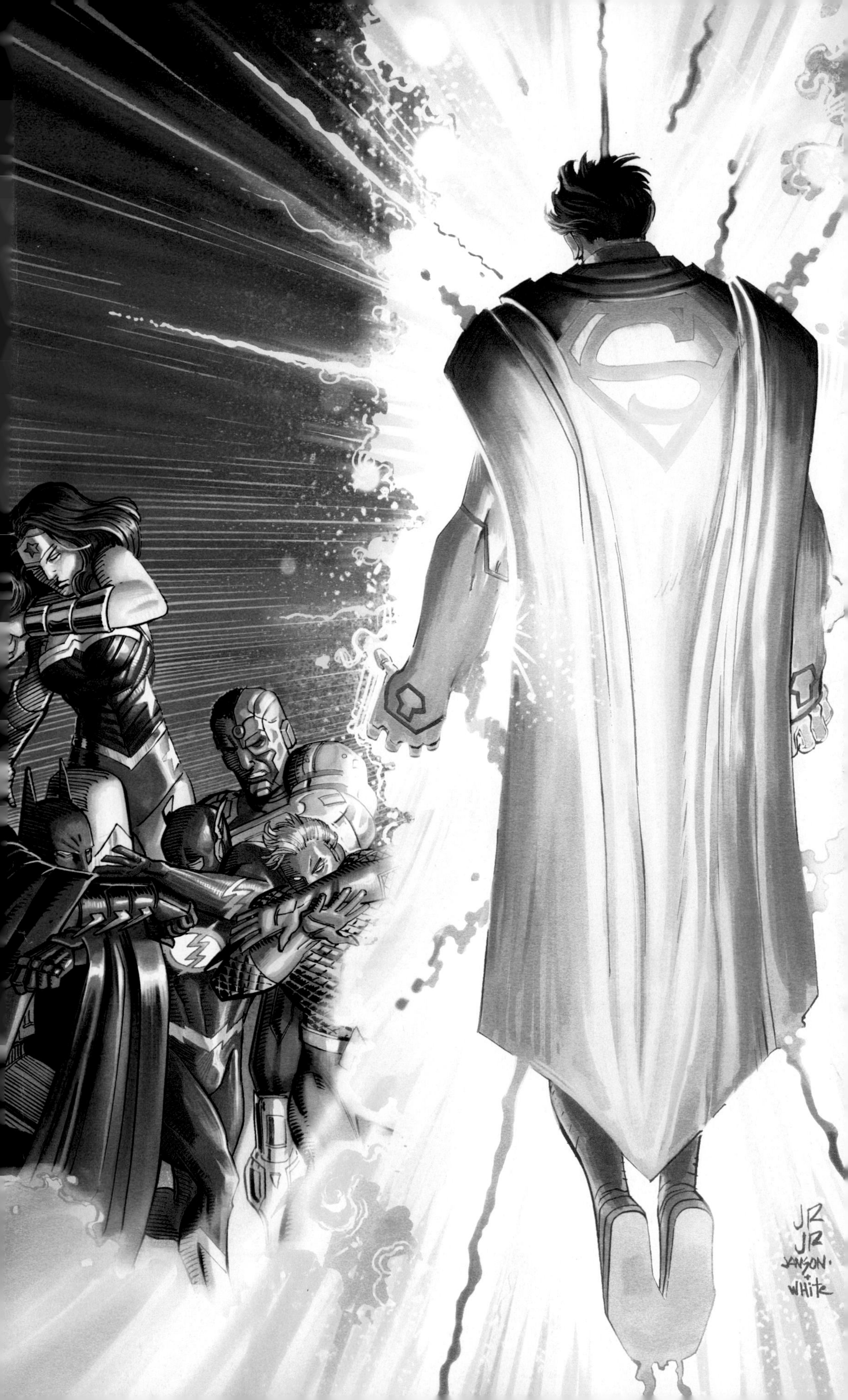
JR
JR
JANSON
+
WHITE

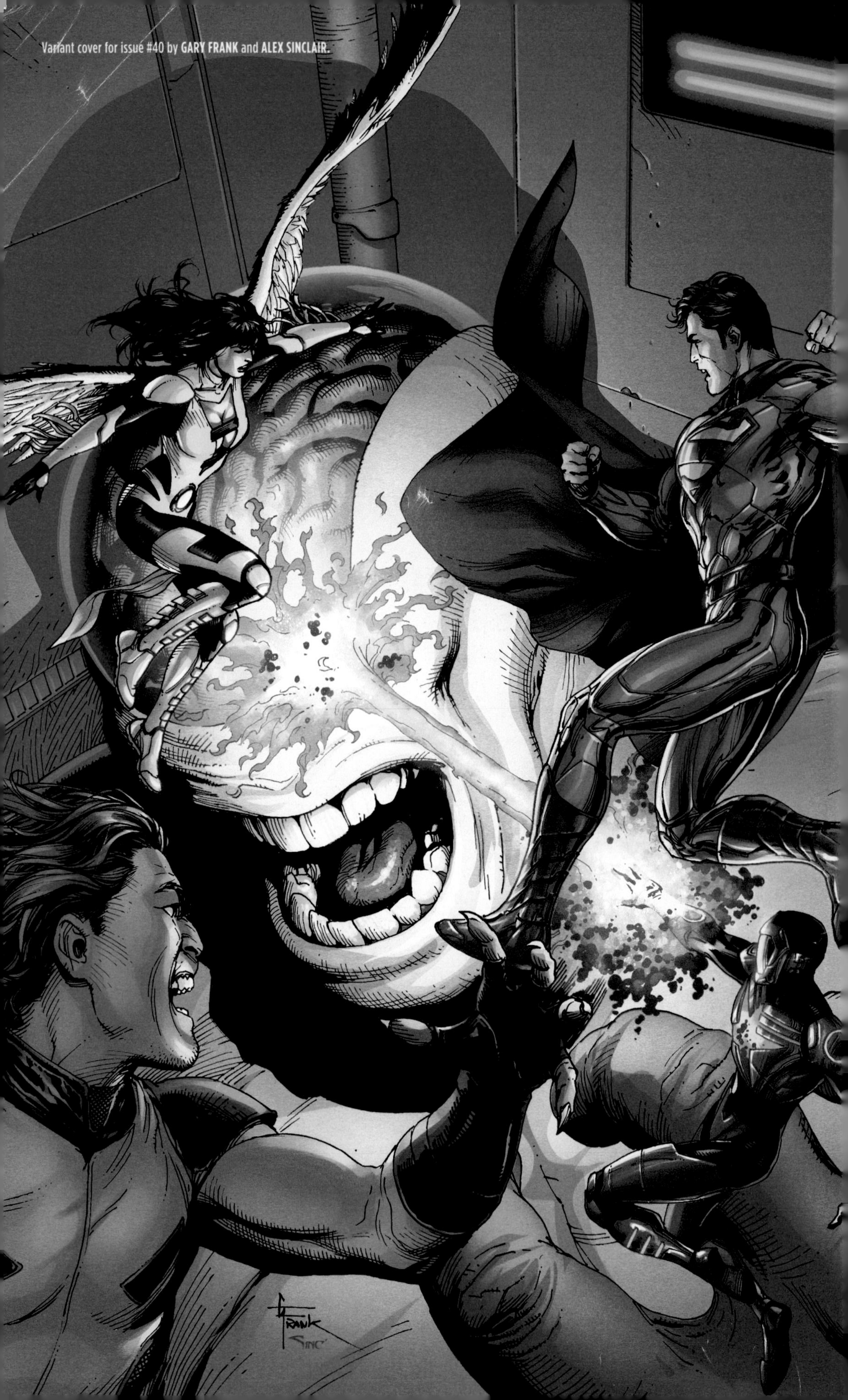
G FRANK
SINC

Variant cover for issue #40 by **GARY FRANK** and **ALEX SINCLAIR.**

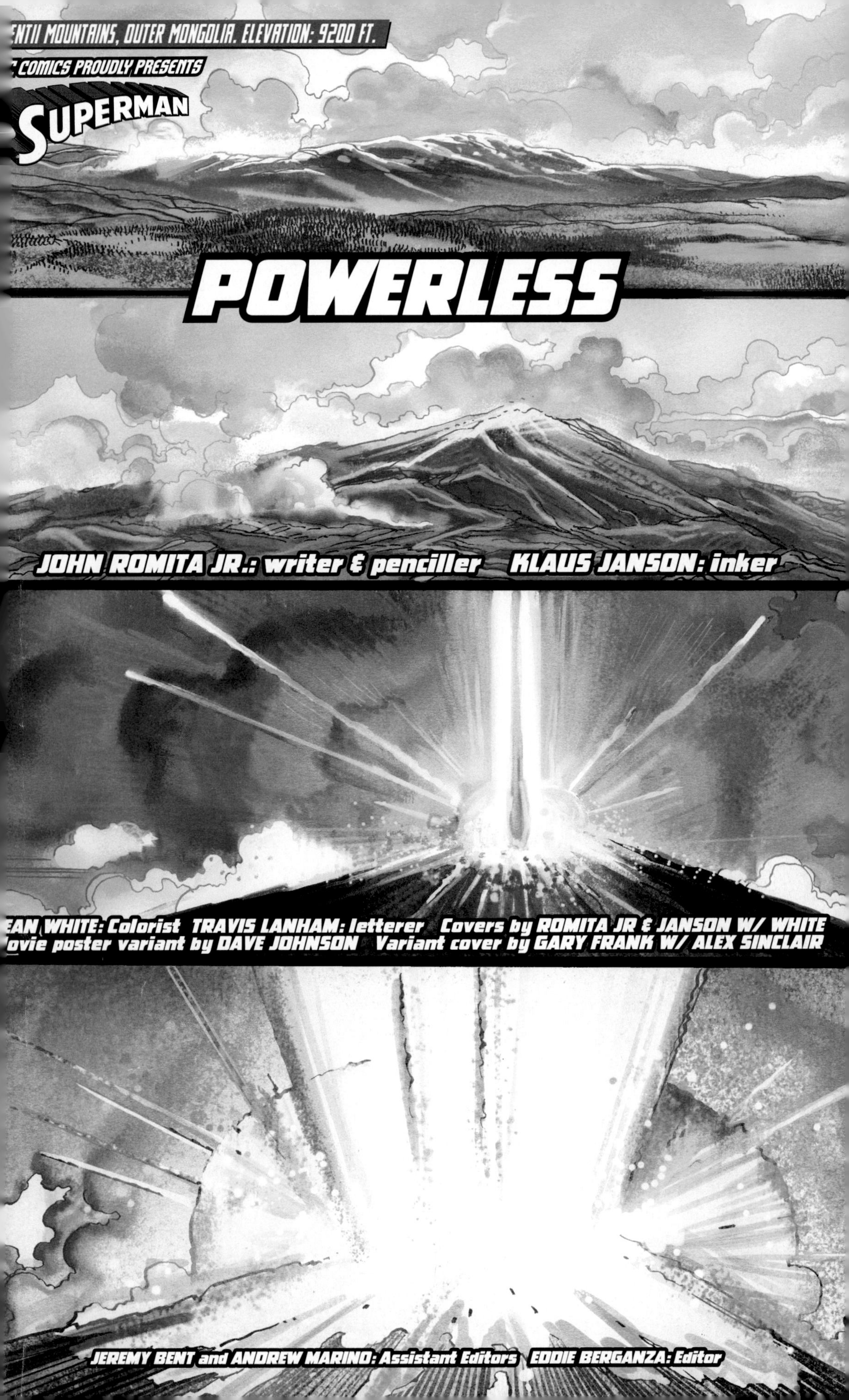
ENTII MOUNTAINS, OUTER MONGOLIA. ELEVATION: 9200 FT.
COMICS PROUDLY PRESENTS
SUPERMAN
POWERLESS
JOHN ROMITA JR.: writer & penciller KLAUS JANSON: inker
EAN WHITE: Colorist TRAVIS LANHAM: letterer Covers by ROMITA JR & JANSON W/ WHITE
ovie poster variant by DAVE JOHNSON Variant cover by GARY FRANK W/ ALEX SINCLAIR
JEREMY BENT and ANDREW MARINO: Assistant Editors EDDIE BERGANZA: Editor

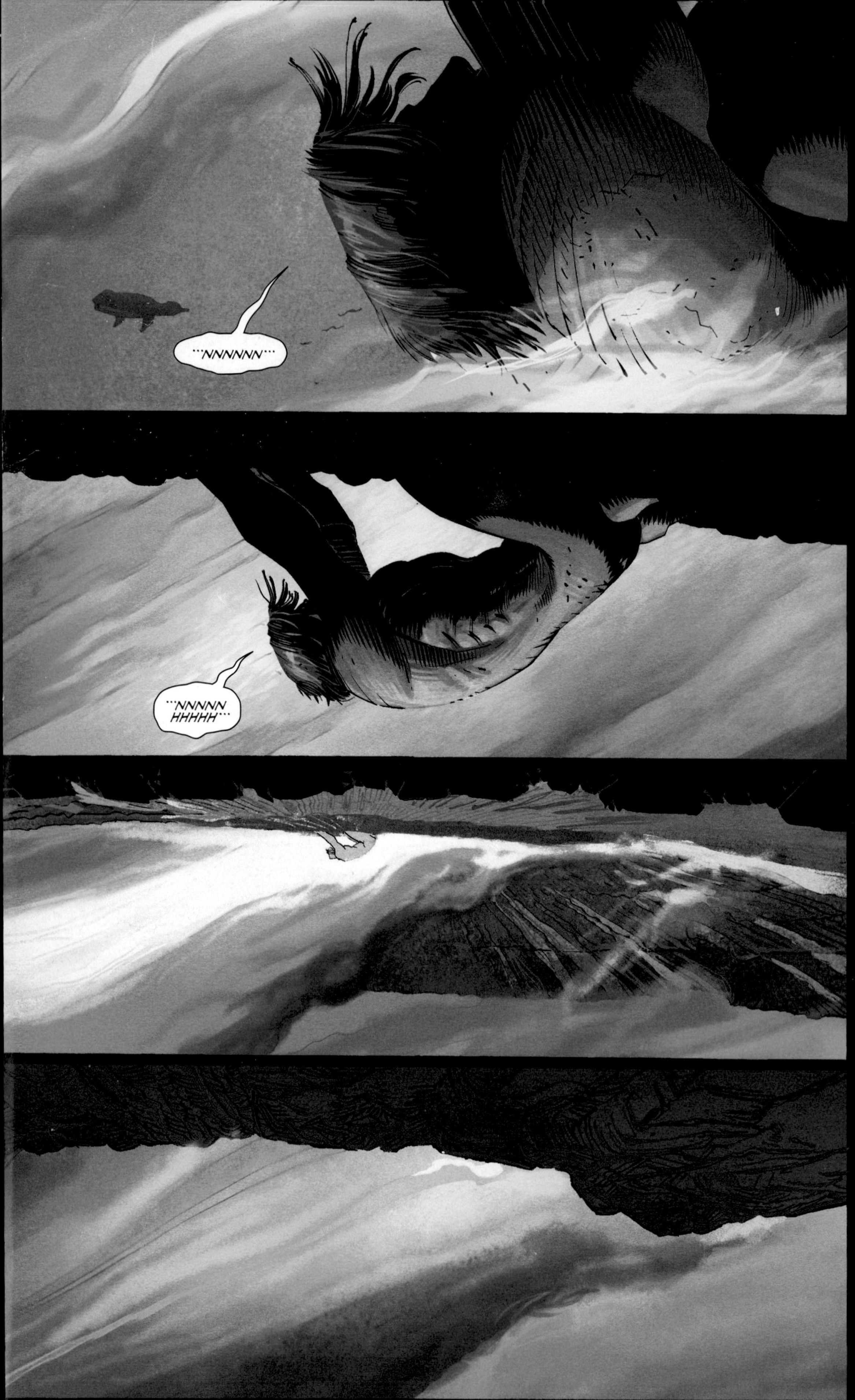
...NNNNNN...
...NNNNN HHHHH...

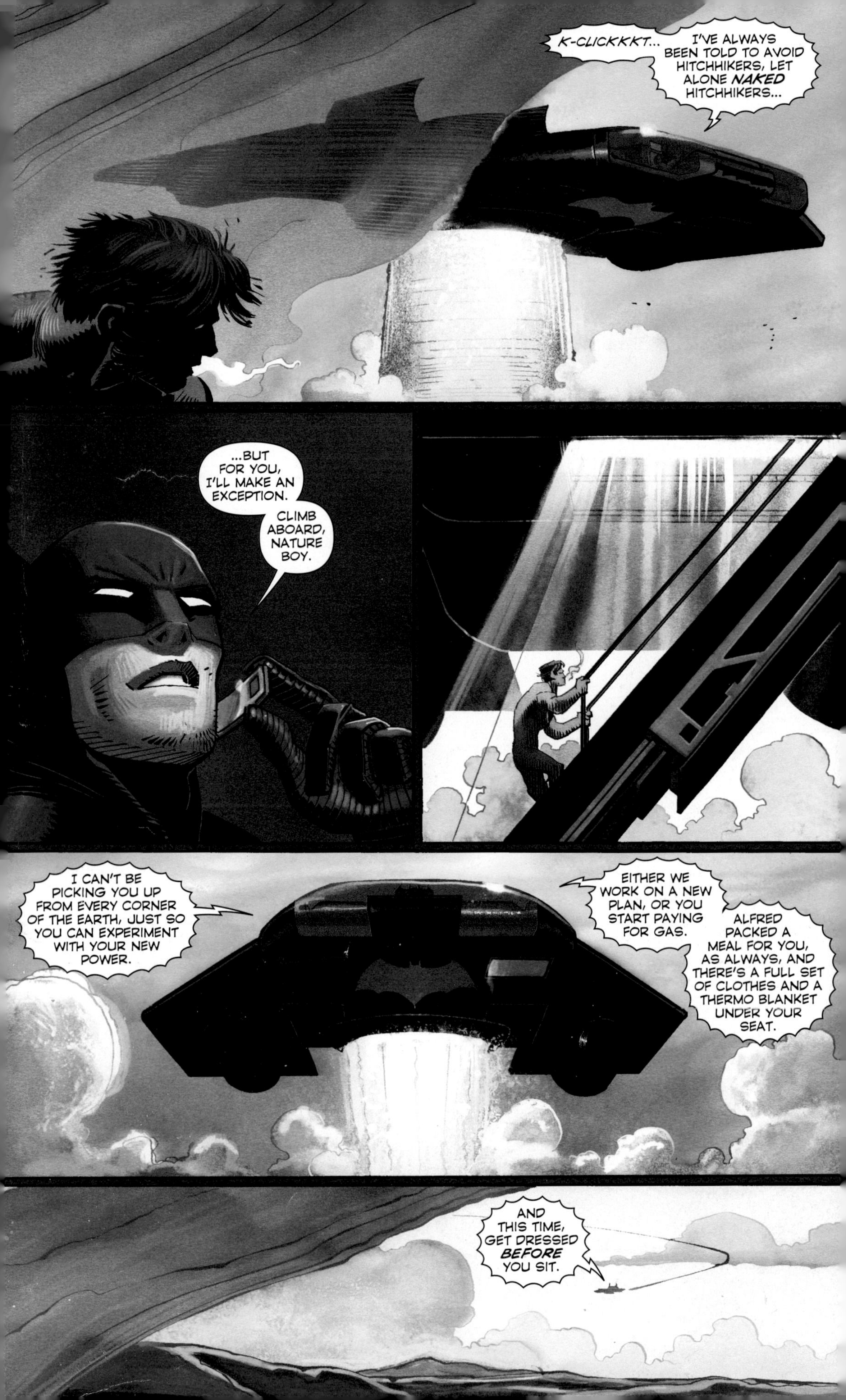
K-CLICKKKT...
I'VE ALWAYS BEEN TOLD TO AVOID HITCHHIKERS, LET ALONE *NAKED* HITCHHIKERS...
...BUT FOR YOU, I'LL MAKE AN EXCEPTION.
CLIMB ABOARD, NATURE BOY.
I CAN'T BE PICKING YOU UP FROM EVERY CORNER OF THE EARTH, JUST SO YOU CAN EXPERIMENT WITH YOUR NEW POWER.
EITHER WE WORK ON A NEW PLAN, OR YOU START PAYING FOR GAS.
ALFRED PACKED A MEAL FOR YOU, AS ALWAYS, AND THERE'S A FULL SET OF CLOTHES AND A THERMO BLANKET UNDER YOUR SEAT.
AND THIS TIME, GET DRESSED *BEFORE* YOU SIT.

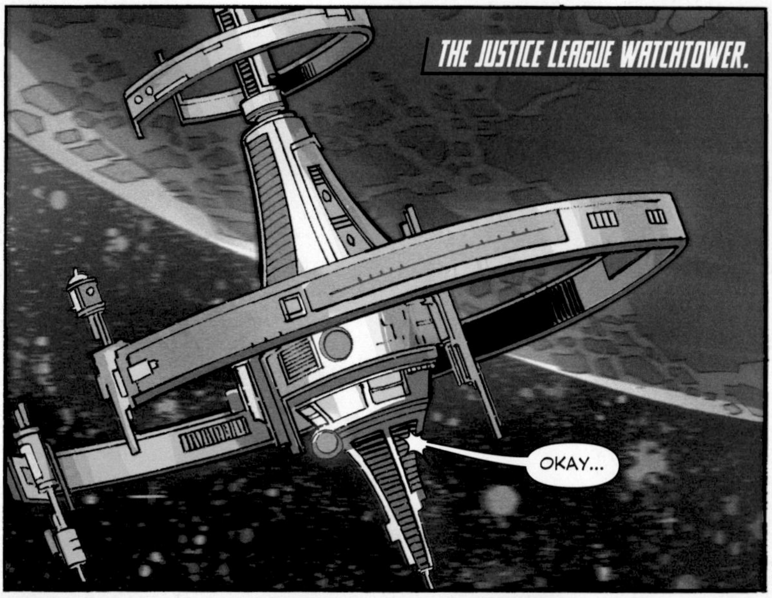
THE JUSTICE LEAGUE WATCHTOWER.
OKAY...

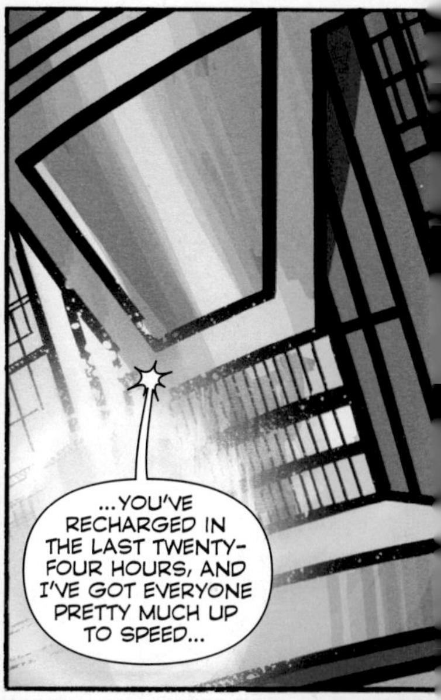
...YOU'VE RECHARGED IN THE LAST TWENTY-FOUR HOURS, AND I'VE GOT EVERYONE PRETTY MUCH UP TO SPEED...

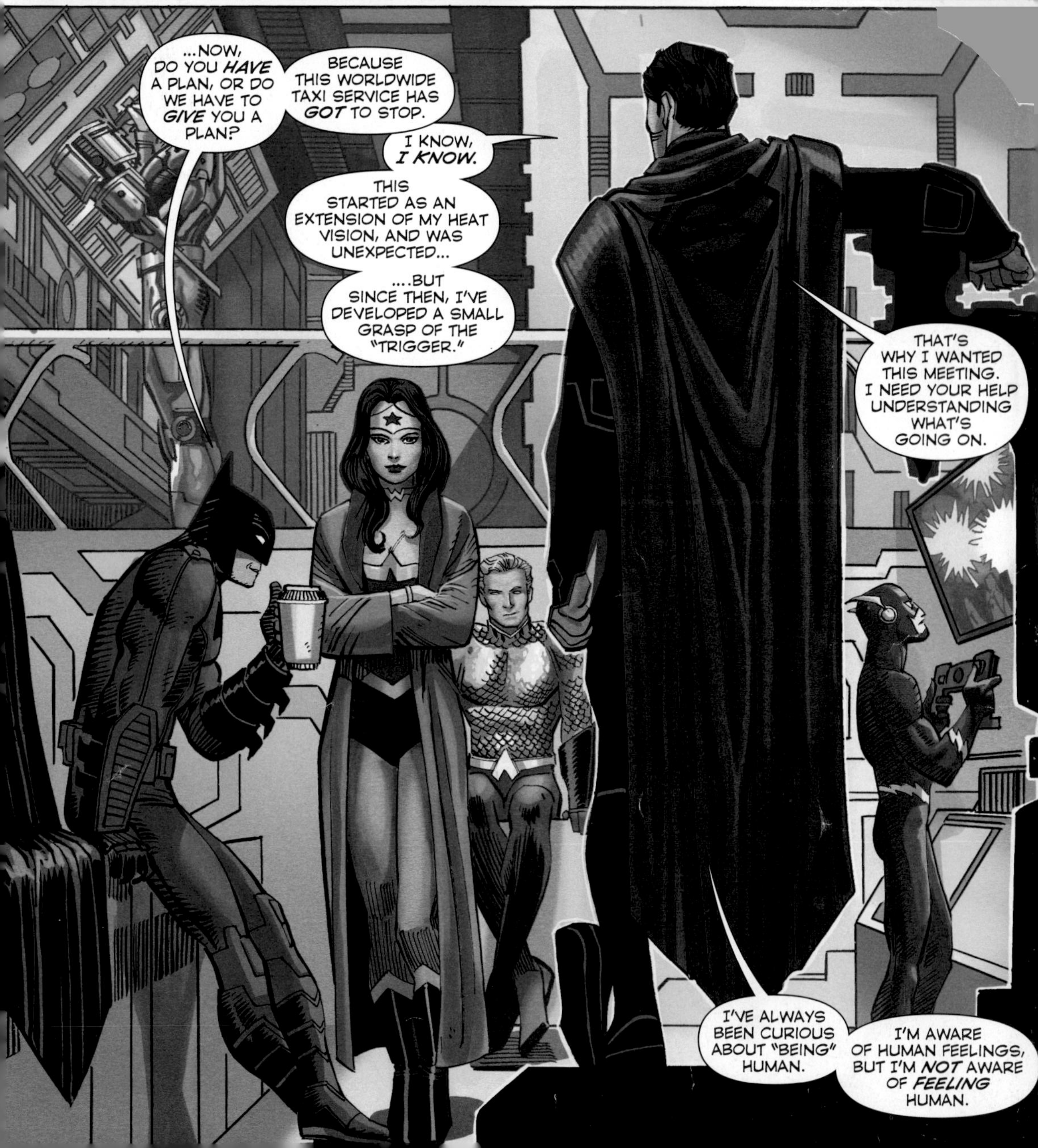
...NOW, DO YOU *HAVE* A PLAN, OR DO WE HAVE TO *GIVE* YOU A PLAN?
BECAUSE THIS WORLDWIDE TAXI SERVICE HAS *GOT* TO STOP.
I KNOW, *I KNOW.*
THIS STARTED AS AN EXTENSION OF MY HEAT VISION, AND WAS UNEXPECTED...
....BUT SINCE THEN, I'VE DEVELOPED A SMALL GRASP OF THE "TRIGGER."
THAT'S WHY I WANTED THIS MEETING. I NEED YOUR HELP UNDERSTANDING WHAT'S GOING ON.
I'VE ALWAYS BEEN CURIOUS ABOUT "BEING" HUMAN.
I'M AWARE OF HUMAN FEELINGS, BUT I'M *NOT* AWARE OF *FEELING* HUMAN.

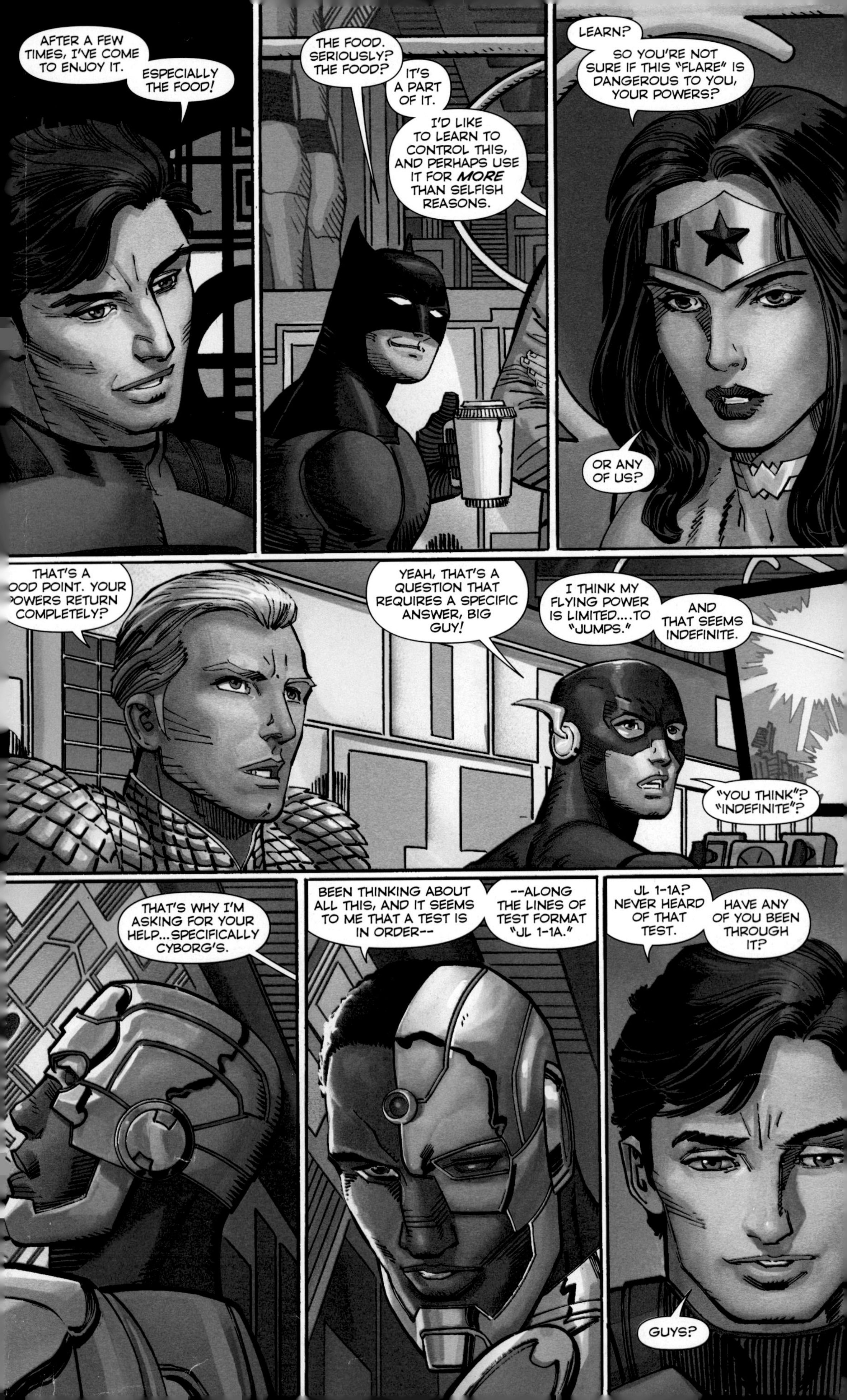
AFTER A FEW TIMES, I'VE COME TO ENJOY IT.
ESPECIALLY THE FOOD!
THE FOOD. SERIOUSLY? THE FOOD?
IT'S A PART OF IT.
I'D LIKE TO LEARN TO CONTROL THIS, AND PERHAPS USE IT FOR MORE THAN SELFISH REASONS.
LEARN?
SO YOU'RE NOT SURE IF THIS "FLARE" IS DANGEROUS TO YOU, YOUR POWERS?
OR ANY OF US?
THAT'S A OOD POINT. YOUR OWERS RETURN COMPLETELY?
YEAH, THAT'S A QUESTION THAT REQUIRES A SPECIFIC ANSWER, BIG GUY!
I THINK MY FLYING POWER IS LIMITED....TO "JUMPS."
AND THAT SEEMS INDEFINITE.
"YOU THINK"? "INDEFINITE"?
THAT'S WHY I'M ASKING FOR YOUR HELP...SPECIFICALLY CYBORG'S.
BEEN THINKING ABOUT ALL THIS, AND IT SEEMS TO ME THAT A TEST IS IN ORDER--
--ALONG THE LINES OF TEST FORMAT "JL 1-1A."
JL 1-1A? NEVER HEARD OF THAT TEST.
HAVE ANY OF YOU BEEN THROUGH IT?
GUYS?

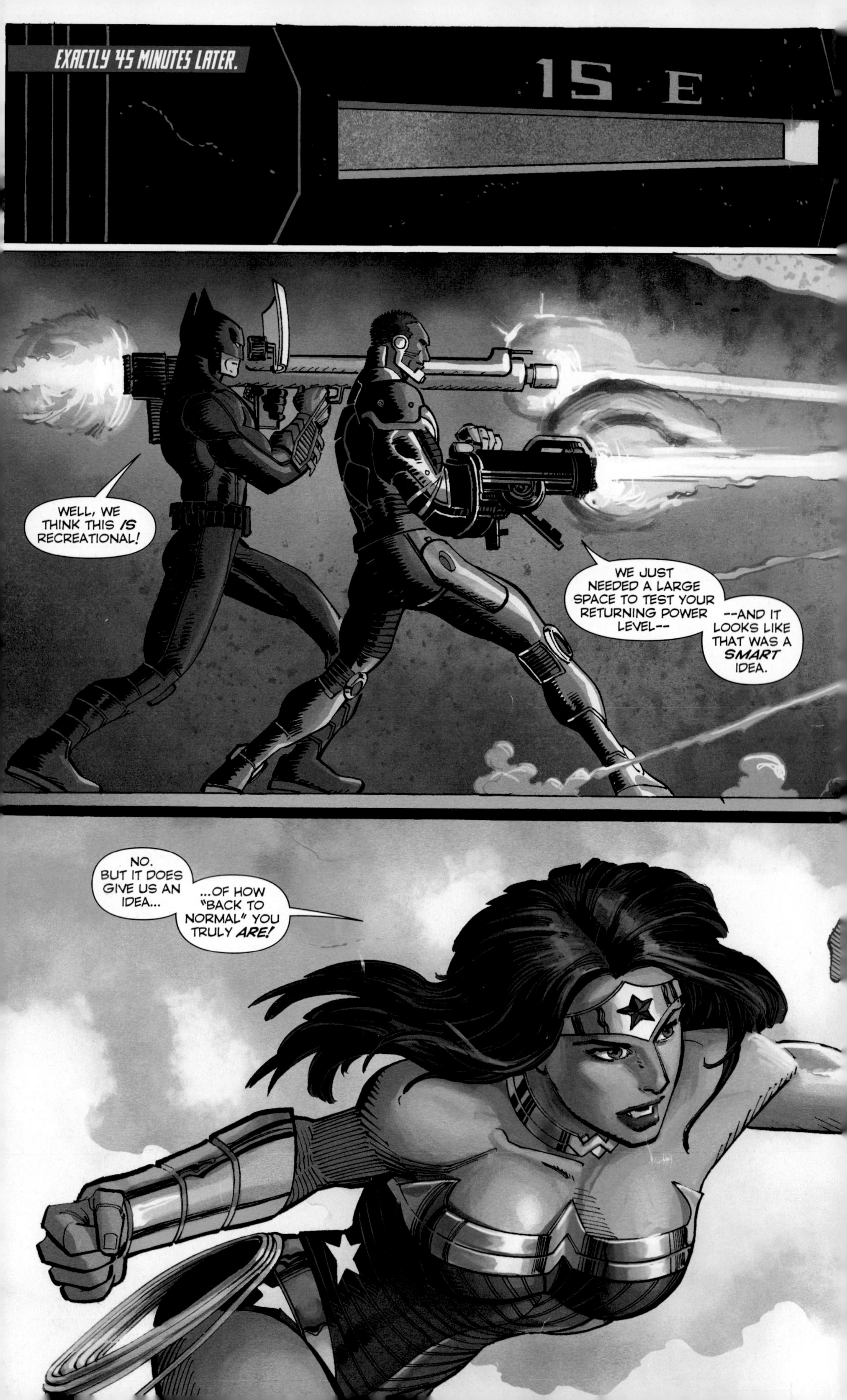
EXACTLY 45 MINUTES LATER.
15 E
WELL, WE THINK THIS *IS* RECREATIONAL!
WE JUST NEEDED A LARGE SPACE TO TEST YOUR RETURNING POWER LEVEL--
--AND IT LOOKS LIKE THAT WAS A *SMART* IDEA.
NO. BUT IT DOES GIVE US AN IDEA...
...OF HOW "BACK TO NORMAL" YOU TRULY *ARE!*

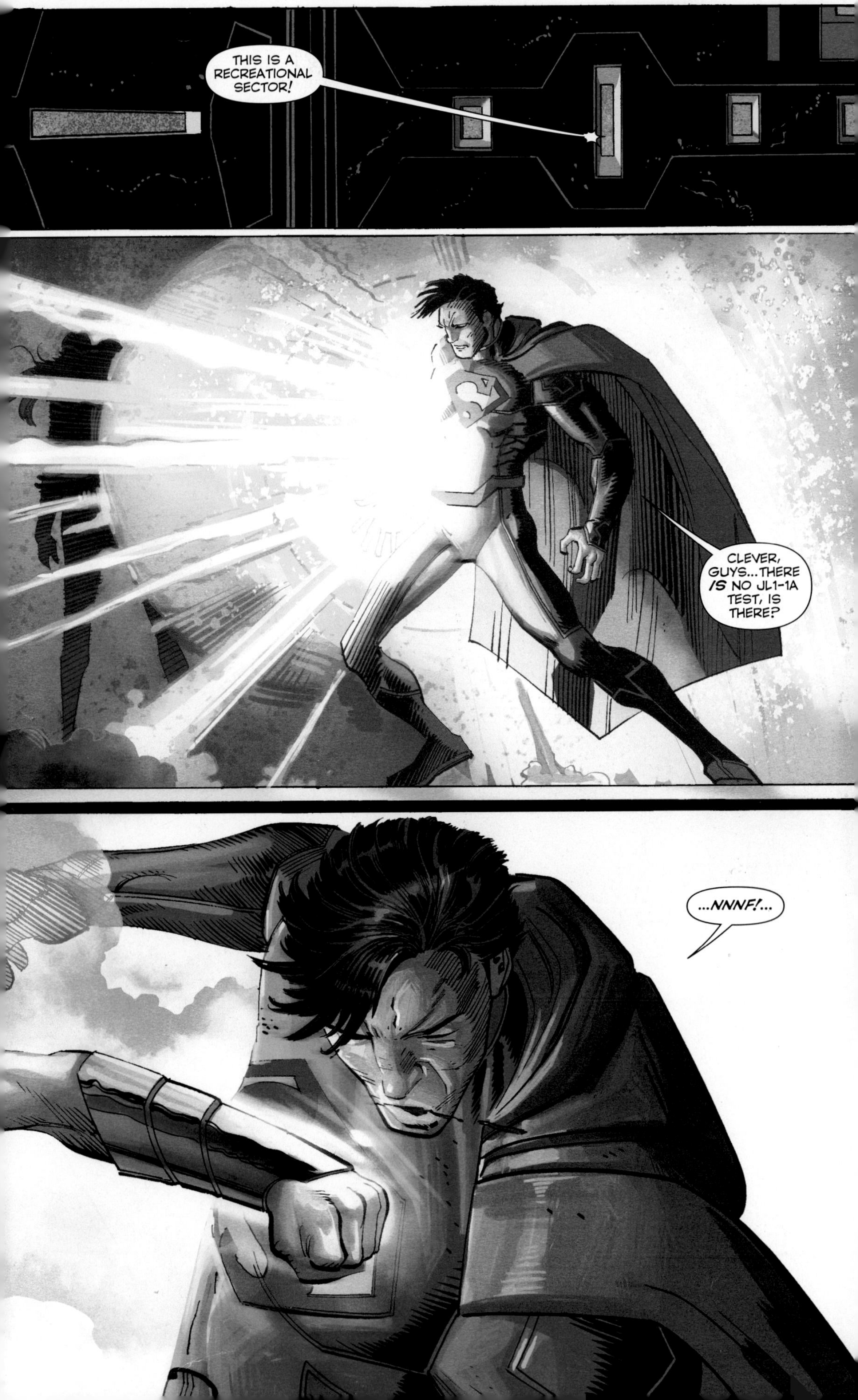
THIS IS A RECREATIONAL SECTOR!
CLEVER, GUYS...THERE *IS* NO JL1-1A TEST, IS THERE?
...*NNNF!*...

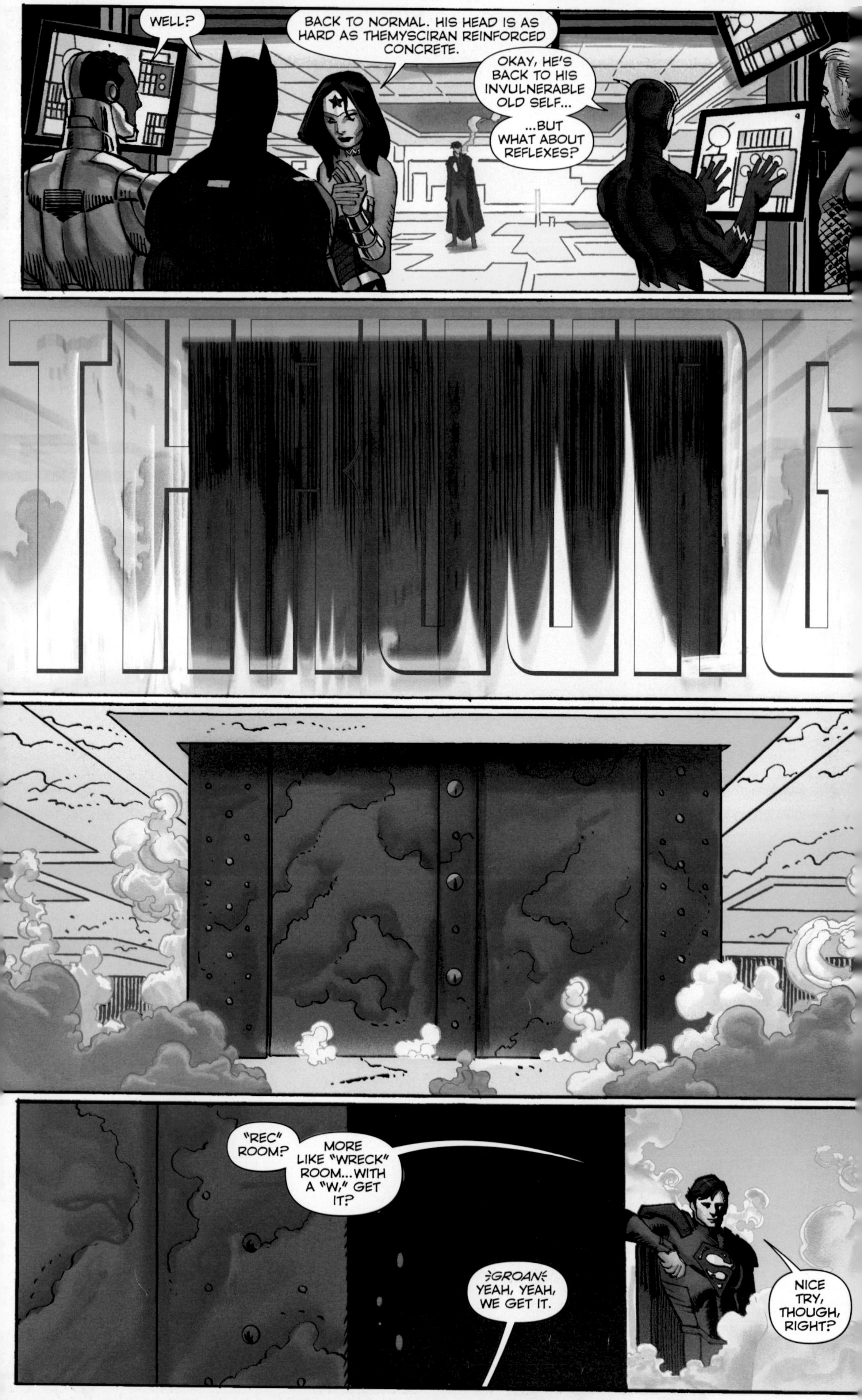
WELL?
BACK TO NORMAL. HIS HEAD IS AS HARD AS THEMYSCIRAN REINFORCED CONCRETE.
OKAY, HE'S BACK TO HIS INVULNERABLE OLD SELF...
...BUT WHAT ABOUT REFLEXES?
THHOOMG
"REC" ROOM?
MORE LIKE "WRECK" ROOM...WITH A "W," GET IT?
GROAN
YEAH, YEAH, WE GET IT.
NICE TRY, THOUGH, RIGHT?

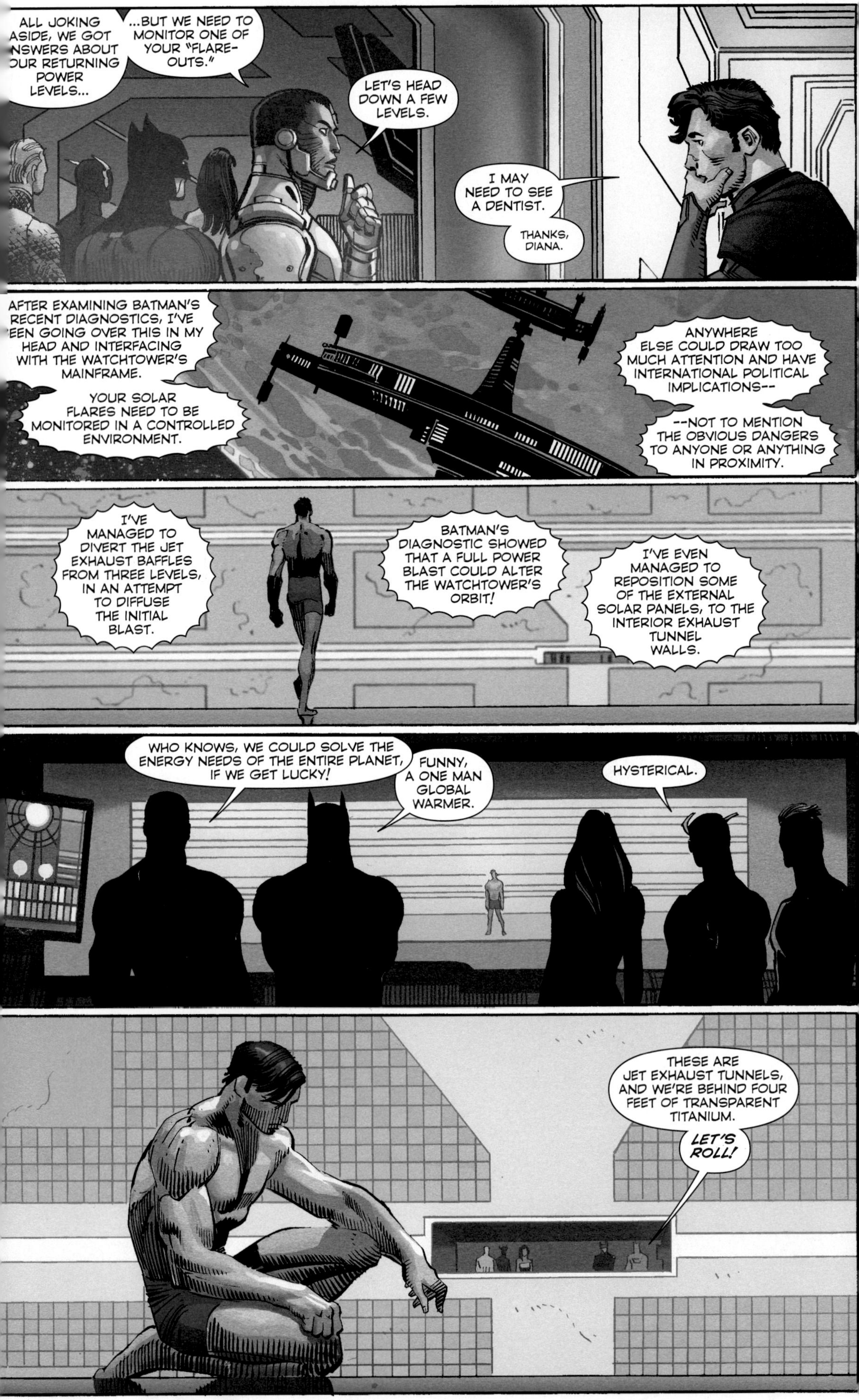

ALL JOKING ASIDE, WE GOT NSWERS ABOUT OUR RETURNING POWER LEVELS...
...BUT WE NEED TO MONITOR ONE OF YOUR "FLARE-OUTS."
LET'S HEAD DOWN A FEW LEVELS.
I MAY NEED TO SEE A DENTIST.
THANKS, DIANA.
AFTER EXAMINING BATMAN'S RECENT DIAGNOSTICS, I'VE EEN GOING OVER THIS IN MY HEAD AND INTERFACING WITH THE WATCHTOWER'S MAINFRAME.
YOUR SOLAR FLARES NEED TO BE MONITORED IN A CONTROLLED ENVIRONMENT.
ANYWHERE ELSE COULD DRAW TOO MUCH ATTENTION AND HAVE INTERNATIONAL POLITICAL IMPLICATIONS--
--NOT TO MENTION THE OBVIOUS DANGERS TO ANYONE OR ANYTHING IN PROXIMITY.
I'VE MANAGED TO DIVERT THE JET EXHAUST BAFFLES FROM THREE LEVELS, IN AN ATTEMPT TO DIFFUSE THE INITIAL BLAST.
BATMAN'S DIAGNOSTIC SHOWED THAT A FULL POWER BLAST COULD ALTER THE WATCHTOWER'S ORBIT!
I'VE EVEN MANAGED TO REPOSITION SOME OF THE EXTERNAL SOLAR PANELS, TO THE INTERIOR EXHAUST TUNNEL WALLS.
WHO KNOWS, WE COULD SOLVE THE ENERGY NEEDS OF THE ENTIRE PLANET, IF WE GET LUCKY!
FUNNY, A ONE MAN GLOBAL WARMER.
HYSTERICAL.
THESE ARE JET EXHAUST TUNNELS, AND WE'RE BEHIND FOUR FEET OF TRANSPARENT TITANIUM.
LET'S ROLL!

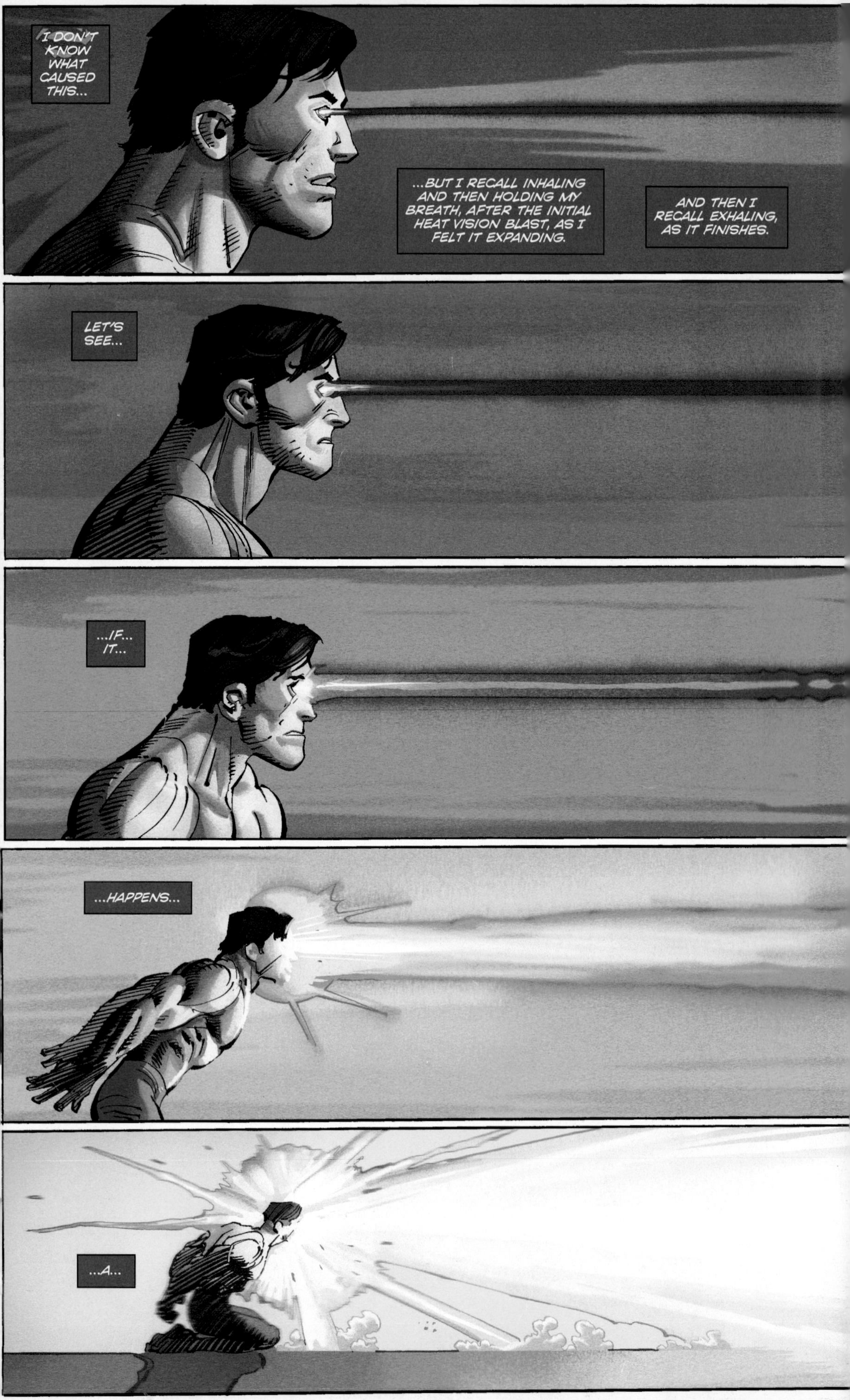
I DON'T KNOW WHAT CAUSED THIS...
...BUT I RECALL INHALING AND THEN HOLDING MY BREATH, AFTER THE INITIAL HEAT VISION BLAST, AS I FELT IT EXPANDING.
AND THEN I RECALL EXHALING, AS IT FINISHES.
LET'S SEE...
...IF... IT...
...HAPPENS...
...A...

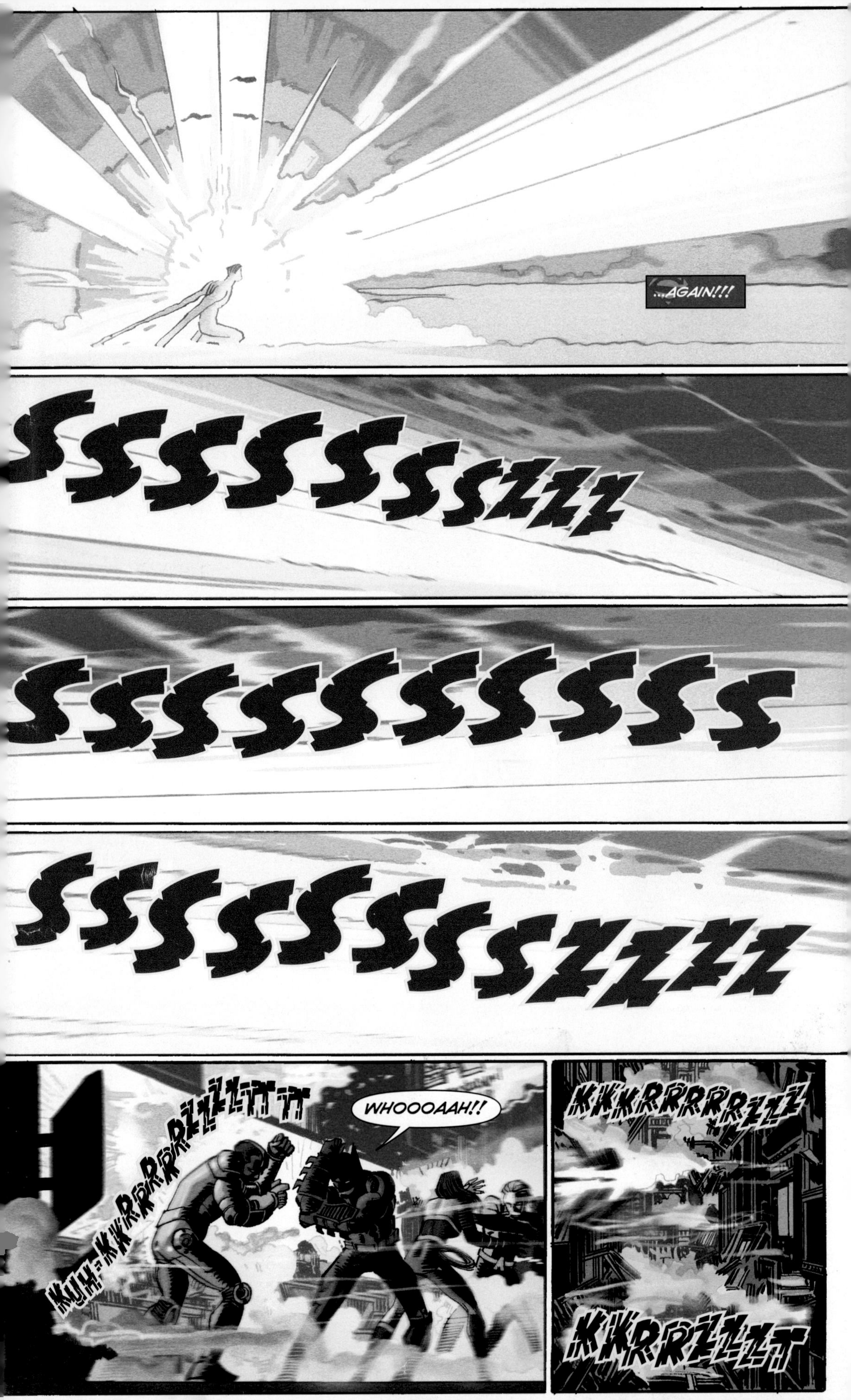
...AGAIN!!!
SSSSSSSZZZZ
SSSSSSSSSSS
SSSSSSSSZZZZZ
KUH-KKRRRRRZZZTTT
WHOOOAAH!!
KKKRRRRRRZZZ
KKRRZZZZT

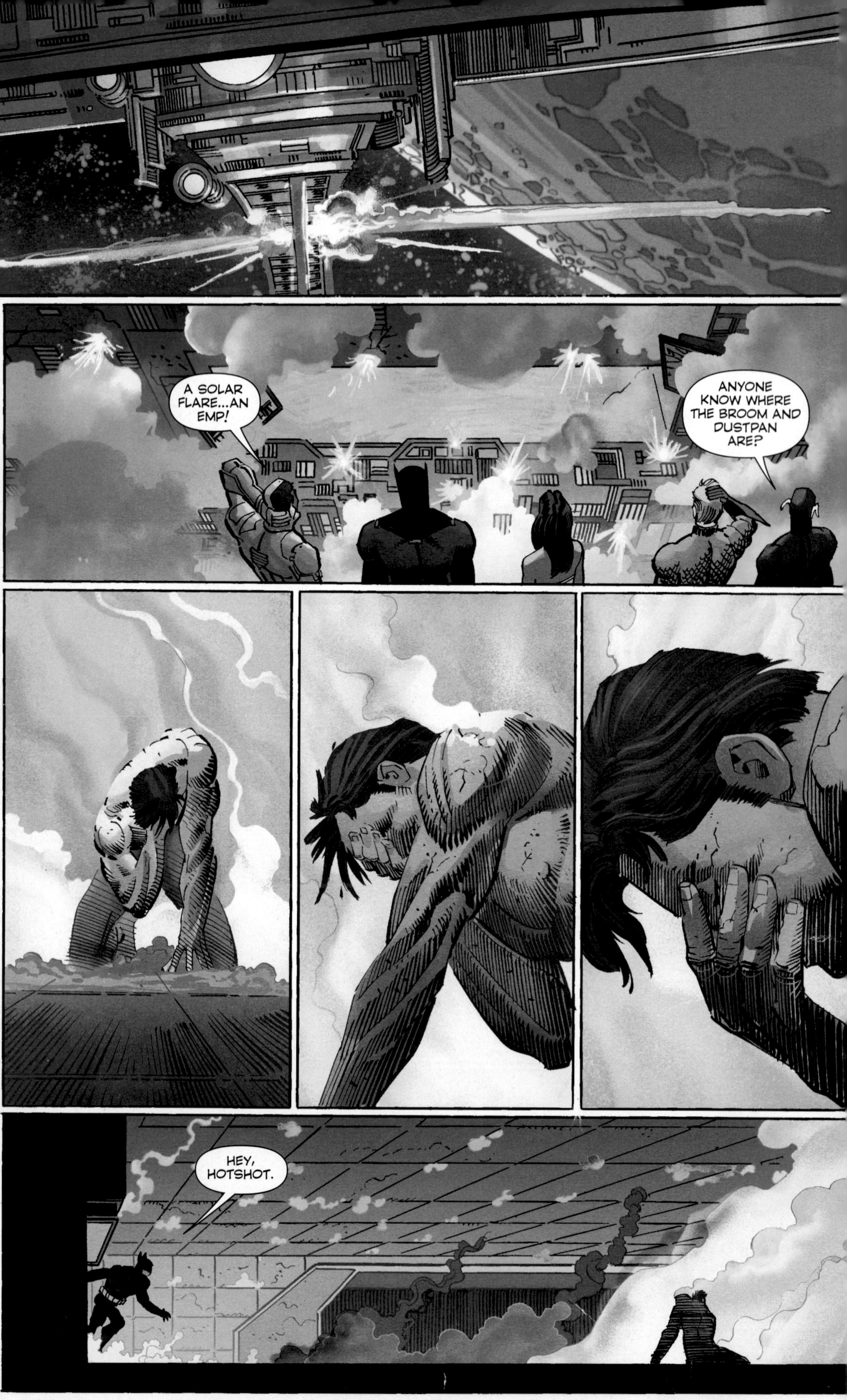
A SOLAR FLARE...AN EMP!
ANYONE KNOW WHERE THE BROOM AND DUSTPAN ARE?
HEY, HOTSHOT.

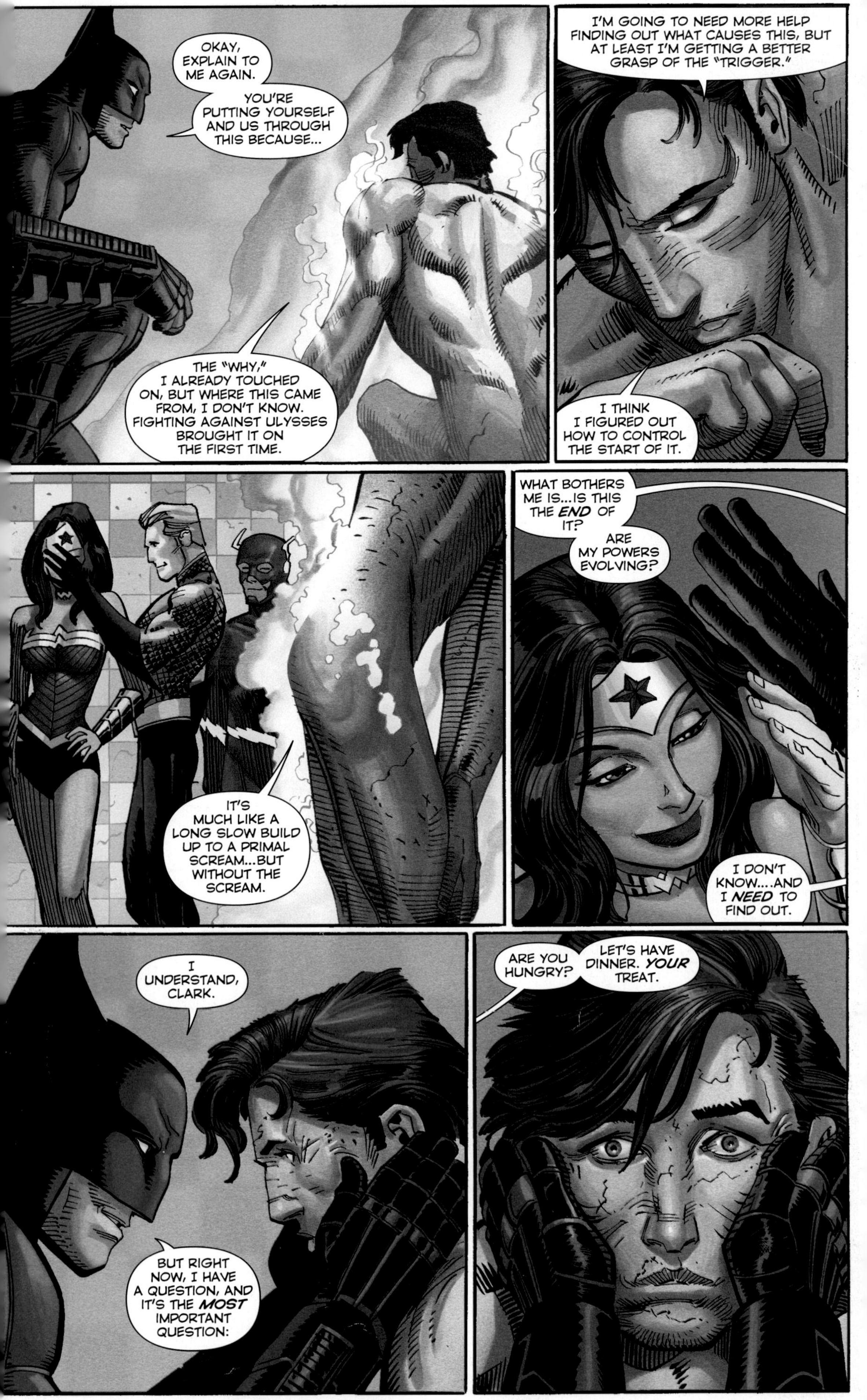
OKAY, EXPLAIN TO ME AGAIN.
YOU'RE PUTTING YOURSELF AND US THROUGH THIS BECAUSE...
THE "WHY," I ALREADY TOUCHED ON, BUT WHERE THIS CAME FROM, I DON'T KNOW. FIGHTING AGAINST ULYSSES BROUGHT IT ON THE FIRST TIME.
I'M GOING TO NEED MORE HELP FINDING OUT WHAT CAUSES THIS, BUT AT LEAST I'M GETTING A BETTER GRASP OF THE "TRIGGER."
I THINK I FIGURED OUT HOW TO CONTROL THE START OF IT.
IT'S MUCH LIKE A LONG SLOW BUILD UP TO A PRIMAL SCREAM...BUT WITHOUT THE SCREAM.
WHAT BOTHERS ME IS...IS THIS THE *END* OF IT?
ARE MY POWERS EVOLVING?
I DON'T KNOW....AND I *NEED* TO FIND OUT.
I UNDERSTAND, CLARK.
BUT RIGHT NOW, I HAVE A QUESTION, AND IT'S THE *MOST* IMPORTANT QUESTION:
ARE YOU HUNGRY?
LET'S HAVE DINNER. *YOUR* TREAT.

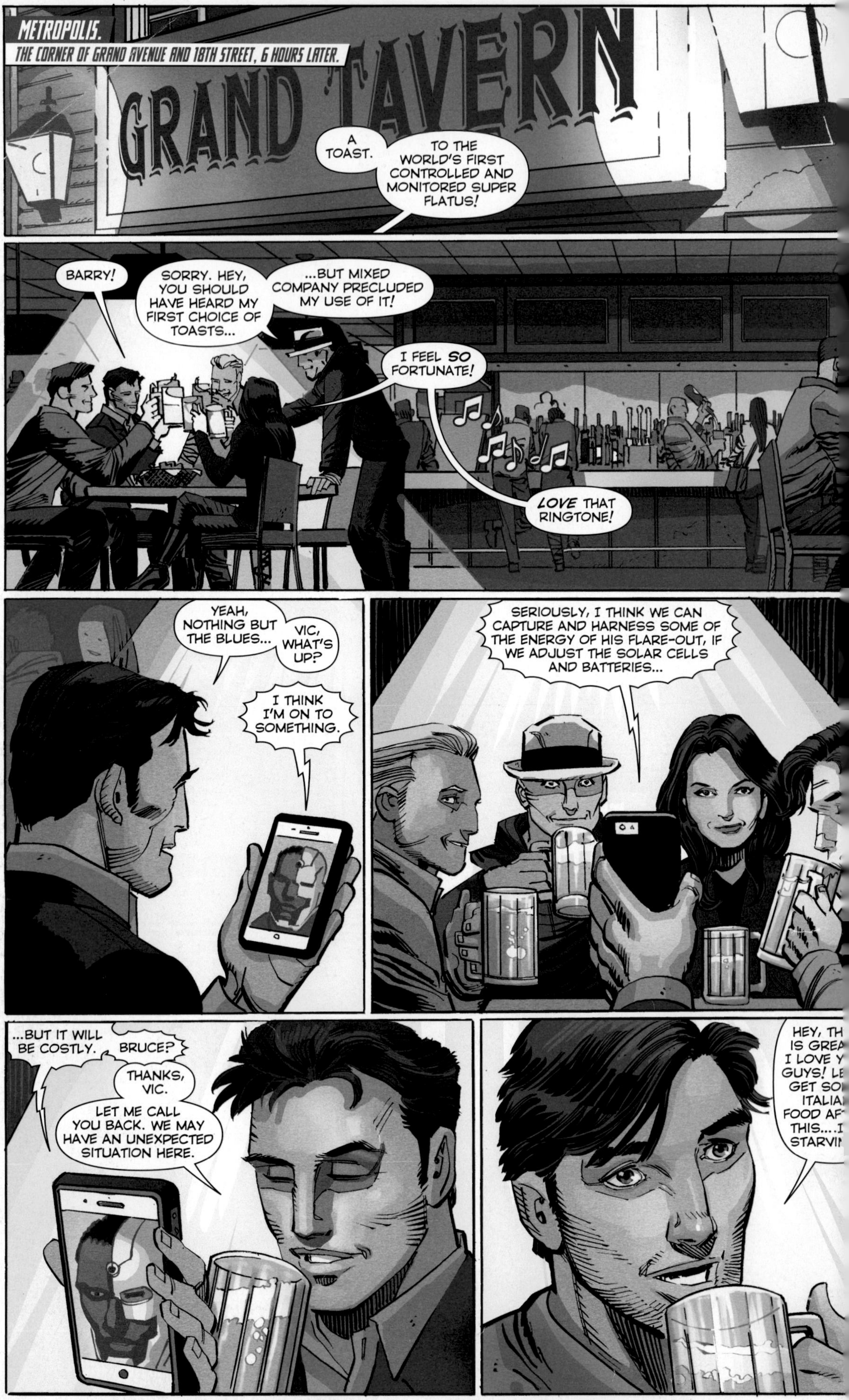
METROPOLIS.
THE CORNER OF GRAND AVENUE AND 18TH STREET, 6 HOURS LATER.
GRAND TAVERN
A TOAST.
TO THE WORLD'S FIRST CONTROLLED AND MONITORED SUPER FLATUS!
BARRY!
SORRY. HEY, YOU SHOULD HAVE HEARD MY FIRST CHOICE OF TOASTS...
...BUT MIXED COMPANY PRECLUDED MY USE OF IT!
I FEEL SO FORTUNATE!
LOVE THAT RINGTONE!
YEAH, NOTHING BUT THE BLUES...
VIC, WHAT'S UP?
I THINK I'M ON TO SOMETHING.
SERIOUSLY, I THINK WE CAN CAPTURE AND HARNESS SOME OF THE ENERGY OF HIS FLARE-OUT, IF WE ADJUST THE SOLAR CELLS AND BATTERIES...
...BUT IT WILL BE COSTLY.
BRUCE?
THANKS, VIC.
LET ME CALL YOU BACK. WE MAY HAVE AN UNEXPECTED SITUATION HERE.
HEY, TH
IS GREA
I LOVE Y
GUYS! LE
GET SO
ITALIA
FOOD AF
THIS....I
STARVI

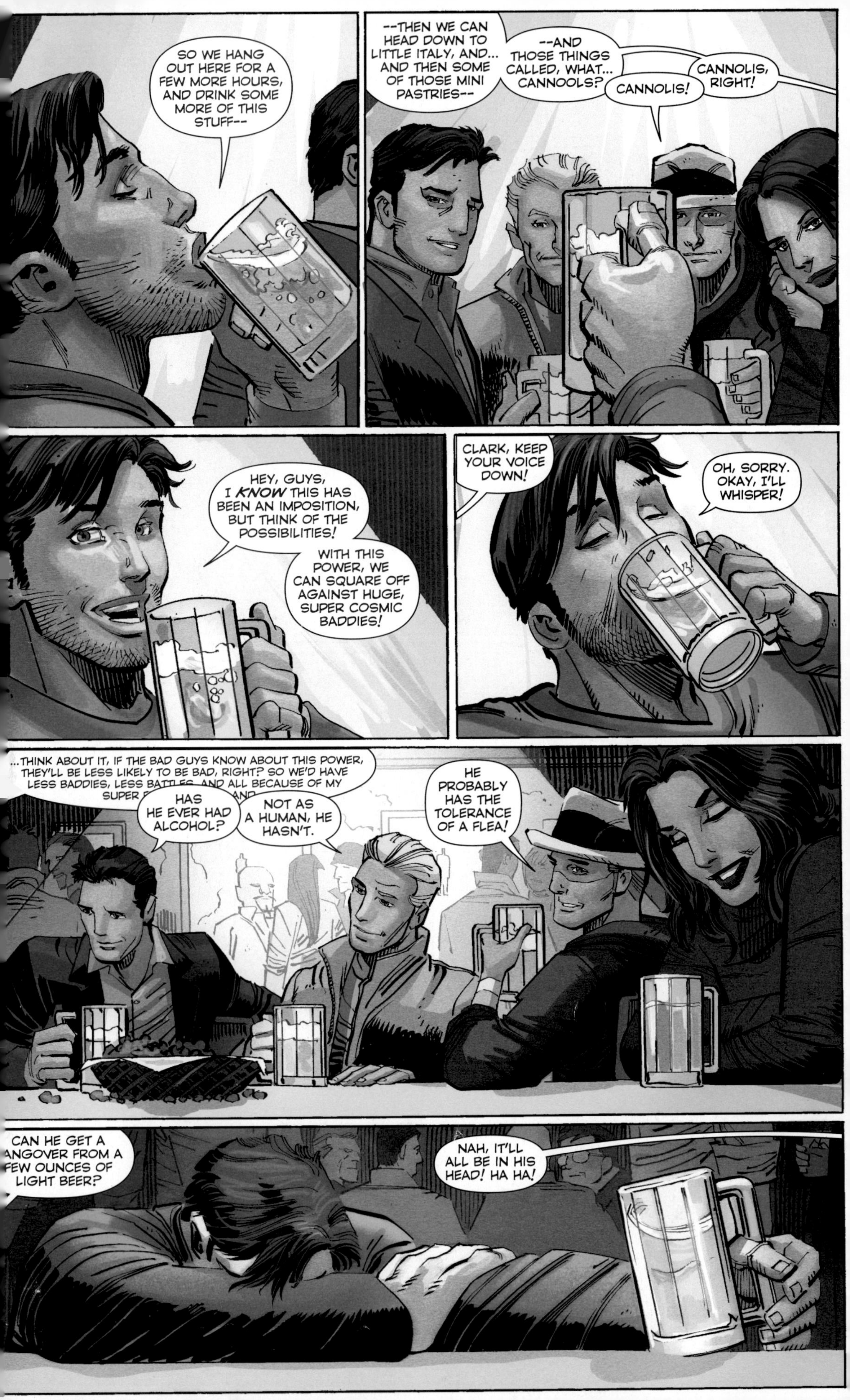
SO WE HANG OUT HERE FOR A FEW MORE HOURS, AND DRINK SOME MORE OF THIS STUFF--
--THEN WE CAN HEAD DOWN TO LITTLE ITALY, AND... AND THEN SOME OF THOSE MINI PASTRIES--
--AND THOSE THINGS CALLED, WHAT... CANNOOLS?
CANNOLIS!
CANNOLIS, RIGHT!
HEY, GUYS, I KNOW THIS HAS BEEN AN IMPOSITION, BUT THINK OF THE POSSIBILITIES!
WITH THIS POWER, WE CAN SQUARE OFF AGAINST HUGE, SUPER COSMIC BADDIES!
CLARK, KEEP YOUR VOICE DOWN!
OH, SORRY. OKAY, I'LL WHISPER!
...THINK ABOUT IT, IF THE BAD GUYS KNOW ABOUT THIS POWER, THEY'LL BE LESS LIKELY TO BE BAD, RIGHT? SO WE'D HAVE LESS BADDIES, LESS BATTLES, AND ALL BECAUSE OF MY
HAS HE EVER HAD ALCOHOL?
NOT AS A HUMAN, HE HASN'T.
HE PROBABLY HAS THE TOLERANCE OF A FLEA!
CAN HE GET A ANGOVER FROM A FEW OUNCES OF LIGHT BEER?
NAH, IT'LL ALL BE IN HIS HEAD! HA HA!

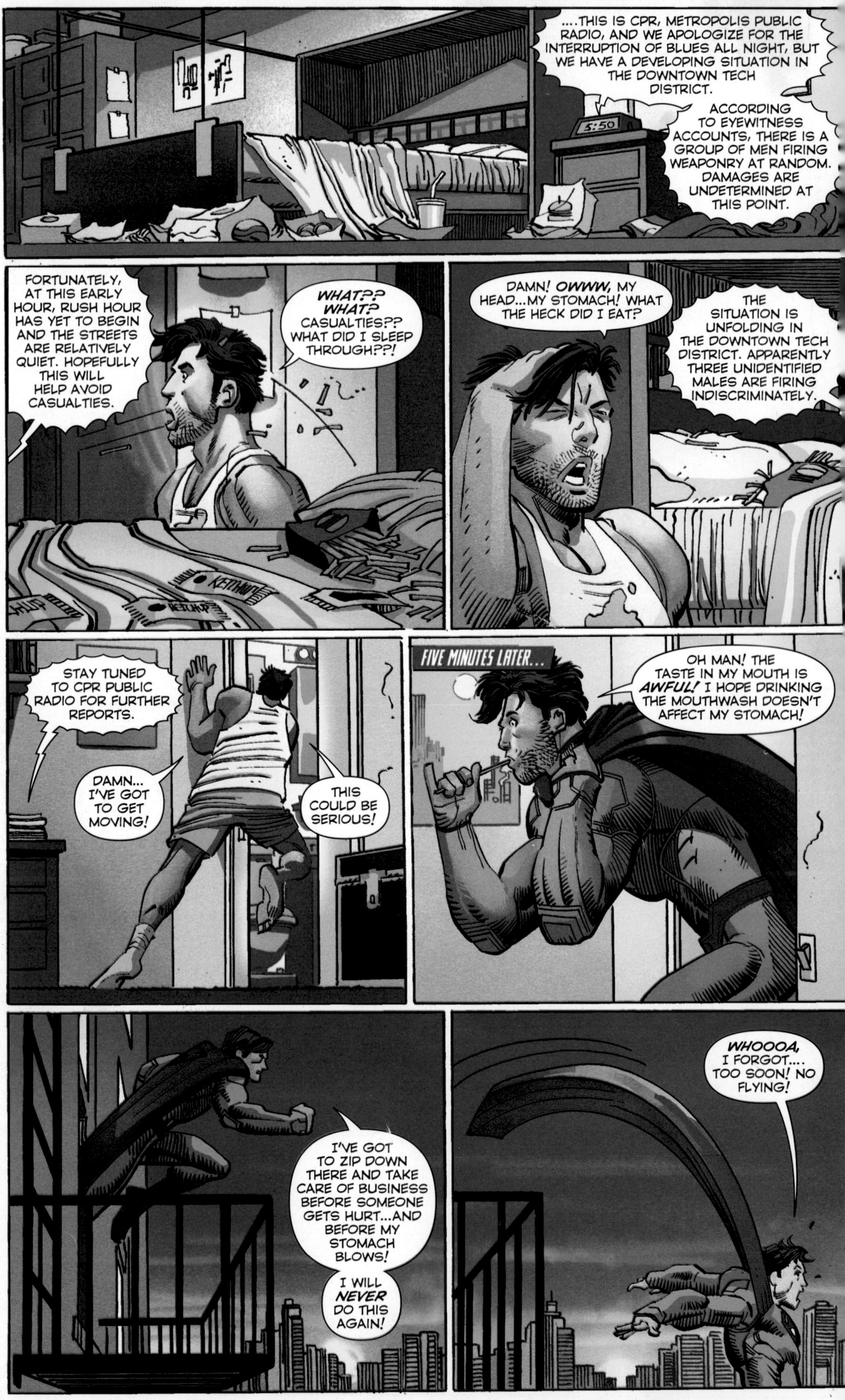
....THIS IS CPR, METROPOLIS PUBLIC RADIO, AND WE APOLOGIZE FOR THE INTERRUPTION OF BLUES ALL NIGHT, BUT WE HAVE A DEVELOPING SITUATION IN THE DOWNTOWN TECH DISTRICT.
ACCORDING TO EYEWITNESS ACCOUNTS, THERE IS A GROUP OF MEN FIRING WEAPONRY AT RANDOM. DAMAGES ARE UNDETERMINED AT THIS POINT.
5:50
FORTUNATELY, AT THIS EARLY HOUR, RUSH HOUR HAS YET TO BEGIN AND THE STREETS ARE RELATIVELY QUIET. HOPEFULLY THIS WILL HELP AVOID CASUALTIES.
WHAT?? WHAT? CASUALTIES?? WHAT DID I SLEEP THROUGH??!
DAMN! OWWW, MY HEAD...MY STOMACH! WHAT THE HECK DID I EAT?
THE SITUATION IS UNFOLDING IN THE DOWNTOWN TECH DISTRICT. APPARENTLY THREE UNIDENTIFIED MALES ARE FIRING INDISCRIMINATELY.
STAY TUNED TO CPR PUBLIC RADIO FOR FURTHER REPORTS.
DAMN... I'VE GOT TO GET MOVING!
THIS COULD BE SERIOUS!
FIVE MINUTES LATER...
OH MAN! THE TASTE IN MY MOUTH IS AWFUL! I HOPE DRINKING THE MOUTHWASH DOESN'T AFFECT MY STOMACH!
I'VE GOT TO ZIP DOWN THERE AND TAKE CARE OF BUSINESS BEFORE SOMEONE GETS HURT...AND BEFORE MY STOMACH BLOWS!
I WILL NEVER DO THIS AGAIN!
WHOOOA, I FORGOT.... TOO SOON! NO FLYING!

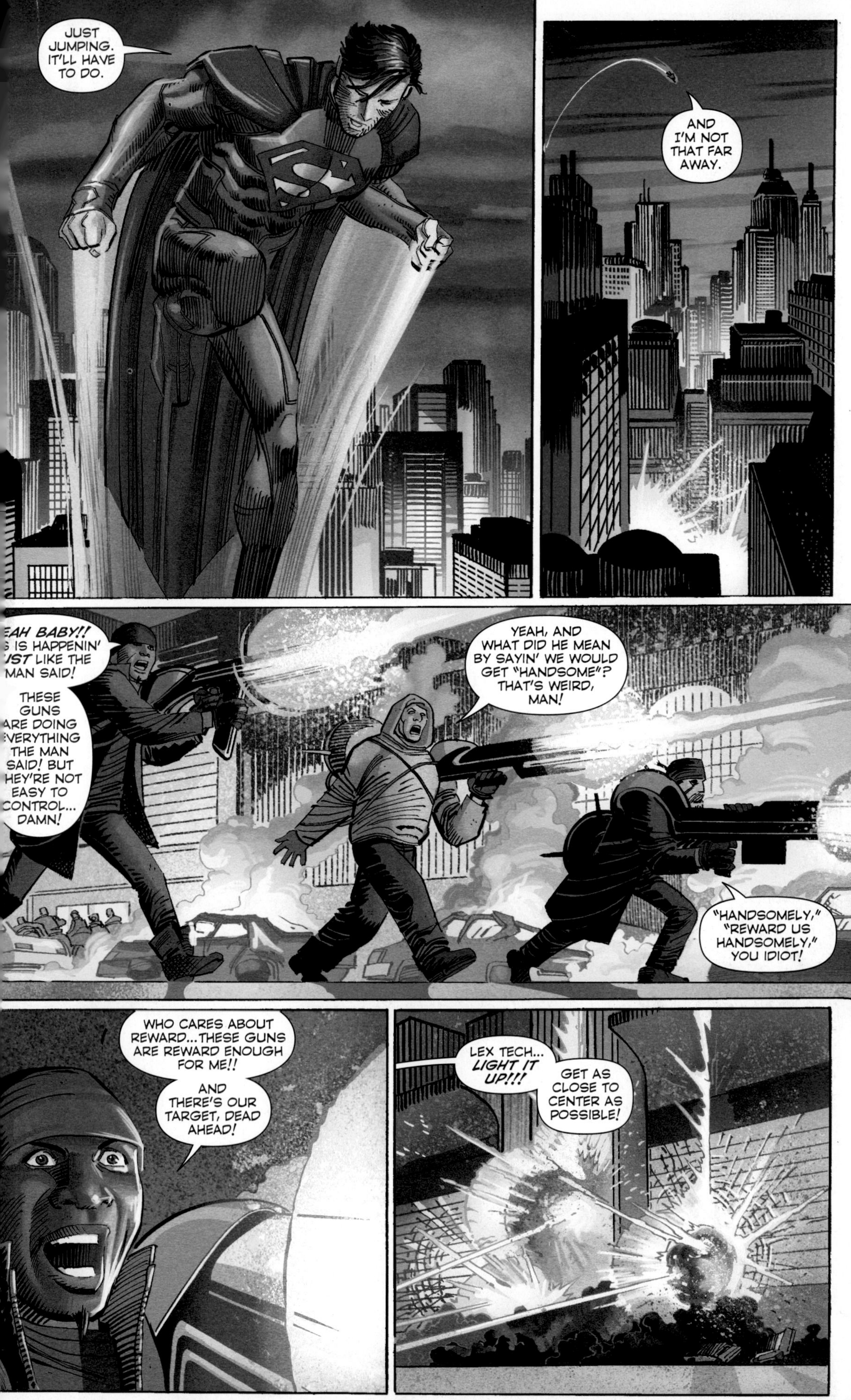
JUST JUMPING. IT'LL HAVE TO DO.
AND I'M NOT THAT FAR AWAY.
EAH BABY!! S IS HAPPENIN' UST LIKE THE MAN SAID!
THESE GUNS ARE DOING EVERYTHING THE MAN SAID! BUT HEY'RE NOT EASY TO CONTROL... DAMN!
YEAH, AND WHAT DID HE MEAN BY SAYIN' WE WOULD GET "HANDSOME"? THAT'S WEIRD, MAN!
"HANDSOMELY," "REWARD US HANDSOMELY," YOU IDIOT!
WHO CARES ABOUT REWARD...THESE GUNS ARE REWARD ENOUGH FOR ME!!
AND THERE'S OUR TARGET, DEAD AHEAD!
LEX TECH... LIGHT IT UP!!!
GET AS CLOSE TO CENTER AS POSSIBLE!

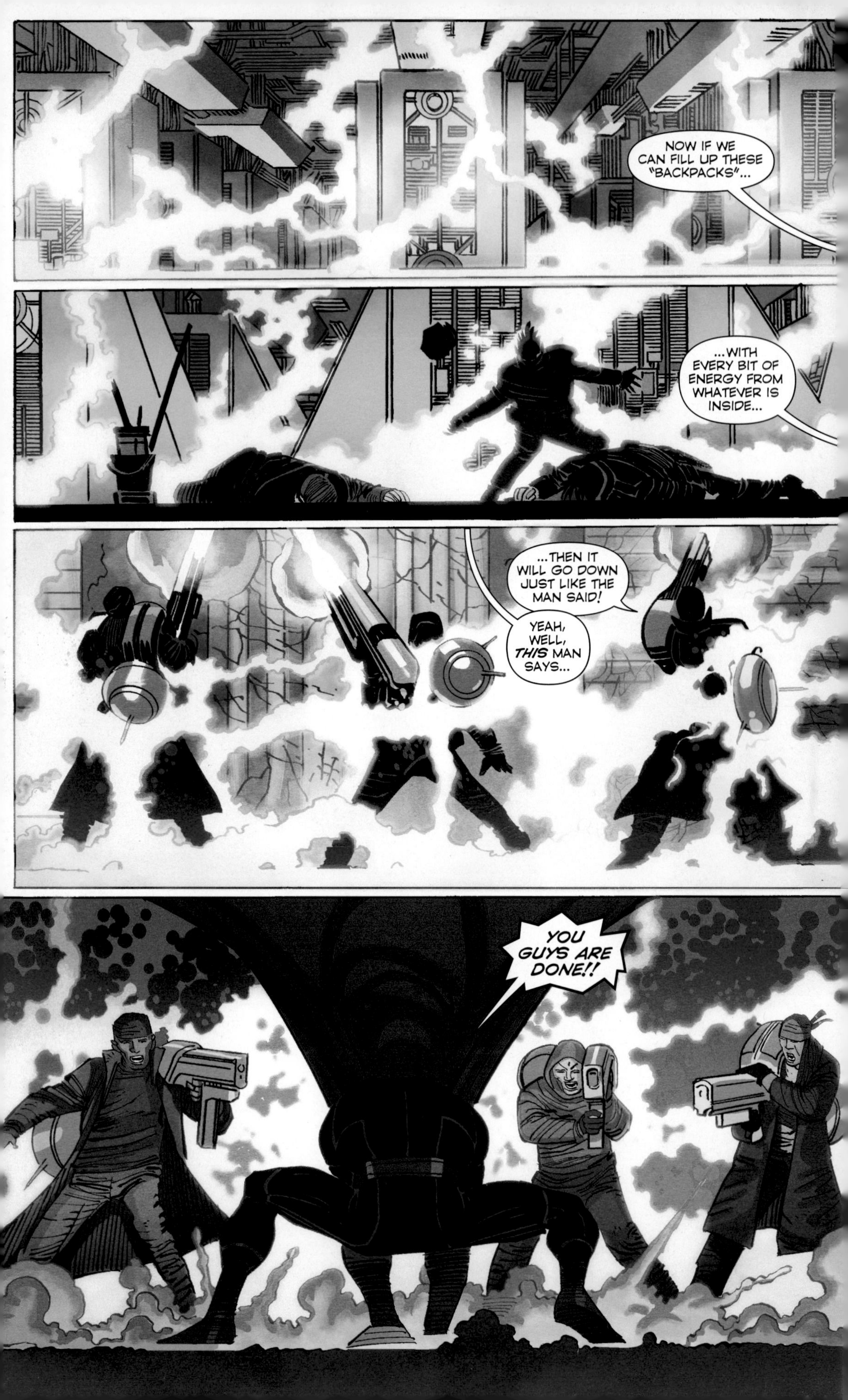
NOW IF WE CAN FILL UP THESE "BACKPACKS"...
...WITH EVERY BIT OF ENERGY FROM WHATEVER IS INSIDE...
...THEN IT WILL GO DOWN JUST LIKE THE MAN SAID!
YEAH, WELL, *THIS* MAN SAYS...
YOU GUYS ARE DONE!!

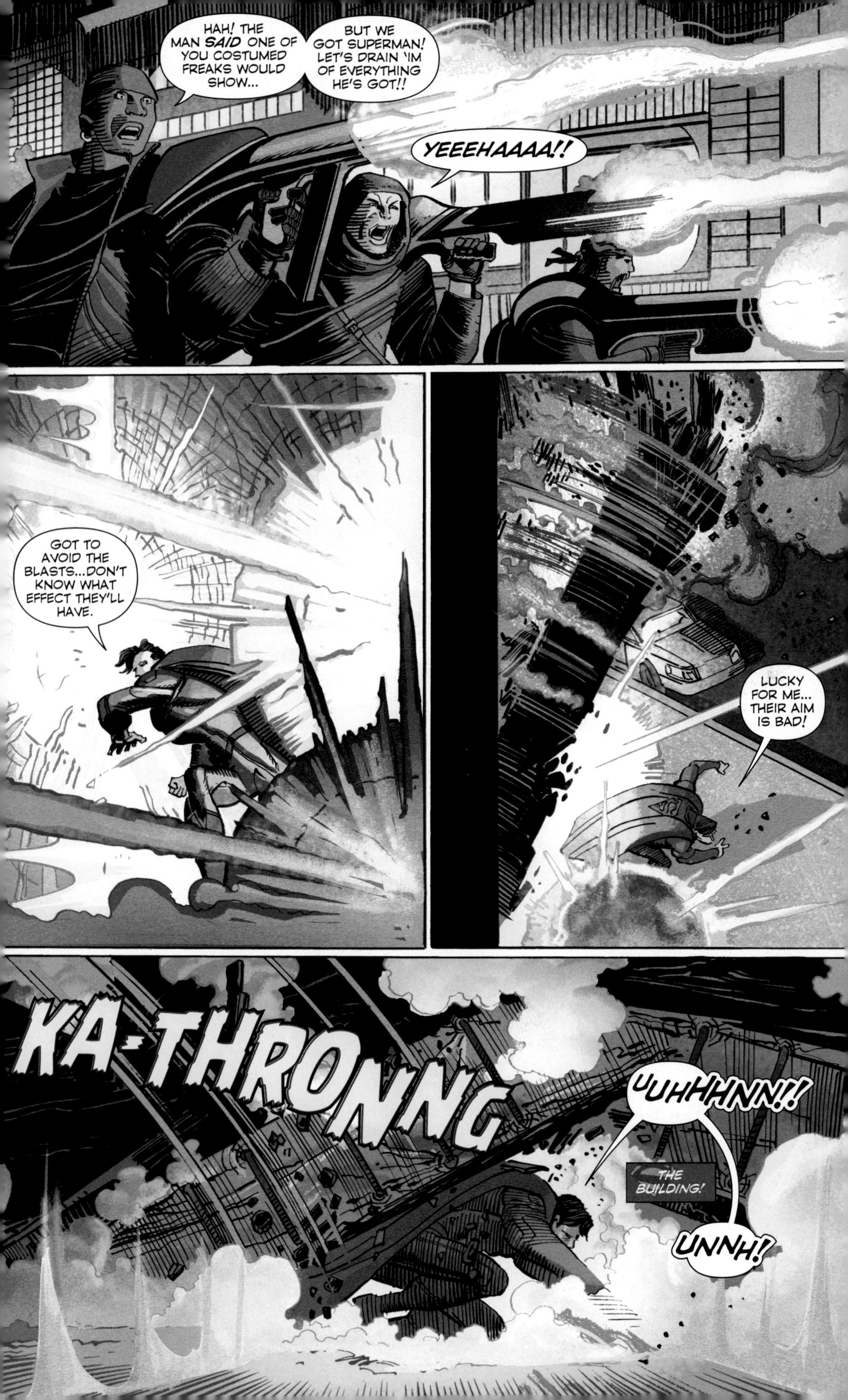
HAH! THE MAN SAID ONE OF YOU COSTUMED FREAKS WOULD SHOW...
BUT WE GOT SUPERMAN! LET'S DRAIN 'IM OF EVERYTHING HE'S GOT!!
YEEEHAAAA!!
GOT TO AVOID THE BLASTS...DON'T KNOW WHAT EFFECT THEY'LL HAVE.
LUCKY FOR ME... THEIR AIM IS BAD!
KA-THRONNG
UUHHHNN!!
THE BUILDING!
UNNH!

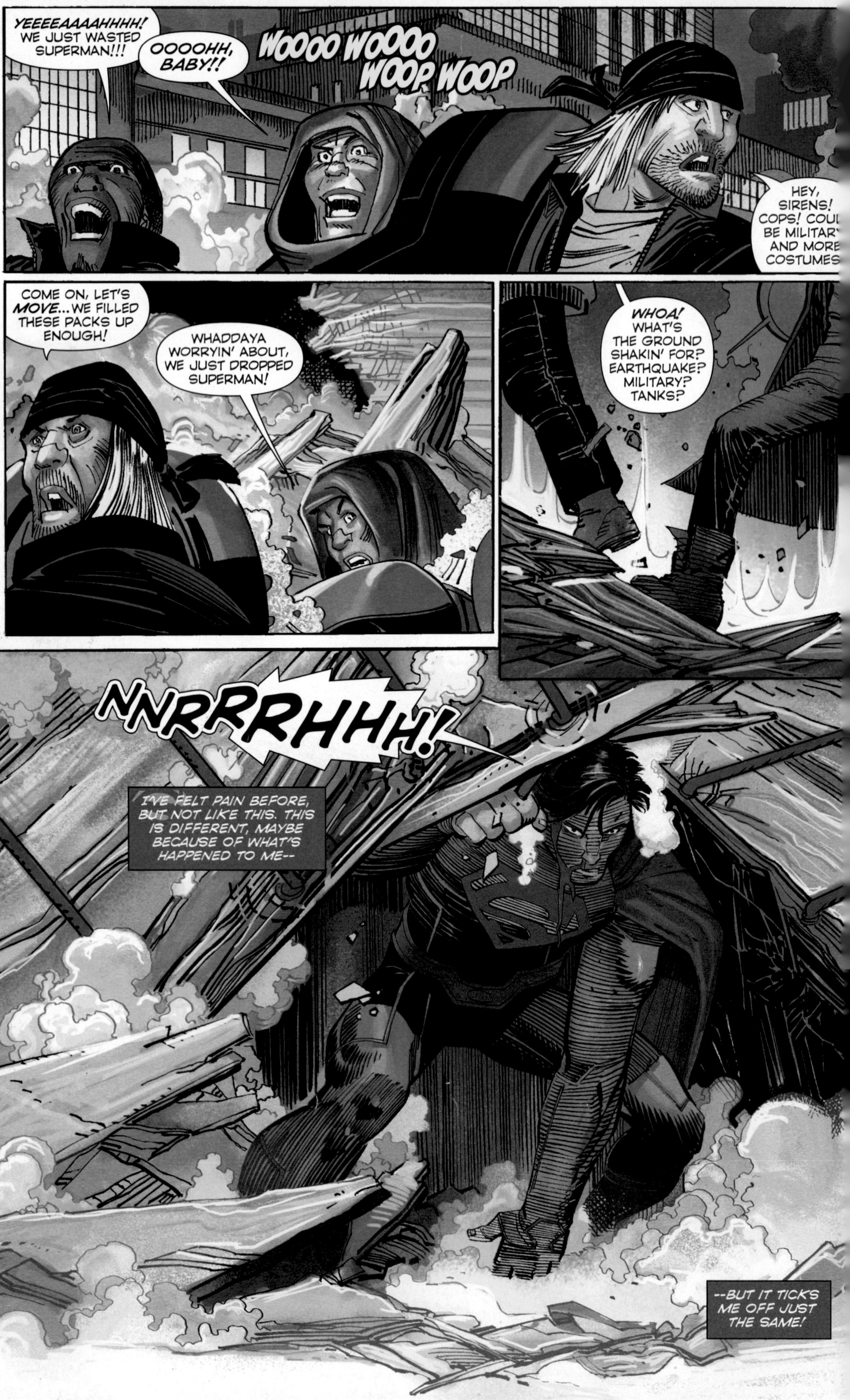
YEEEEAAAAHHHH! WE JUST WASTED SUPERMAN!!!
OOOOHH, BABY!!
WOOOO WOOOO WOOP WOOP
HEY, SIRENS! COPS! COUL BE MILITARY AND MORE COSTUMES
COME ON, LET'S MOVE...WE FILLED THESE PACKS UP ENOUGH!
WHADDAYA WORRYIN' ABOUT, WE JUST DROPPED SUPERMAN!
WHOA! WHAT'S THE GROUND SHAKIN' FOR? EARTHQUAKE? MILITARY? TANKS?
NNRRRRHHH!
I'VE FELT PAIN BEFORE, BUT NOT LIKE THIS. THIS IS DIFFERENT, MAYBE BECAUSE OF WHAT'S HAPPENED TO ME--
--BUT IT TICKS ME OFF JUST THE SAME!

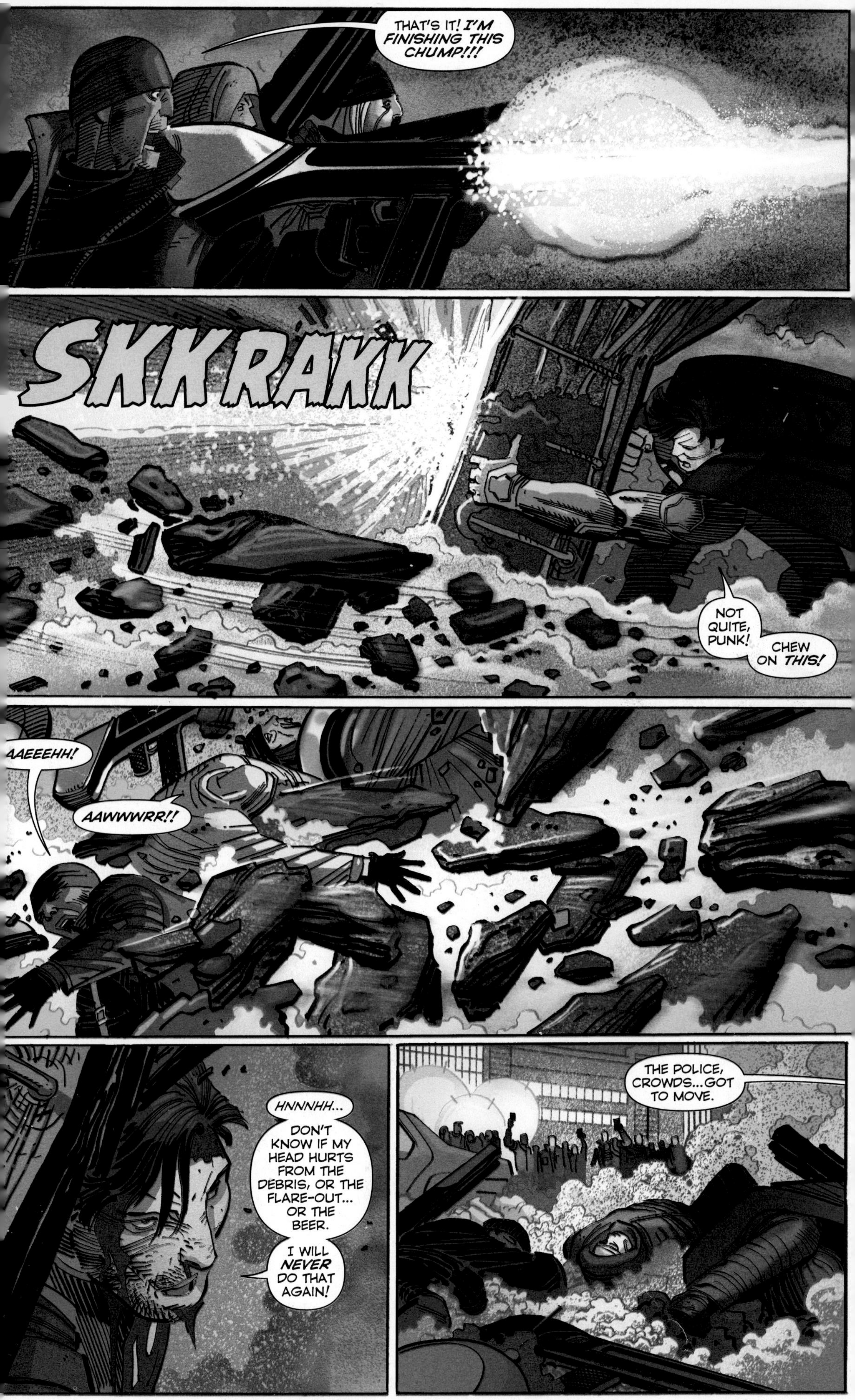
THAT'S IT! *I'M FINISHING THIS CHUMP!!!*
SKKRAKK
NOT QUITE, PUNK!
CHEW ON *THIS!*
AAEEEHH!
*AAWWWRR!!*
*HNNNHH...*
DON'T KNOW IF MY HEAD HURTS FROM THE DEBRIS, OR THE FLARE-OUT... OR THE BEER.
I WILL ***NEVER*** DO THAT AGAIN!
THE POLICE, CROWDS...GOT TO MOVE.

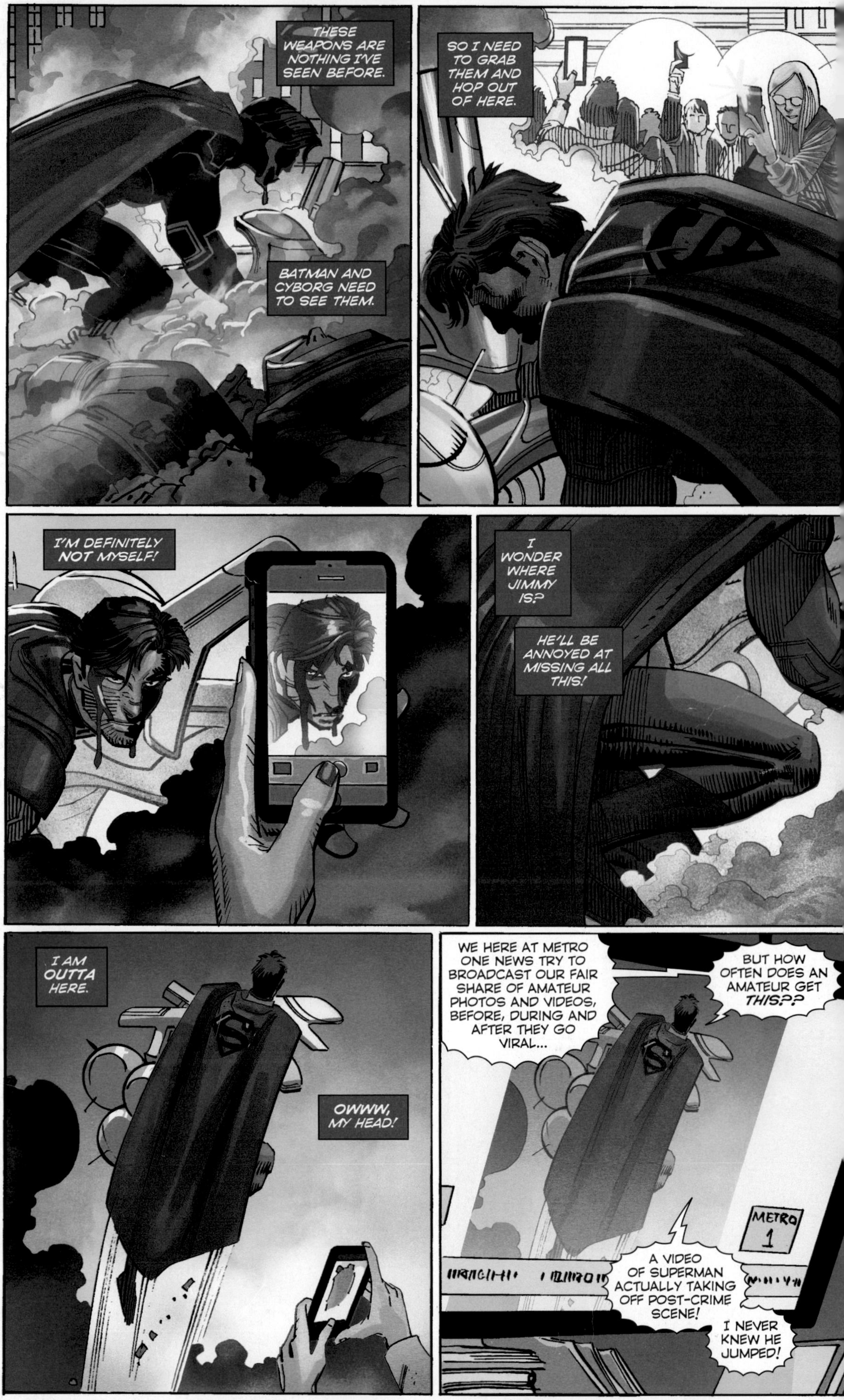
THESE WEAPONS ARE NOTHING I'VE SEEN BEFORE.
BATMAN AND CYBORG NEED TO SEE THEM.
SO I NEED TO GRAB THEM AND HOP OUT OF HERE.
I'M DEFINITELY NOT MYSELF!
I WONDER WHERE JIMMY IS?
HE'LL BE ANNOYED AT MISSING ALL THIS!
I AM OUTTA HERE.
OWWW, MY HEAD!
WE HERE AT METRO ONE NEWS TRY TO BROADCAST OUR FAIR SHARE OF AMATEUR PHOTOS AND VIDEOS, BEFORE, DURING AND AFTER THEY GO VIRAL...
BUT HOW OFTEN DOES AN AMATEUR GET THIS??
METRO 1
A VIDEO OF SUPERMAN ACTUALLY TAKING OFF POST-CRIME SCENE!
I NEVER KNEW HE JUMPED!

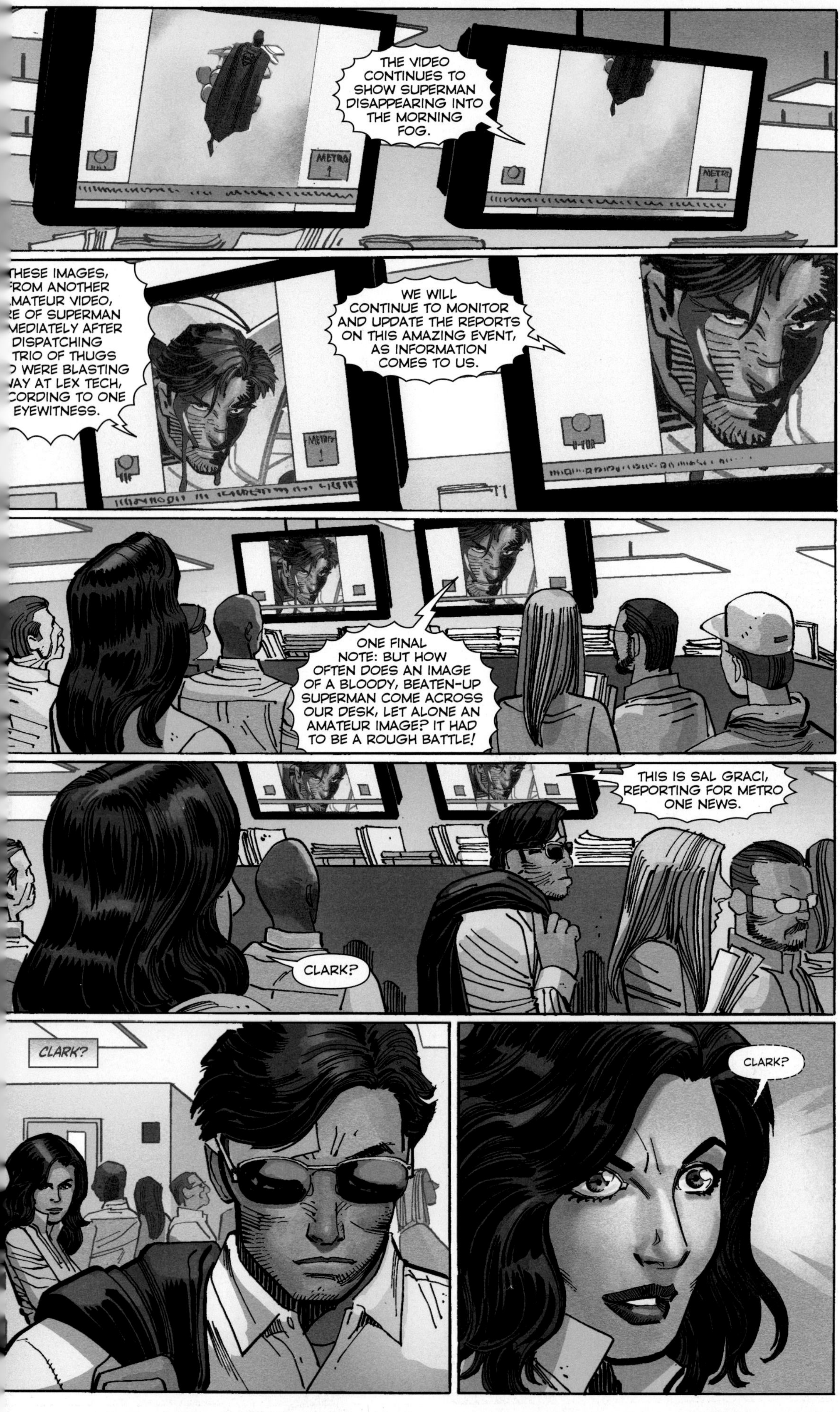
THE VIDEO CONTINUES TO SHOW SUPERMAN DISAPPEARING INTO THE MORNING FOG.
THESE IMAGES, FROM ANOTHER AMATEUR VIDEO, RE OF SUPERMAN MEDIATELY AFTER DISPATCHING TRIO OF THUGS WERE BLASTING WAY AT LEX TECH, CORDING TO ONE EYEWITNESS.
WE WILL CONTINUE TO MONITOR AND UPDATE THE REPORTS ON THIS AMAZING EVENT, AS INFORMATION COMES TO US.
ONE FINAL NOTE: BUT HOW OFTEN DOES AN IMAGE OF A BLOODY, BEATEN-UP SUPERMAN COME ACROSS OUR DESK, LET ALONE AN AMATEUR IMAGE? IT HAD TO BE A ROUGH BATTLE!
THIS IS SAL GRACI, REPORTING FOR METRO ONE NEWS.
CLARK?
CLARK?
CLARK?

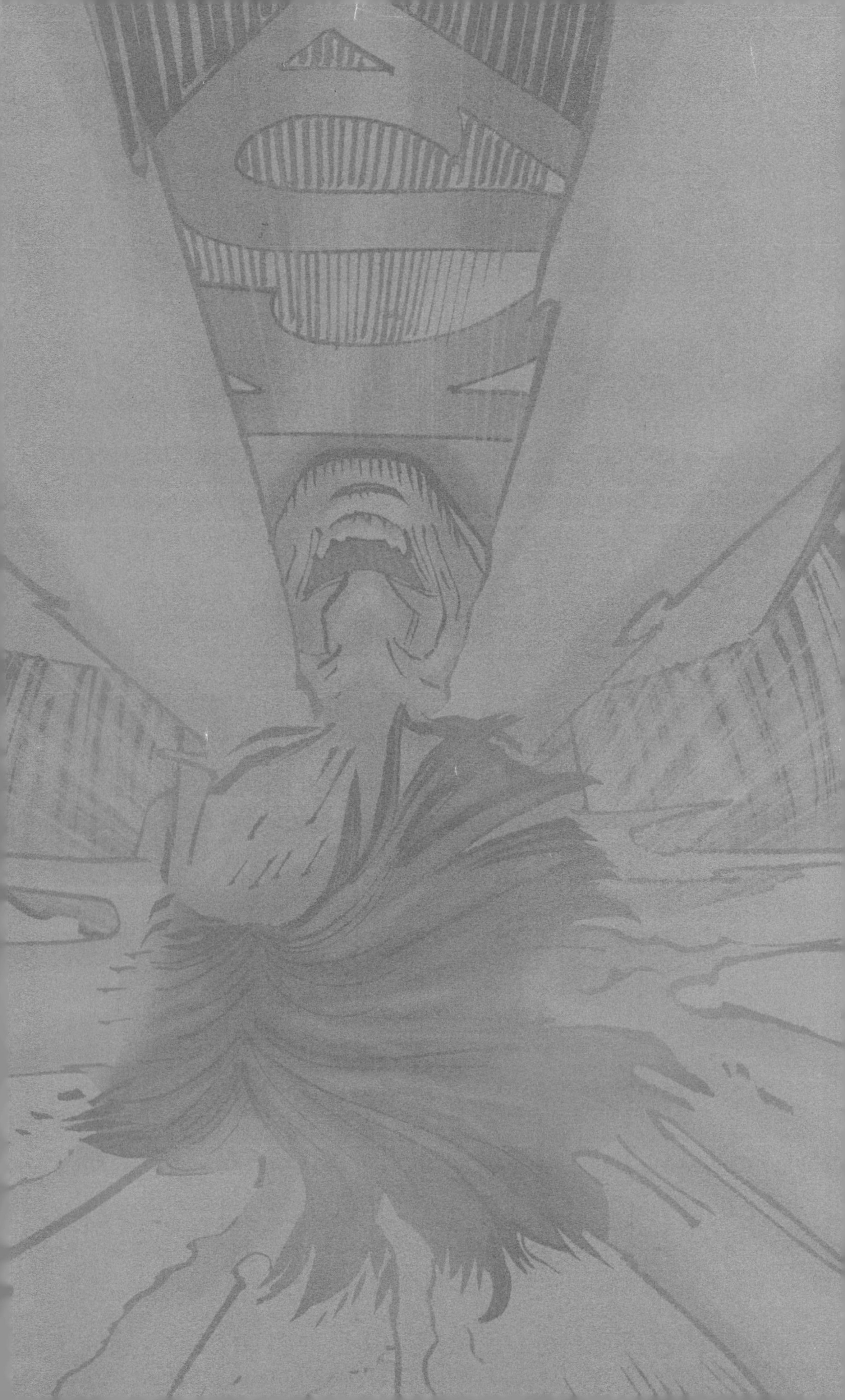

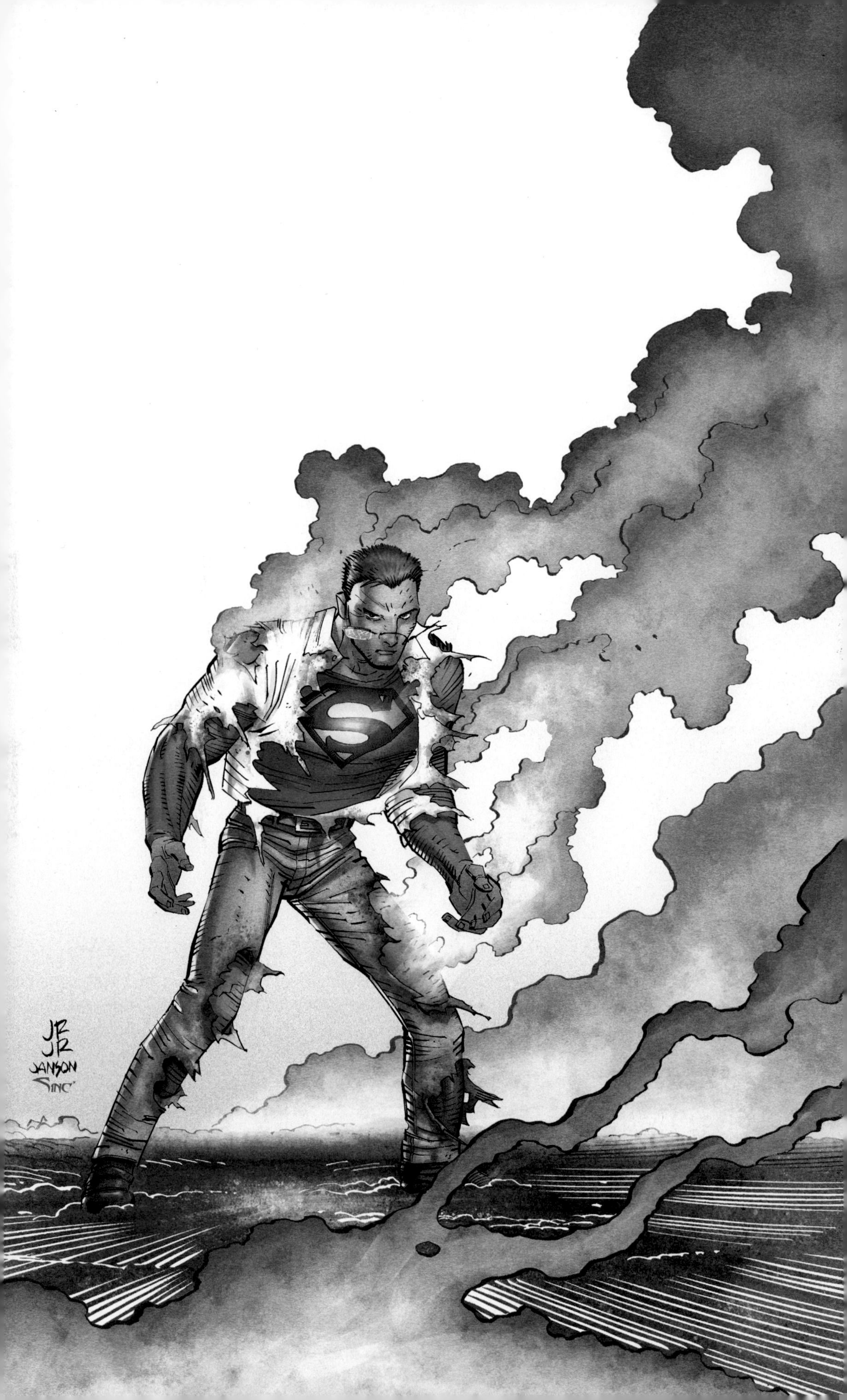
JR JR
JANSON
SINC'

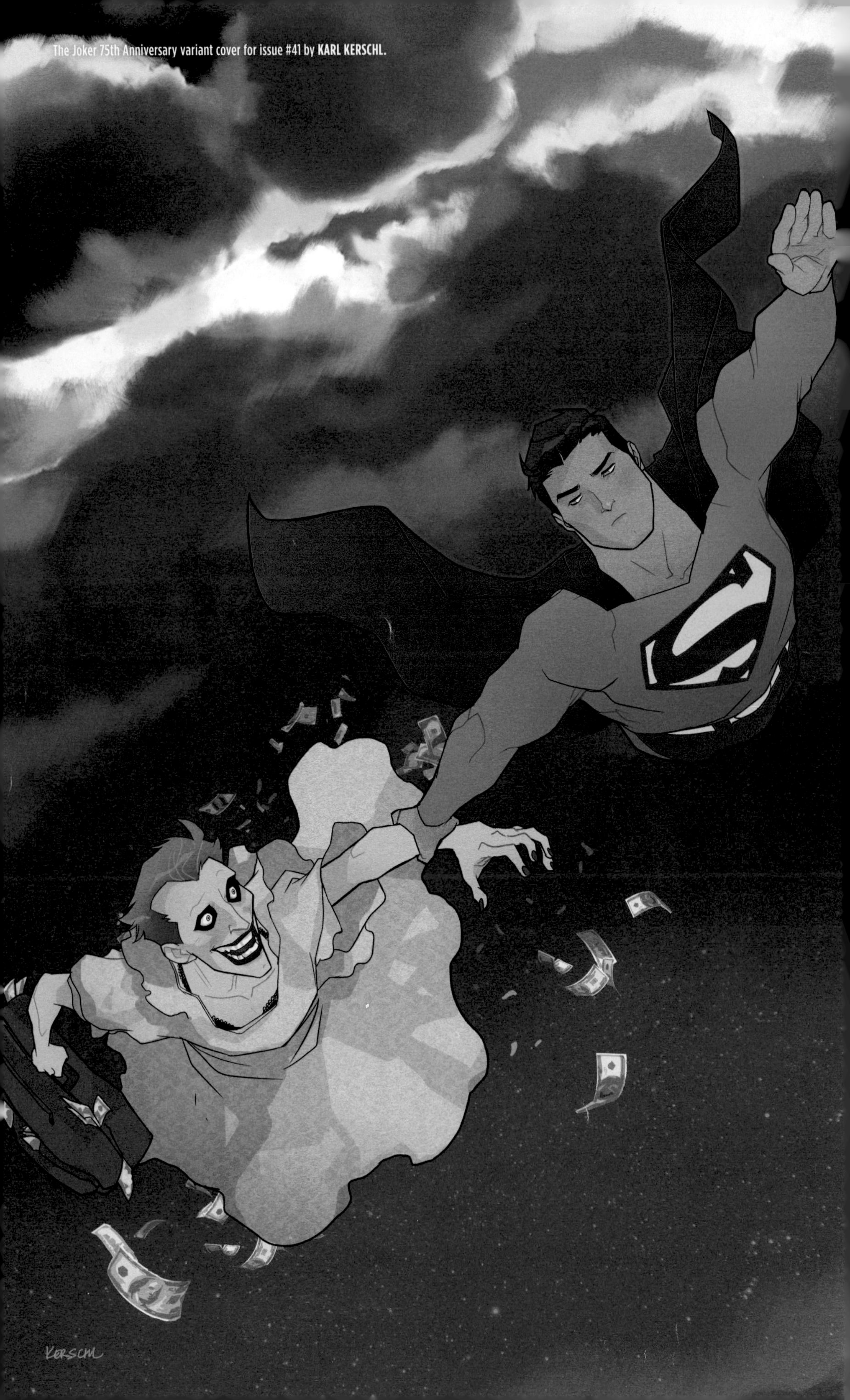
KERSCHL

The Joker 75th Anniversary variant cover for issue #41 by **KARL KERSCHL.**

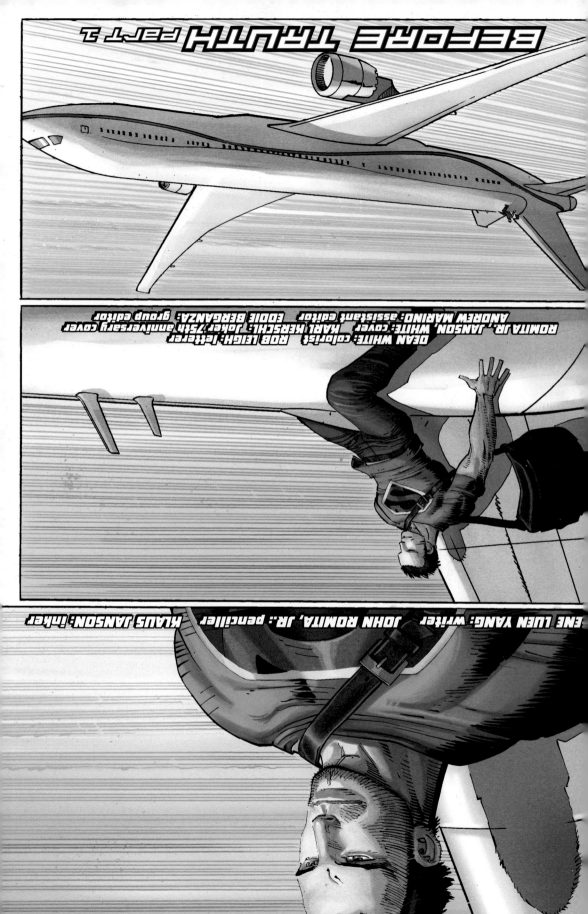

# BEFORE TRUTH Part 1

GENE LUEN YANG: writer    JOHN ROMITA, JR.: penciller    KLAUS JANSON: inker

DEAN WHITE: colorist    ROB LEIGH: letterer
ROMITA JR., JANSON, WHITE: cover    KARL KERSCHL: Joker 75th anniversary cover
ANDREW MARINO: assistant editor    EDDIE BERGANZA: group editor

AFTER EVERYTHING CHANGED.

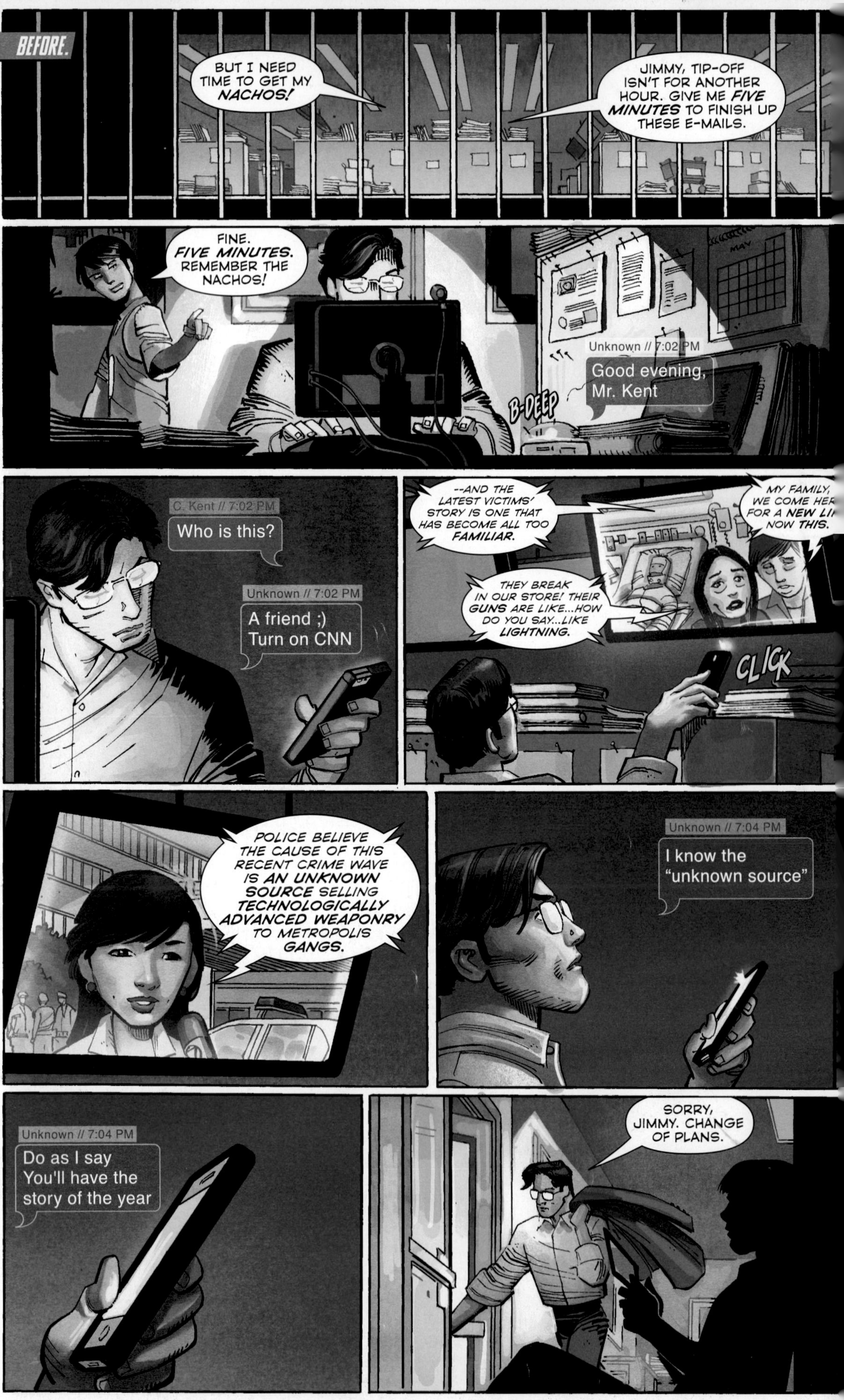
BEFORE.
BUT I NEED TIME TO GET MY *NACHOS!*
JIMMY, TIP-OFF ISN'T FOR ANOTHER HOUR. GIVE ME *FIVE MINUTES* TO FINISH UP THESE E-MAILS.
FINE. *FIVE MINUTES.* REMEMBER THE NACHOS!
Unknown // 7:02 PM
Good evening, Mr. Kent
B-DEEP
C. Kent // 7:02 PM
Who is this?
Unknown // 7:02 PM
A friend ;) Turn on CNN
--AND THE LATEST VICTIMS' STORY IS ONE THAT HAS BECOME ALL TOO *FAMILIAR.*
MY FAMILY, WE COME HER FOR A *NEW LI* NOW *THIS.*
THEY BREAK IN OUR STORE! THEIR *GUNS* ARE LIKE...HOW DO YOU SAY...LIKE *LIGHTNING.*
CLICK
POLICE BELIEVE THE CAUSE OF THIS RECENT CRIME WAVE IS *AN UNKNOWN SOURCE* SELLING *TECHNOLOGICALLY ADVANCED WEAPONRY* TO METROPOLIS *GANGS.*
Unknown // 7:04 PM
I know the "unknown source"
Unknown // 7:04 PM
Do as I say You'll have the story of the year
SORRY, JIMMY. CHANGE OF PLANS.

ZZZ-KRAT-KRACK

HA HA! IMPRESSIVE!

YOUR STAFF SENT US YOUR SPECIFICATIONS. GIVE IT A TRY.

COME. I HAVE A GIFT FOR YOU.

MY DEAR GENERAL, "SPIDER" IS THE WORLD'S MOST ADVANCED 3D PRINTER. IT ALLOWS US TO CUSTOMIZE EVERY WEAPON TO ITS USER.

WE HAVE TEN SUCH PRINTERS, ALL OPERATING AT DIFFERENT SCALES.

THE LARGEST ONE IS MOBILE. IT'S CAPABLE OF PRINTING A TANK.

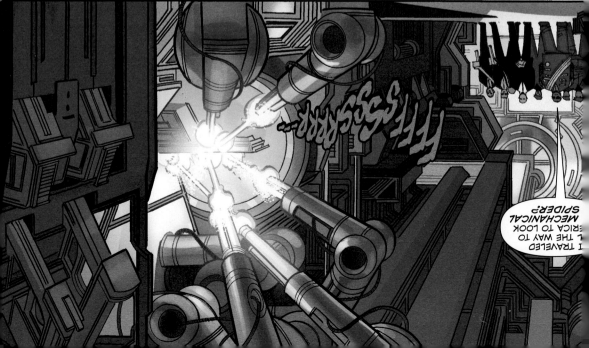

FFFSSSSRRR...

I TRAVELED ALL THE WAY TO AMERICA TO LOOK AT A MECHANICAL SPIDER?

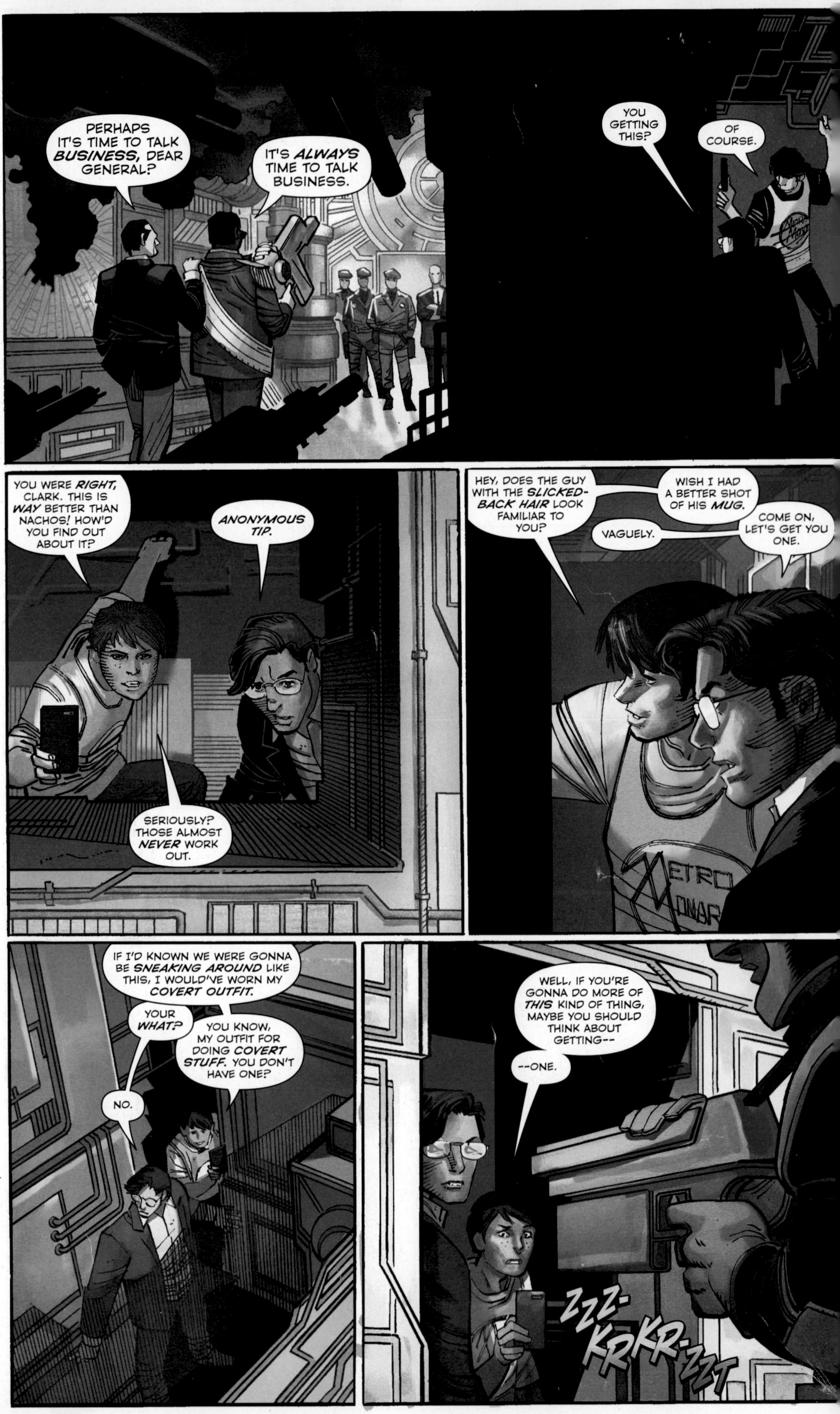
PERHAPS IT'S TIME TO TALK BUSINESS, DEAR GENERAL?
IT'S ALWAYS TIME TO TALK BUSINESS.
YOU GETTING THIS?
OF COURSE.
YOU WERE RIGHT, CLARK. THIS IS WAY BETTER THAN NACHOS! HOW'D YOU FIND OUT ABOUT IT?
ANONYMOUS TIP.
SERIOUSLY? THOSE ALMOST NEVER WORK OUT.
HEY, DOES THE GUY WITH THE SLICKED-BACK HAIR LOOK FAMILIAR TO YOU?
WISH I HAD A BETTER SHOT OF HIS MUG.
VAGUELY.
COME ON, LET'S GET YOU ONE.
IF I'D KNOWN WE WERE GONNA BE SNEAKING AROUND LIKE THIS, I WOULD'VE WORN MY COVERT OUTFIT.
YOUR WHAT?
YOU KNOW, MY OUTFIT FOR DOING COVERT STUFF. YOU DON'T HAVE ONE?
NO.
WELL, IF YOU'RE GONNA DO MORE OF THIS KIND OF THING, MAYBE YOU SHOULD THINK ABOUT GETTING--
--ONE.
ZZZ-KRKR-ZZT

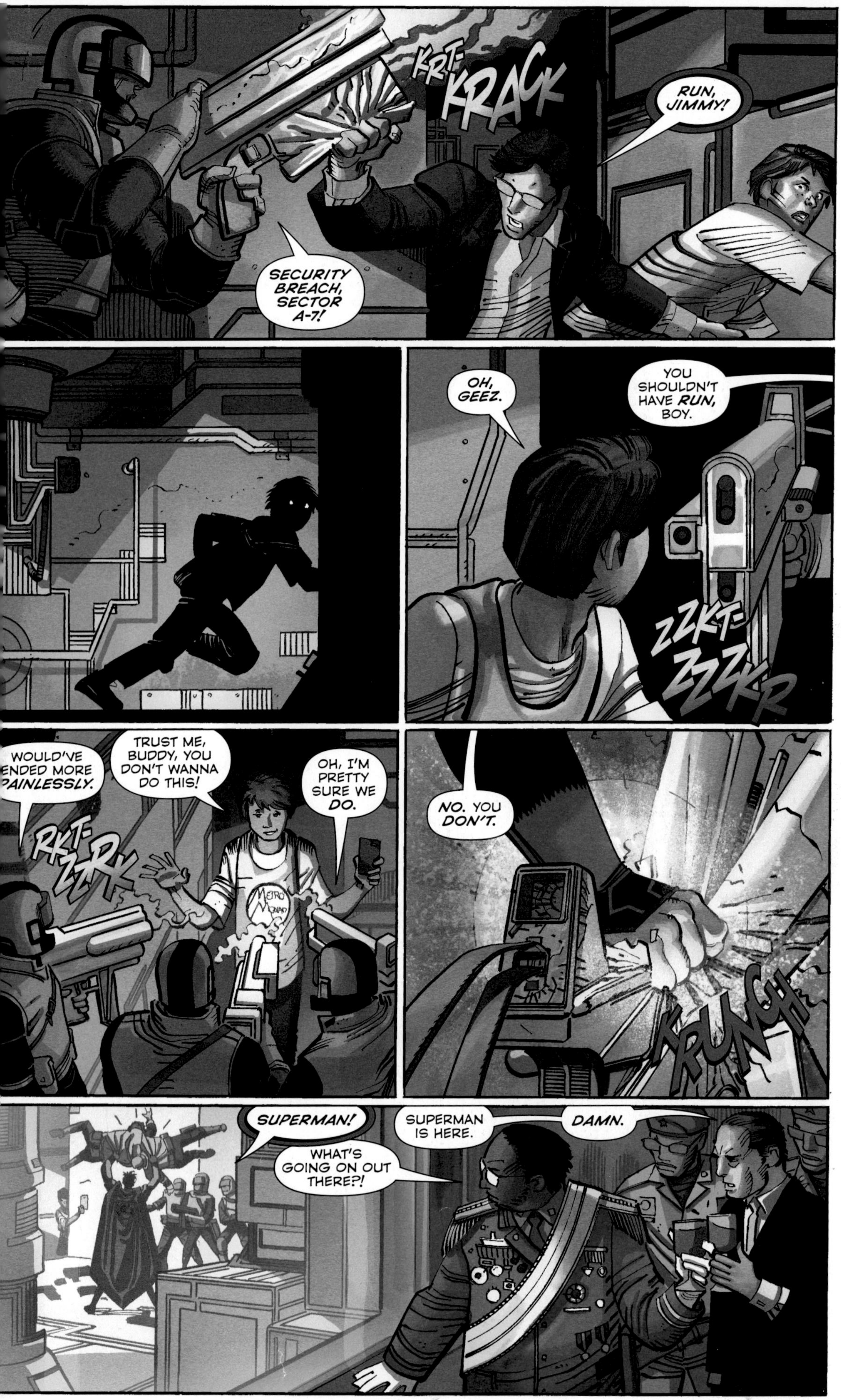
KRT-KRACK
RUN, JIMMY!
SECURITY BREACH, SECTOR A-7!
OH, GEEZ.
YOU SHOULDN'T HAVE RUN, BOY.
ZZKT-ZZZKR
WOULD'VE ENDED MORE PAINLESSLY.
TRUST ME, BUDDY, YOU DON'T WANNA DO THIS!
OH, I'M PRETTY SURE WE DO.
RKT-ZZRK
NO. YOU DON'T.
KRUNCH
SUPERMAN!
WHAT'S GOING ON OUT THERE?!
SUPERMAN IS HERE.
DAMN.

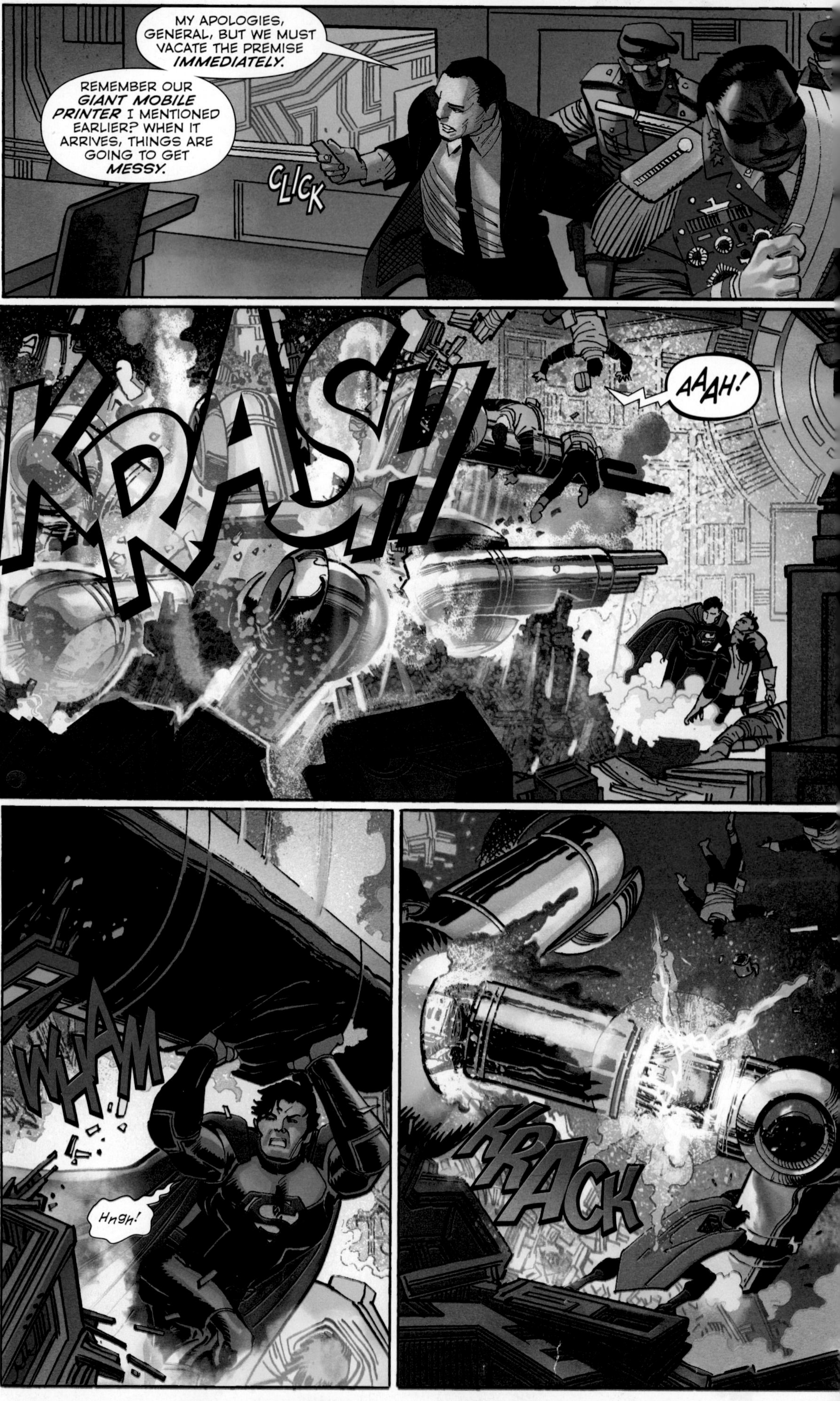
MY APOLOGIES, GENERAL, BUT WE MUST VACATE THE PREMISE IMMEDIATELY.
REMEMBER OUR GIANT MOBILE PRINTER I MENTIONED EARLIER? WHEN IT ARRIVES, THINGS ARE GOING TO GET MESSY.
CLICK
KRASH!
AAAH!
WHAM
Hngh!
KRACK

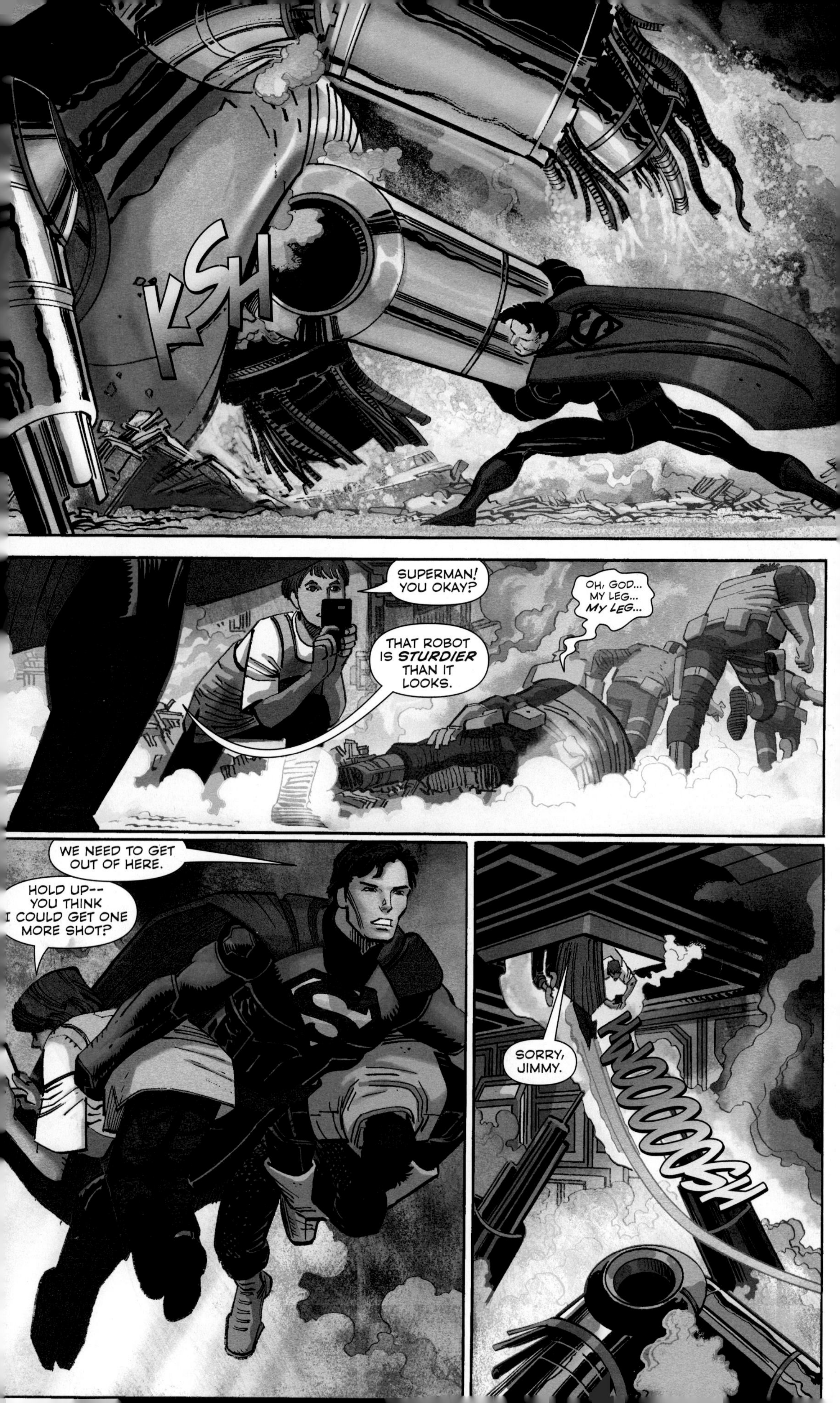
KSH
SUPERMAN! YOU OKAY?
THAT ROBOT IS *STURDIER* THAN IT LOOKS.
OH, GOD... MY LEG... *MY LEG...*
WE NEED TO GET OUT OF HERE.
HOLD UP-- YOU THINK I COULD GET ONE MORE SHOT?
SORRY, JIMMY.
HWOOOOOSH

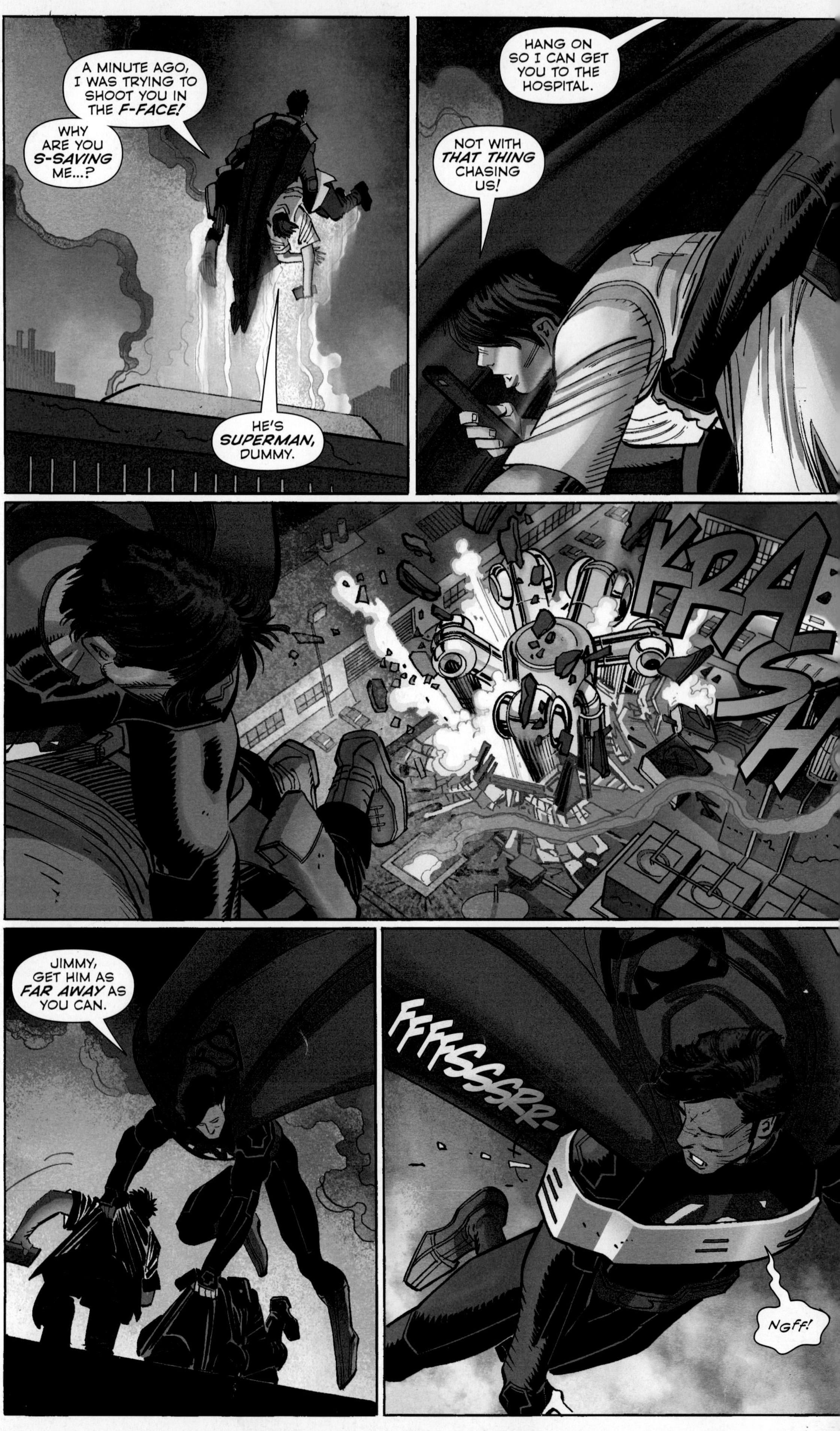

A MINUTE AGO, I WAS TRYING TO SHOOT YOU IN THE *F-FACE!*
WHY ARE YOU *S-SAVING* ME...?
HE'S *SUPERMAN,* DUMMY.
HANG ON SO I CAN GET YOU TO THE HOSPITAL.
NOT WITH *THAT THING* CHASING US!
KRASH
JIMMY, GET HIM AS *FAR AWAY* AS YOU CAN.
FFFSSSRR-
NGff!

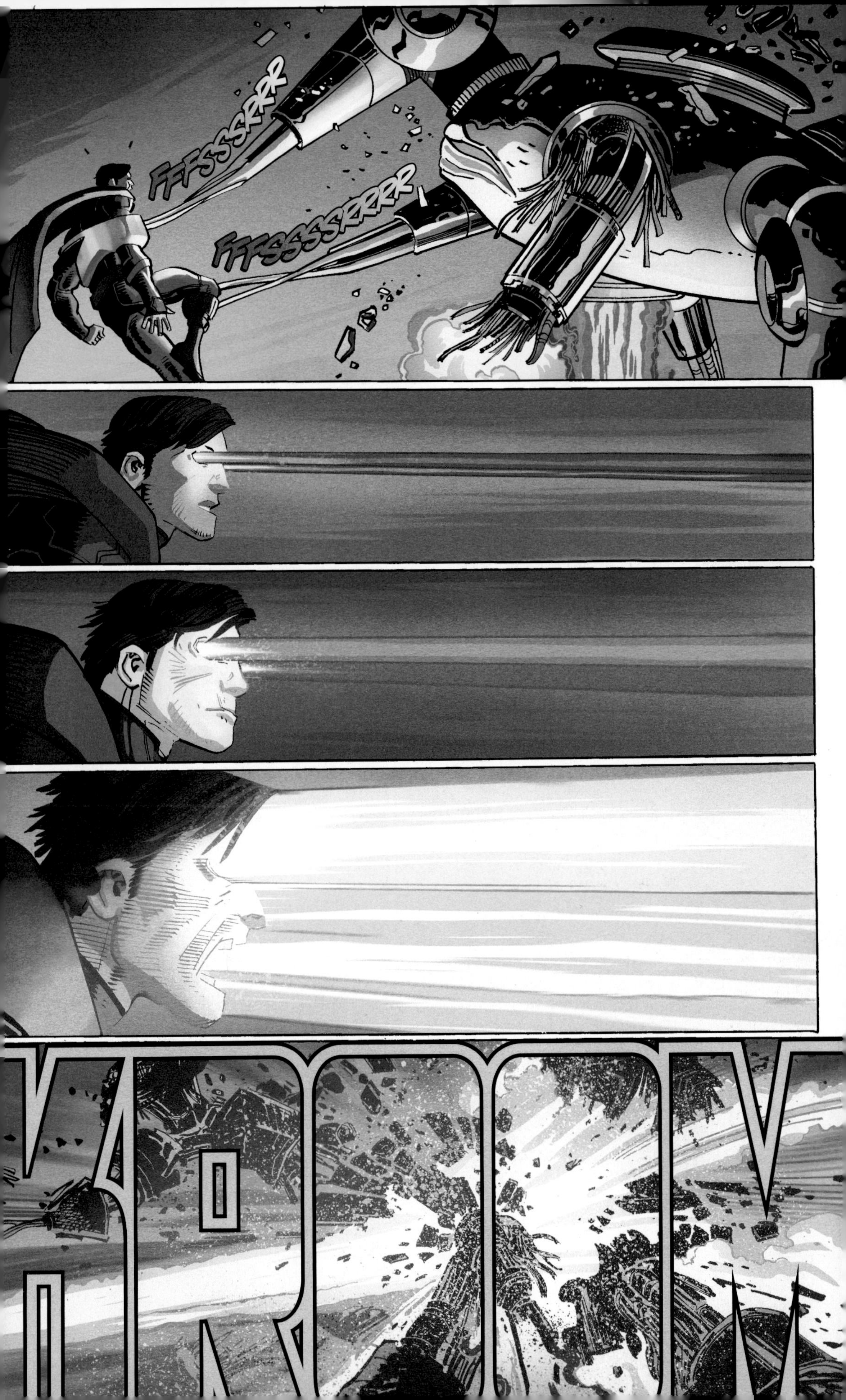
FFFSSSRRR
FFFSSSSSRRRR

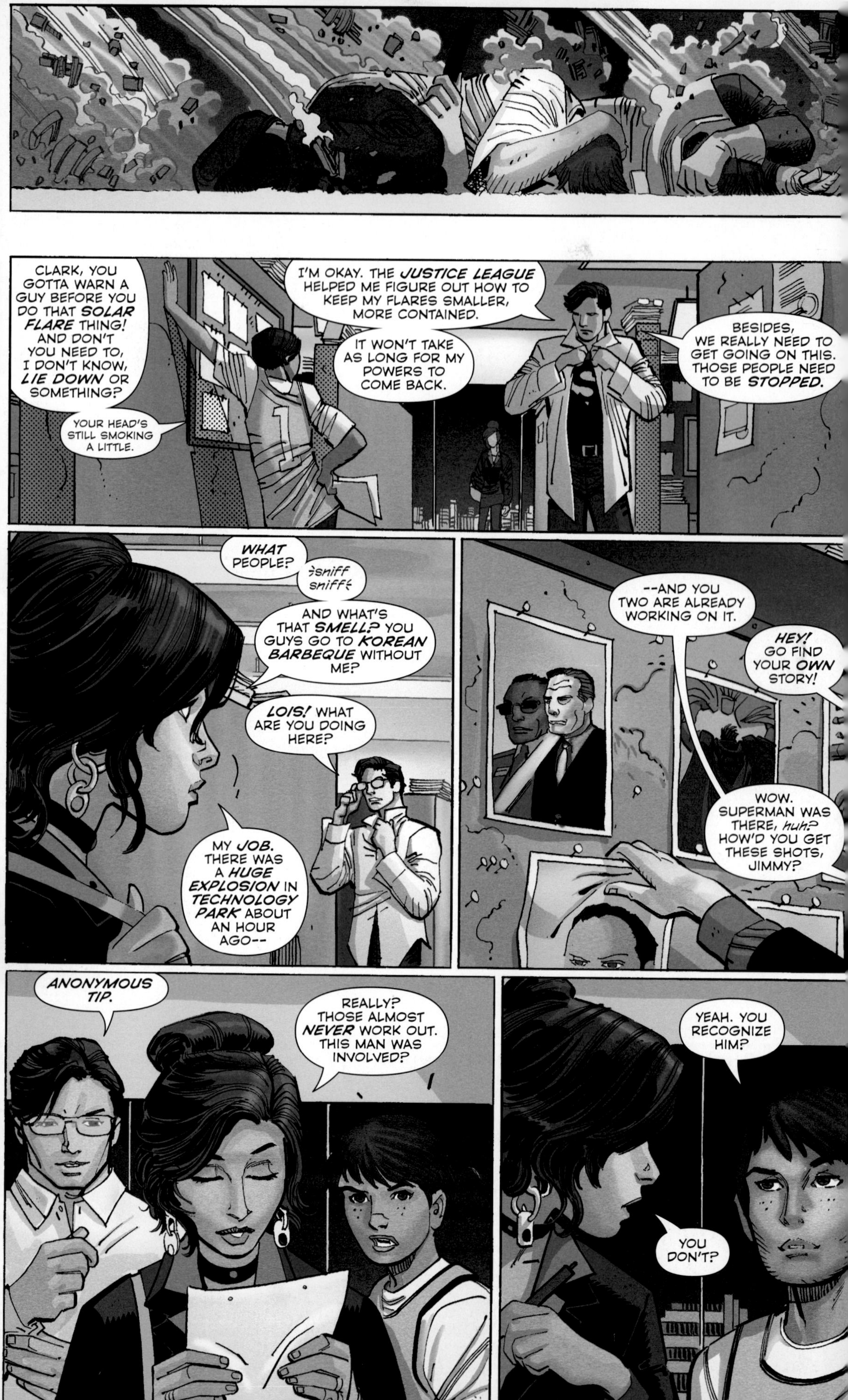
CLARK, YOU GOTTA WARN A GUY BEFORE YOU DO THAT *SOLAR FLARE* THING! AND DON'T YOU NEED TO, I DON'T KNOW, *LIE DOWN* OR SOMETHING?
YOUR HEAD'S STILL SMOKING A LITTLE.
I'M OKAY. THE *JUSTICE LEAGUE* HELPED ME FIGURE OUT HOW TO KEEP MY FLARES SMALLER, MORE CONTAINED.
IT WON'T TAKE AS LONG FOR MY POWERS TO COME BACK.
BESIDES, WE REALLY NEED TO GET GOING ON THIS. THOSE PEOPLE NEED TO BE *STOPPED.*
*WHAT* PEOPLE?
⋟sniff sniff⋞
AND WHAT'S THAT *SMELL?* YOU GUYS GO TO *KOREAN BARBEQUE* WITHOUT ME?
*LOIS!* WHAT ARE YOU DOING HERE?
MY *JOB.* THERE WAS A *HUGE EXPLOSION* IN *TECHNOLOGY PARK* ABOUT AN HOUR AGO--
--AND YOU TWO ARE ALREADY WORKING ON IT.
*HEY!* GO FIND YOUR *OWN* STORY!
WOW. SUPERMAN WAS THERE, *huh?* HOW'D YOU GET THESE SHOTS, JIMMY?
*ANONYMOUS TIP.*
REALLY? THOSE ALMOST *NEVER* WORK OUT. THIS MAN WAS INVOLVED?
YEAH. YOU RECOGNIZE HIM?
YOU DON'T?

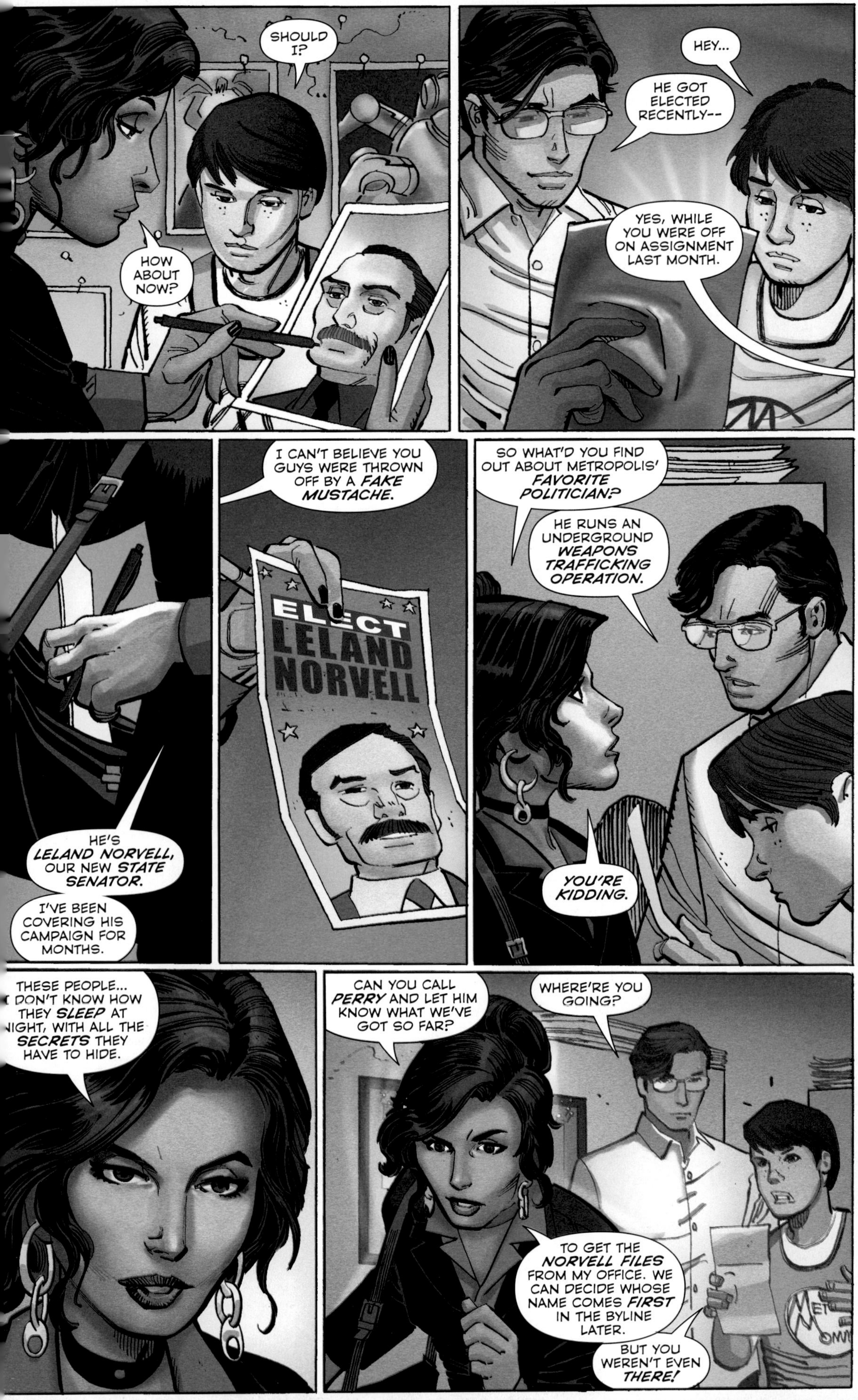
SHOULD I?
HOW ABOUT NOW?
HEY...
HE GOT ELECTED RECENTLY--
YES, WHILE YOU WERE OFF ON ASSIGNMENT LAST MONTH.
HE'S *LELAND NORVELL,* OUR NEW *STATE SENATOR.*
I'VE BEEN COVERING HIS CAMPAIGN FOR MONTHS.
I CAN'T BELIEVE YOU GUYS WERE THROWN OFF BY A *FAKE MUSTACHE.*
ELECT LELAND NORVELL
SO WHAT'D YOU FIND OUT ABOUT METROPOLIS' *FAVORITE POLITICIAN?*
HE RUNS AN UNDERGROUND *WEAPONS TRAFFICKING OPERATION.*
*YOU'RE KIDDING.*
THESE PEOPLE... I DON'T KNOW HOW THEY *SLEEP* AT NIGHT, WITH ALL THE *SECRETS* THEY HAVE TO HIDE.
CAN YOU CALL *PERRY* AND LET HIM KNOW WHAT WE'VE GOT SO FAR?
WHERE'RE YOU GOING?
TO GET THE *NORVELL FILES* FROM MY OFFICE. WE CAN DECIDE WHOSE NAME COMES *FIRST* IN THE BYLINE LATER.
BUT YOU WEREN'T EVEN *THERE!*

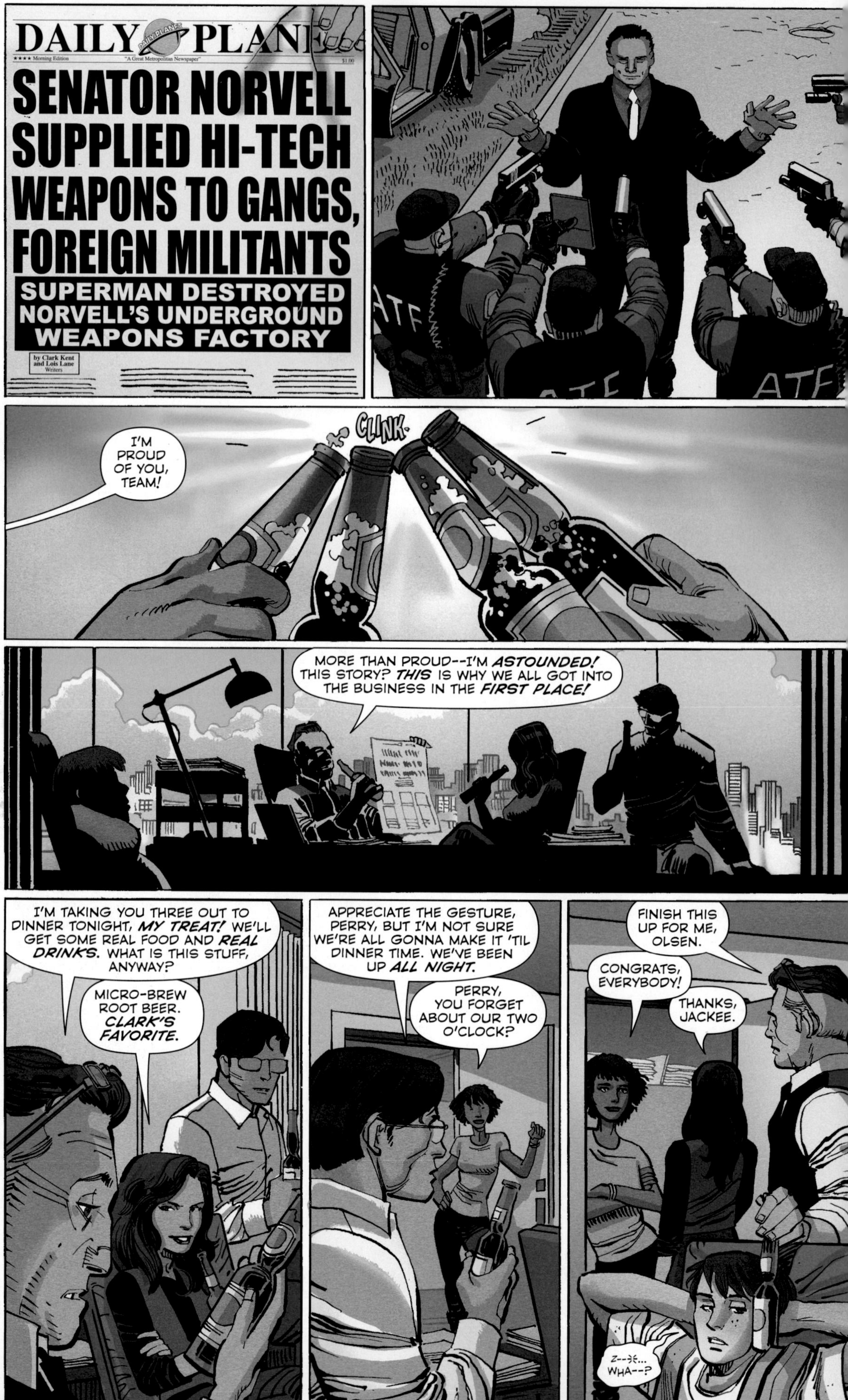
DAILY PLANET
★★★★ Morning Edition
"A Great Metropolitan Newspaper"
$1.00
SENATOR NORVELL SUPPLIED HI-TECH WEAPONS TO GANGS, FOREIGN MILITANTS
SUPERMAN DESTROYED NORVELL'S UNDERGROUND WEAPONS FACTORY
by Clark Kent and Lois Lane Writers
ATF
ATF
ATF
CLINK
I'M PROUD OF YOU, TEAM!
MORE THAN PROUD--I'M ASTOUNDED! THIS STORY? THIS IS WHY WE ALL GOT INTO THE BUSINESS IN THE FIRST PLACE!
I'M TAKING YOU THREE OUT TO DINNER TONIGHT, MY TREAT! WE'LL GET SOME REAL FOOD AND REAL DRINKS. WHAT IS THIS STUFF, ANYWAY?
MICRO-BREW ROOT BEER. CLARK'S FAVORITE.
APPRECIATE THE GESTURE, PERRY, BUT I'M NOT SURE WE'RE ALL GONNA MAKE IT 'TIL DINNER TIME. WE'VE BEEN UP ALL NIGHT.
PERRY, YOU FORGET ABOUT OUR TWO O'CLOCK?
FINISH THIS UP FOR ME, OLSEN.
CONGRATS, EVERYBODY!
THANKS, JACKEE.
Z--✳... WHA--?

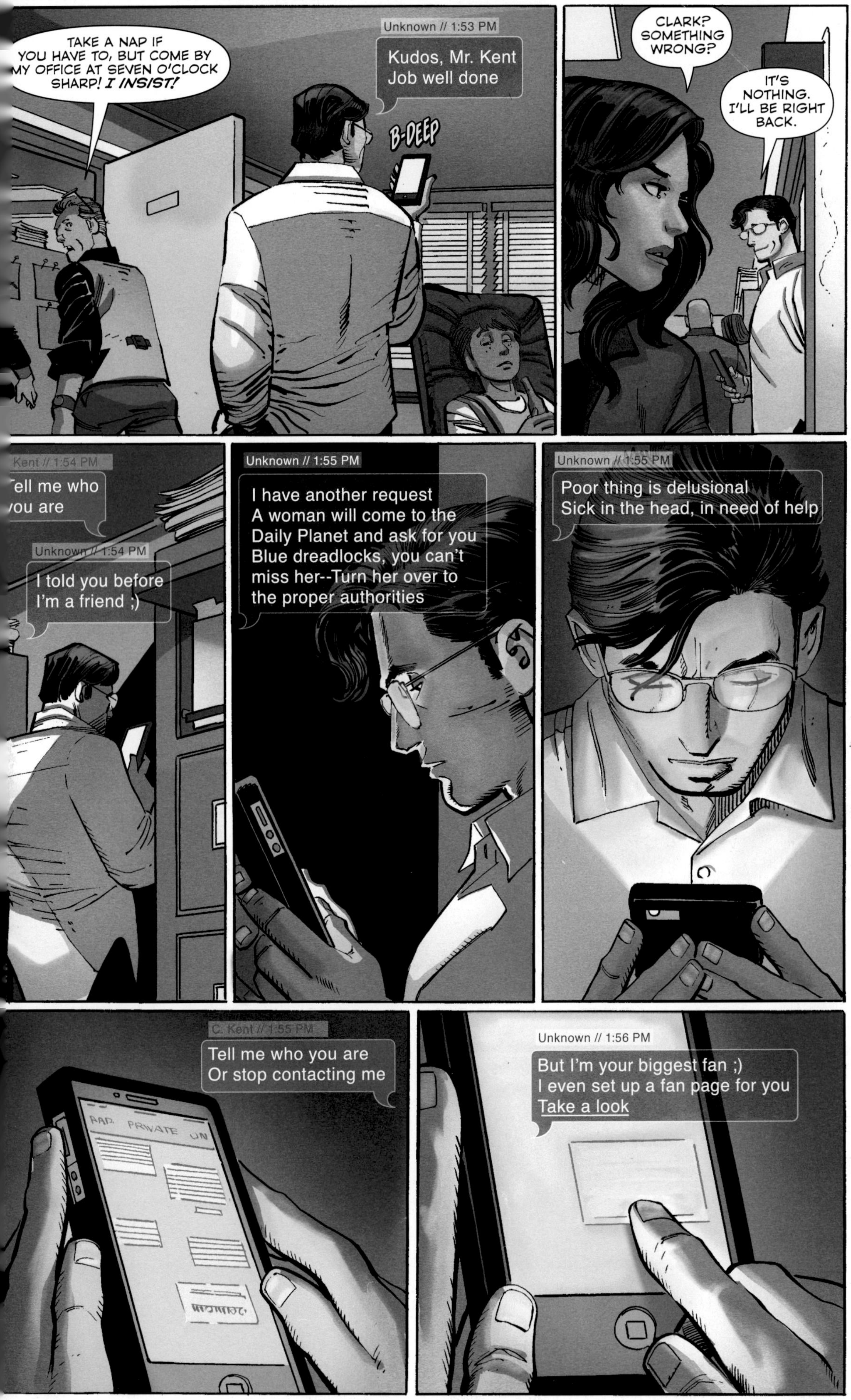
TAKE A NAP IF YOU HAVE TO, BUT COME BY MY OFFICE AT SEVEN O'CLOCK SHARP! I INSIST!
Unknown // 1:53 PM
Kudos, Mr. Kent
Job well done
B-DEEP
CLARK? SOMETHING WRONG?
IT'S NOTHING. I'LL BE RIGHT BACK.
Kent // 1:54 PM
Tell me who you are
Unknown // 1:54 PM
I told you before
I'm a friend ;)
Unknown // 1:55 PM
I have another request
A woman will come to the Daily Planet and ask for you
Blue dreadlocks, you can't miss her--Turn her over to the proper authorities
Unknown // 1:55 PM
Poor thing is delusional
Sick in the head, in need of help
C. Kent // 1:55 PM
Tell me who you are
Or stop contacting me
Unknown // 1:56 PM
But I'm your biggest fan ;)
I even set up a fan page for you
Take a look

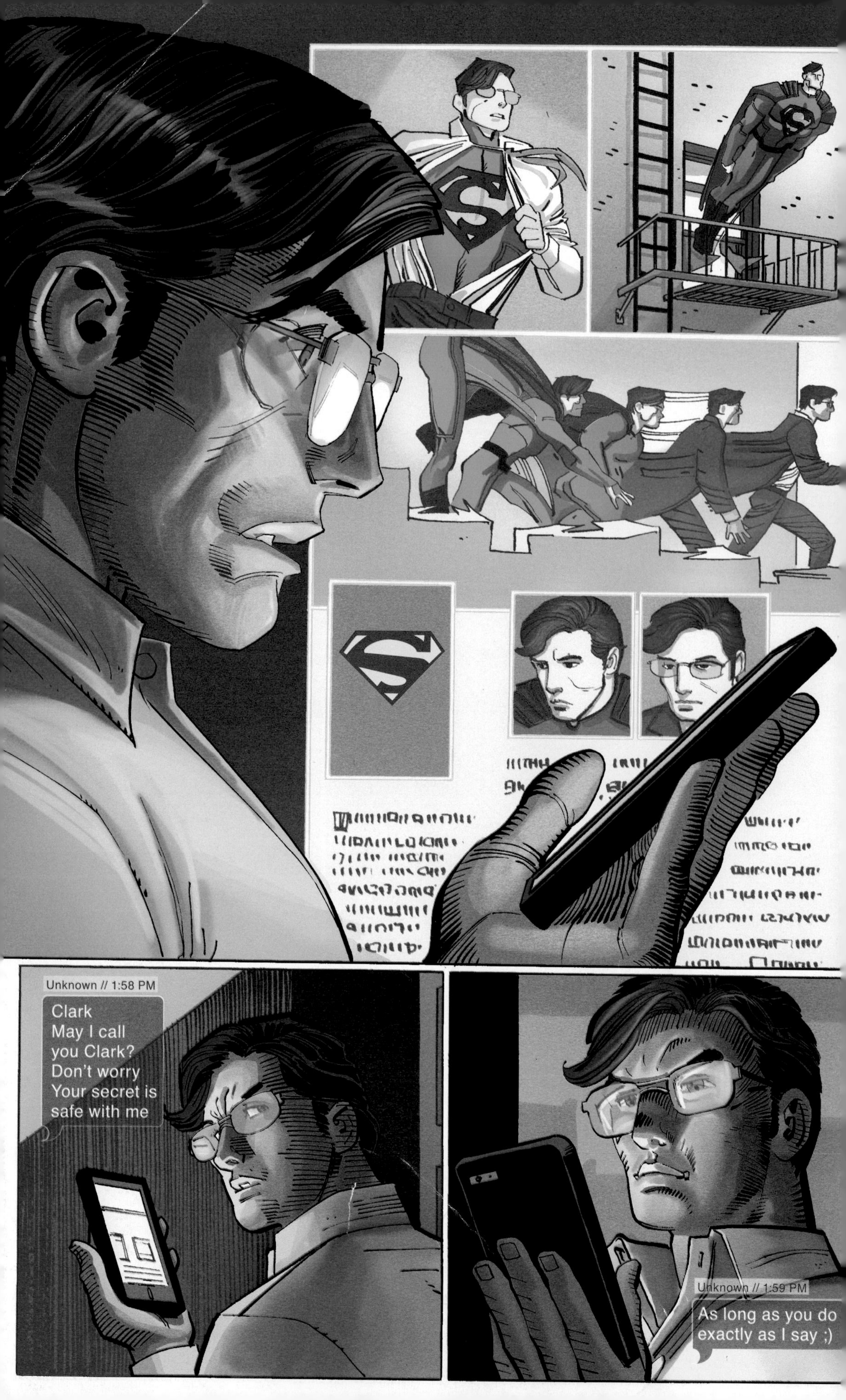
Unknown // 1:58 PM
Clark
May I call
you Clark?
Don't worry
Your secret is
safe with me
Unknown // 1:59 PM
As long as you do
exactly as I say ;)

CLARK KENT

JIMMY, I NEED A FAVOR.

MR. KENT? SOMEONE'S HERE TO SEE YOU.

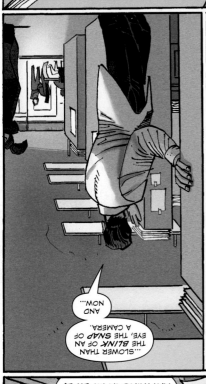

...AND NOW...

"...SLOWER THAN THE BLINK OF AN EYE, THE SNAP OF A CAMERA.

WHAT'S GOING ON?

MAYBE IT'S MY FAULT...EVER SINCE I STARTED FLARING, I'VE BEEN SLOWER...

COME ON, CLARK, YOU GOTTA BELIEVE ME.

I'M YOUR BEST FRIEND.

YOU KNOW HOW DANGEROUS IT'D BE IF THE WRONG PEOPLE FIND OUT!

NO, OF COURSE NOT!

THINK HARD! DID YOU EVER SLIP UP! ACCIDENTALLY TIP SOMEBODY OFF?

I SWEAR, I'VE NEVER BEEN SO CAREFUL ABOUT ANYTHING IN MY LIFE!

JIMMY, WAKE UP!

WHAT...?

ABOUT ME! DID YOU TELL ANYONE?!

JIMMY, DID YOU TELL ANYONE?!

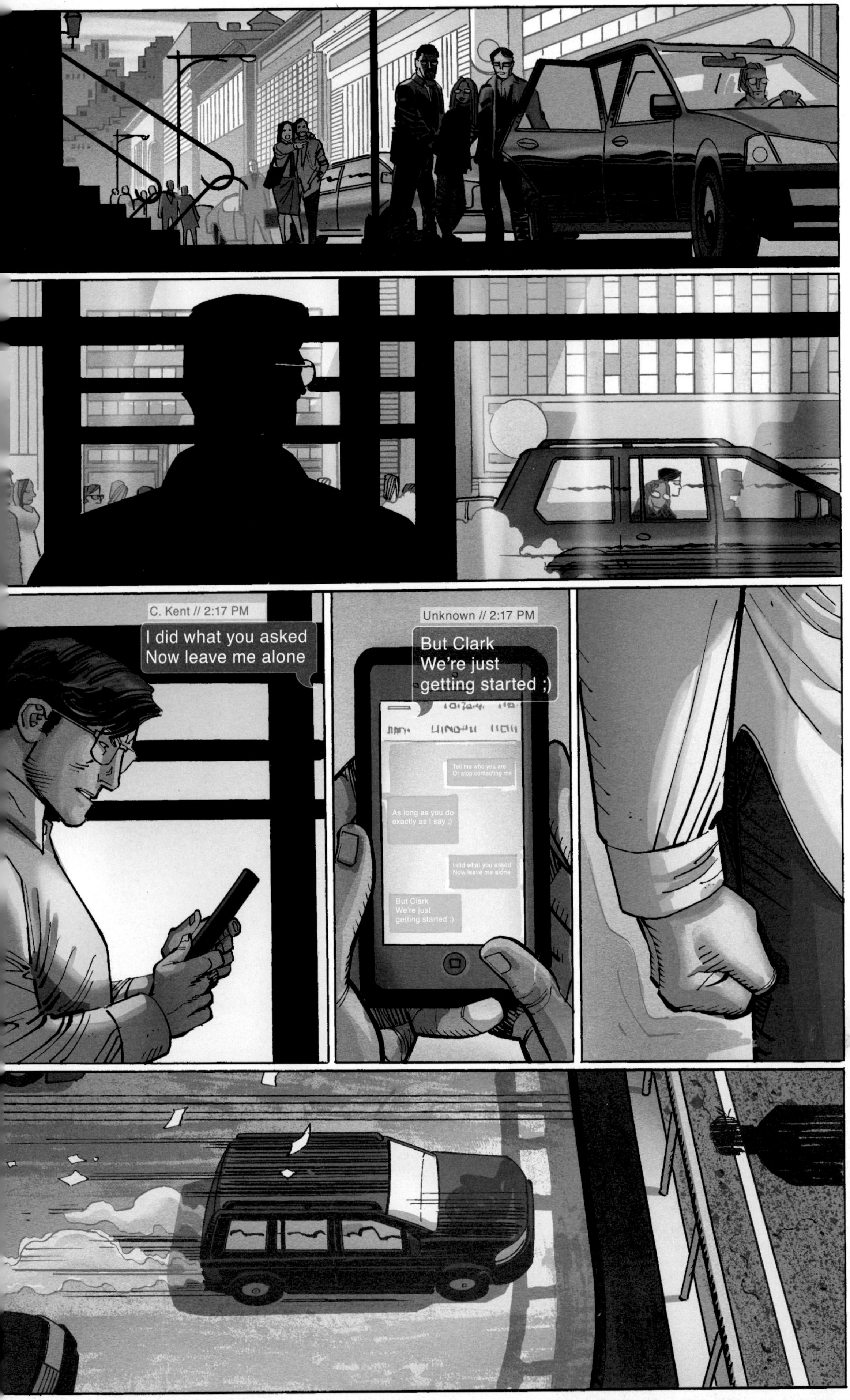
C. Kent // 2:17 PM
I did what you asked
Now leave me alone
Unknown // 2:17 PM
But Clark
We're just
getting started ;)
Tell me who you are
Or stop contacting me
As long as you do
exactly as I say ;)
I did what you asked
Now leave me alone
But Clark
We're just
getting started ;)

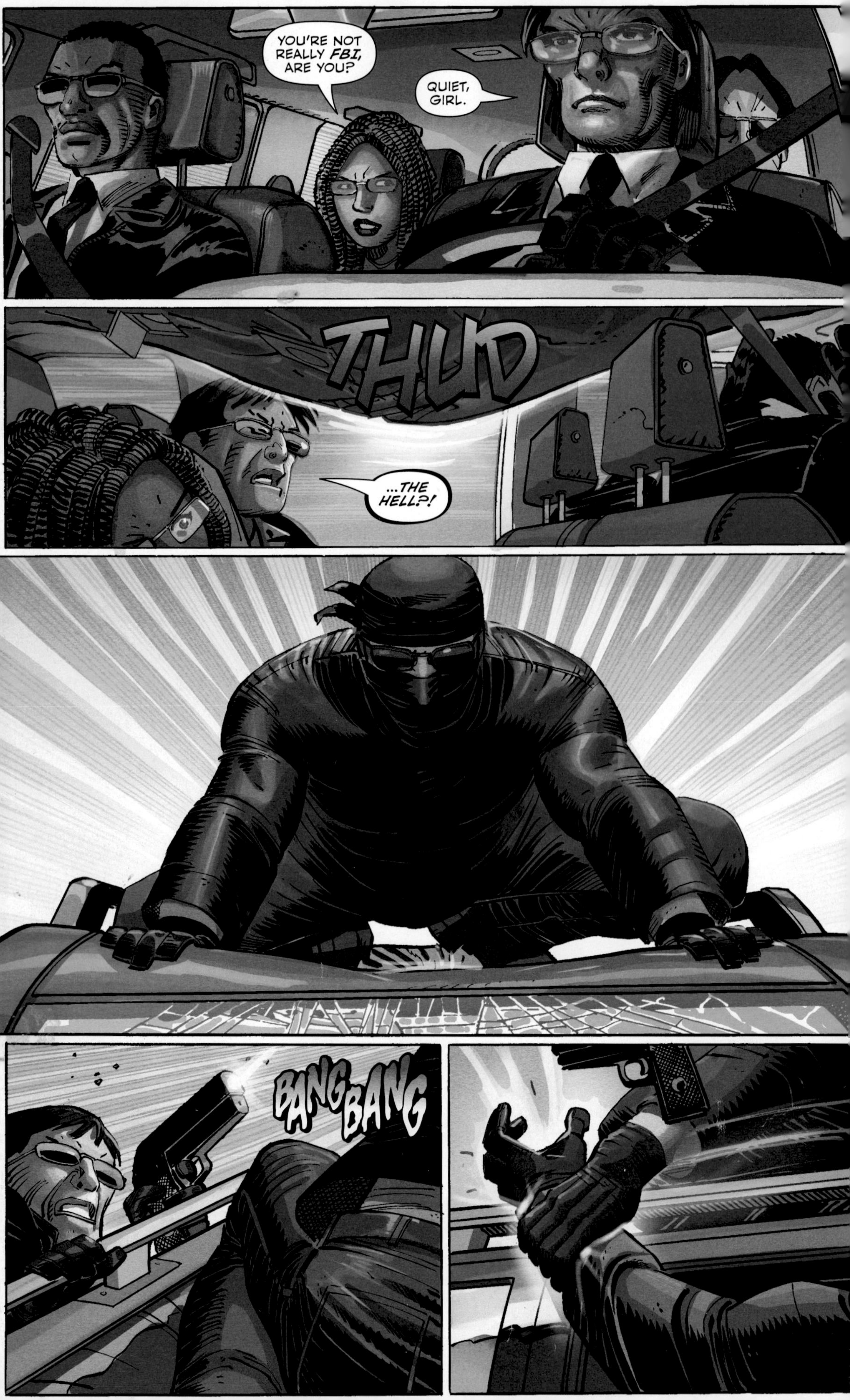
YOU'RE NOT REALLY FBI, ARE YOU?
QUIET, GIRL.
THUD
...THE HELL?!
BANG BANG

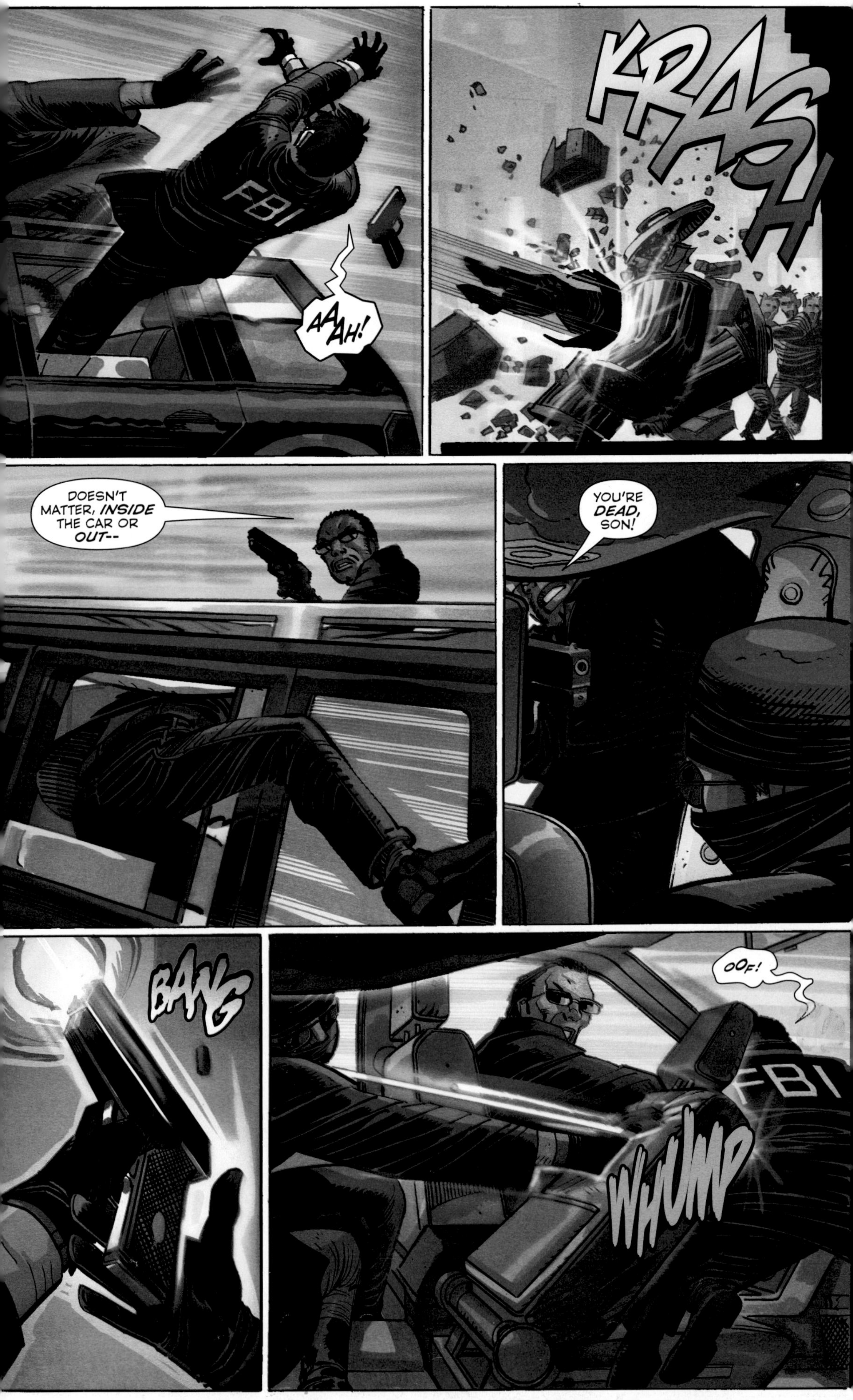
AAAH!
KRASH
DOESN'T MATTER, *INSIDE* THE CAR OR *OUT*--
YOU'RE *DEAD*, SON!
BANG
OOF!
WHUMP

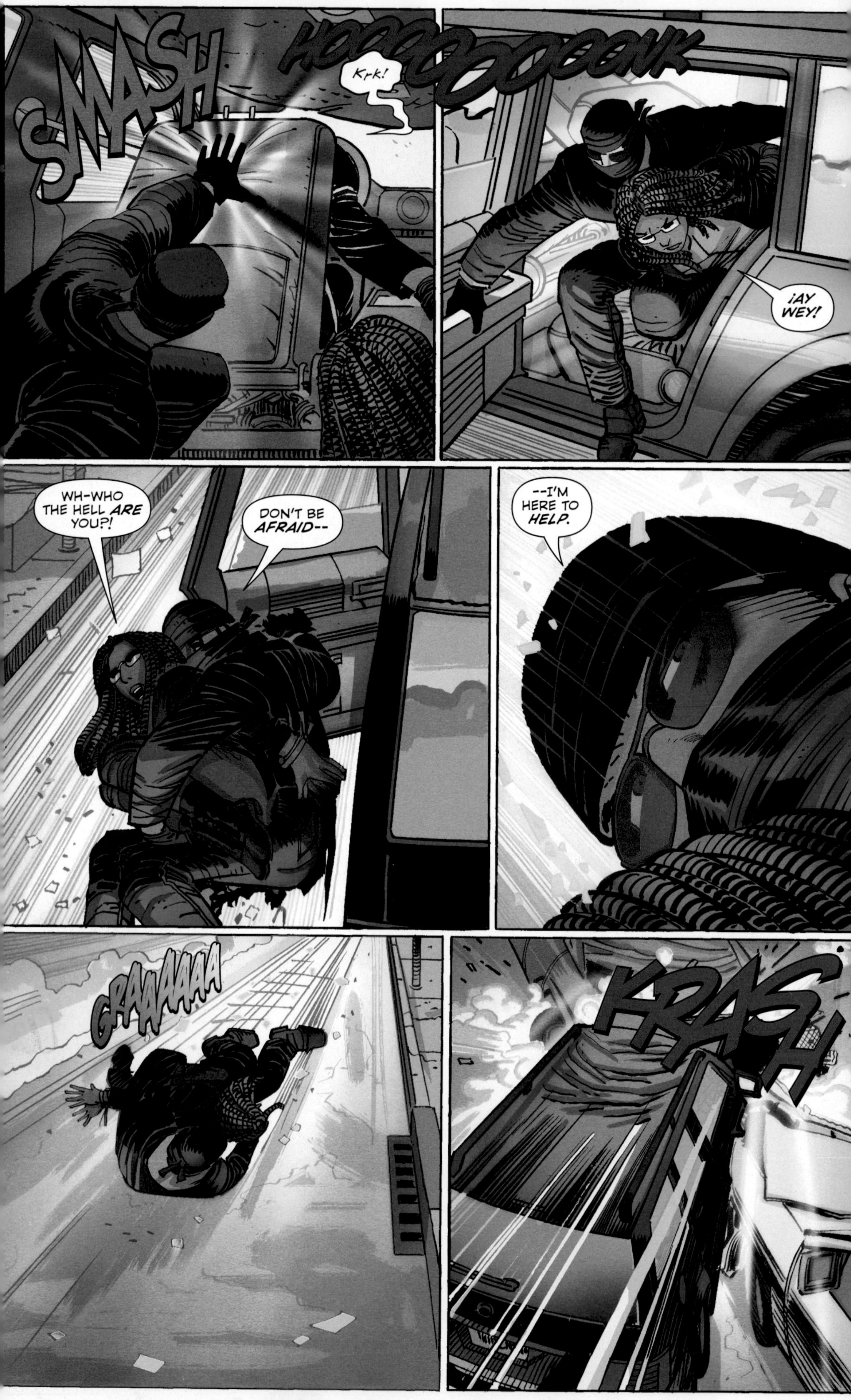
SMASH
Krk!
HOOOOOOOONK
¡AY WEY!
WH-WHO THE HELL ARE YOU?!
DON'T BE AFRAID--
--I'M HERE TO HELP.
GRAAAAAA
KRASH

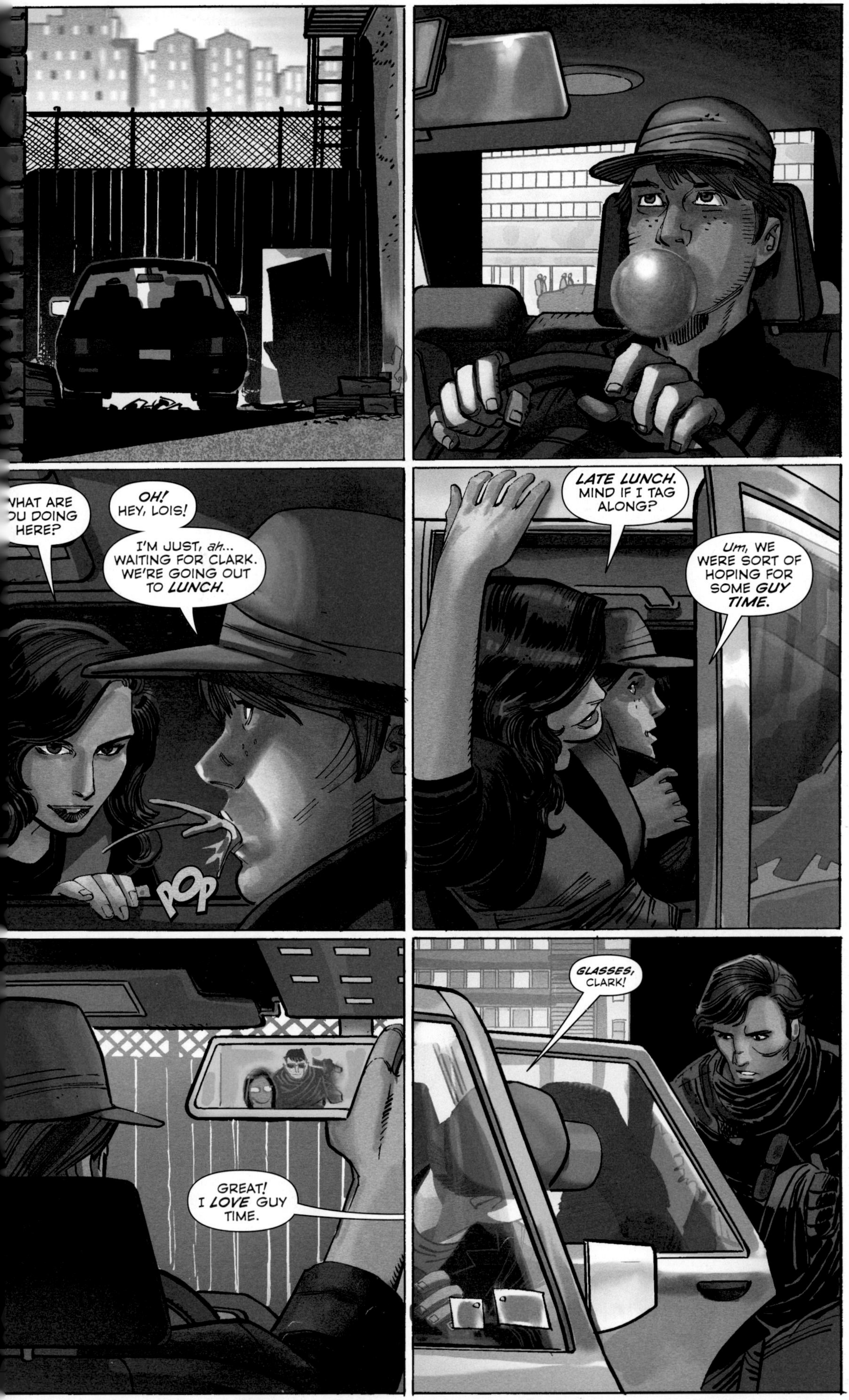
WHAT ARE
OU DOING
HERE?
OH!
HEY, LOIS!
I'M JUST, ah...
WAITING FOR CLARK.
WE'RE GOING OUT
TO LUNCH.
POP
LATE LUNCH.
MIND IF I TAG
ALONG?
Um, WE
WERE SORT OF
HOPING FOR
SOME GUY
TIME.
GREAT!
I LOVE GUY
TIME.
GLASSES,
CLARK!

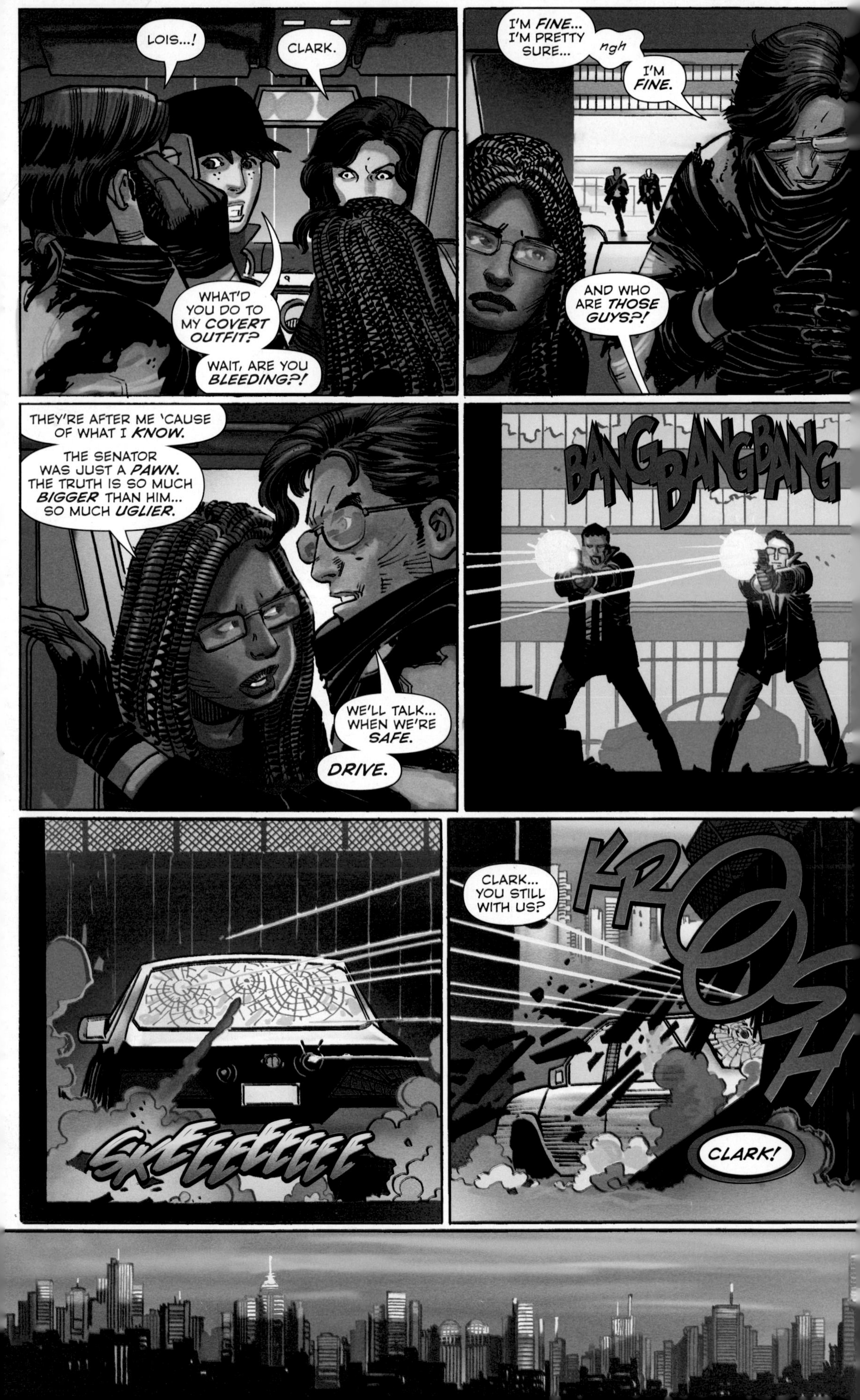

LOIS...!
CLARK.
WHAT'D YOU DO TO MY COVERT OUTFIT?
WAIT, ARE YOU BLEEDING?!
I'M FINE... I'M PRETTY SURE...
ngh
I'M FINE.
AND WHO ARE THOSE GUYS?!
THEY'RE AFTER ME 'CAUSE OF WHAT I KNOW.
THE SENATOR WAS JUST A PAWN. THE TRUTH IS SO MUCH BIGGER THAN HIM... SO MUCH UGLIER.
WE'LL TALK... WHEN WE'RE SAFE.
DRIVE.
BANG BANGBANGBANG
SKEEEEEEEE
CLARK... YOU STILL WITH US?
KROOSH
CLARK!

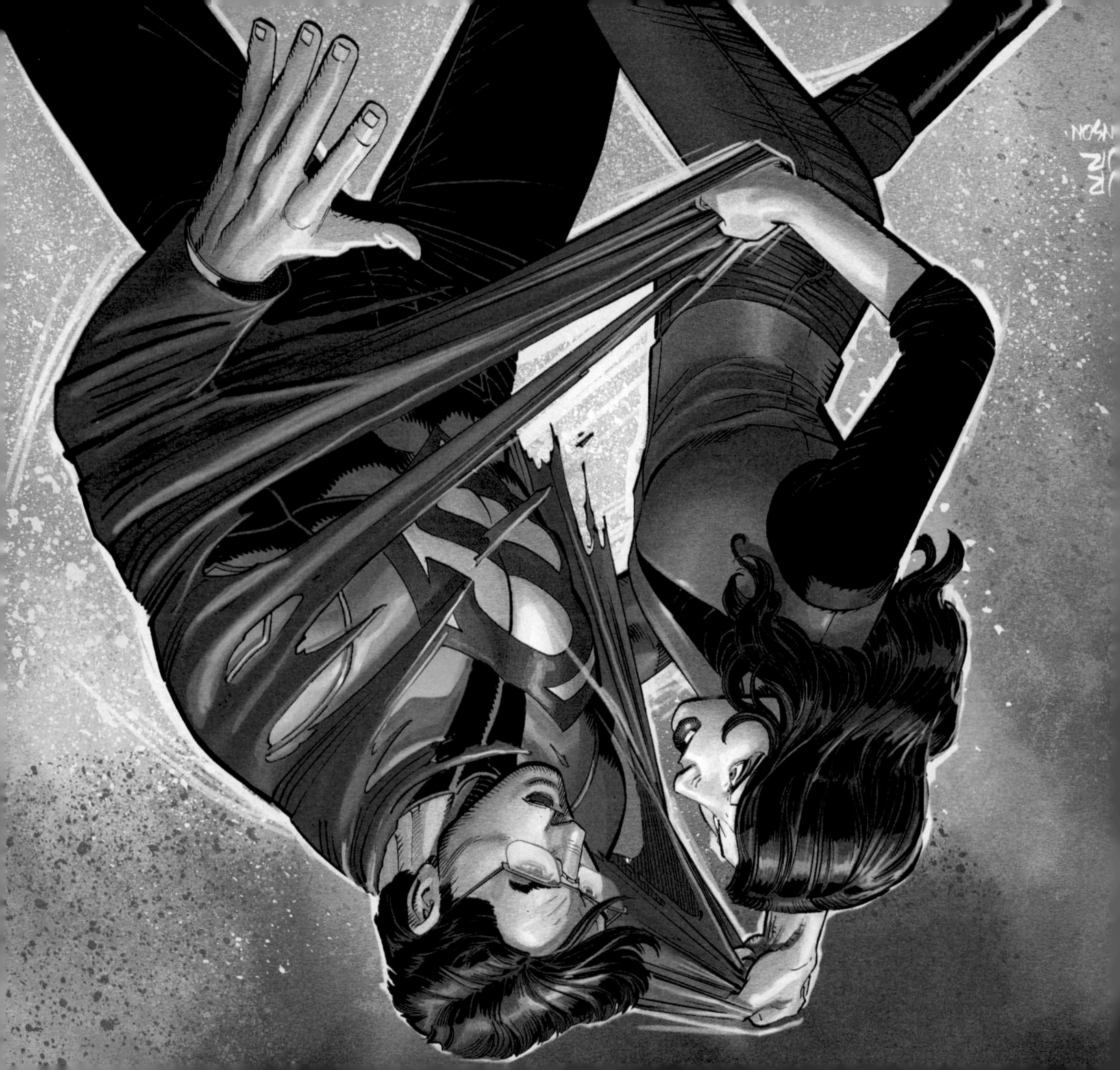

HOW DO YOU KNOW ALL THIS?

I WORK FOR HORDR. OR I *USED TO,* ANYWAY.

*UH...*CLARK? YOU KNOW HOW *WE'RE ALONE?*

I'M THINKING MAYBE YOU'RE *WRONG.*

*Nah,* LEXCORP IS *LAST CENTURY.* LOIS, LUTHOR'S STILL TRYING TO MAKE MONEY FROM *ATOMS.*

THE REAL CASH COMES FROM *INFORMATION,* FROM *SECRETS.*

HORDR'S ALL ABOUT *BITS,* WEAPONS ARE JUST A *SIDE BUSINESS.*

THEY FIGURE OUT THE WORLD'S BIGGEST *SECRETS,* THEN SELL 'EM OR USE 'EM AS *LEVERAGE.*

I DON'T CARE HOW *POWERFUL* YOU ARE--YOU GOT A BIG ENOUGH *SECRET,* HORDR WILL GET TO YOU.

*Um,* ACTUALLY, IT *WAS.*

IT WASN'T *THAT BAD,* JIMMY.

SOUNDS LIKE *LEXCORP.*

THEY'RE KINDA LIKE A *TECH COMPANY* KINDA GONE DOWN--IS A *CRIME SYNDICATE* CALLED *HORDR.*

BEHIND THE *SENATOR* AND THE *GUNS*--BEHIND *EVERYTHING* THAT'S LIKE A *GANG.*

*WE'RE ALONE.* SAY *CONDESA.* SAY WHAT YOU NEED TO SAY.

THE ONLY *HEARTBEATS* WITHIN A MILE ARE *OURS.*

SO YOU'VE GOT YOUR *POWERS* AGAIN?

TOO BAD THEY DIDN'T COME BACK AN *HOUR AGO,* CLARK. YOU COULD'VE SAVED YOURSELF FROM GETTING *SHOT.*

MAN, ALL THAT *BLEEDING* IN THE CAR HAD US *WORRIED.*

*OUTSIDE METROPOLIS.*

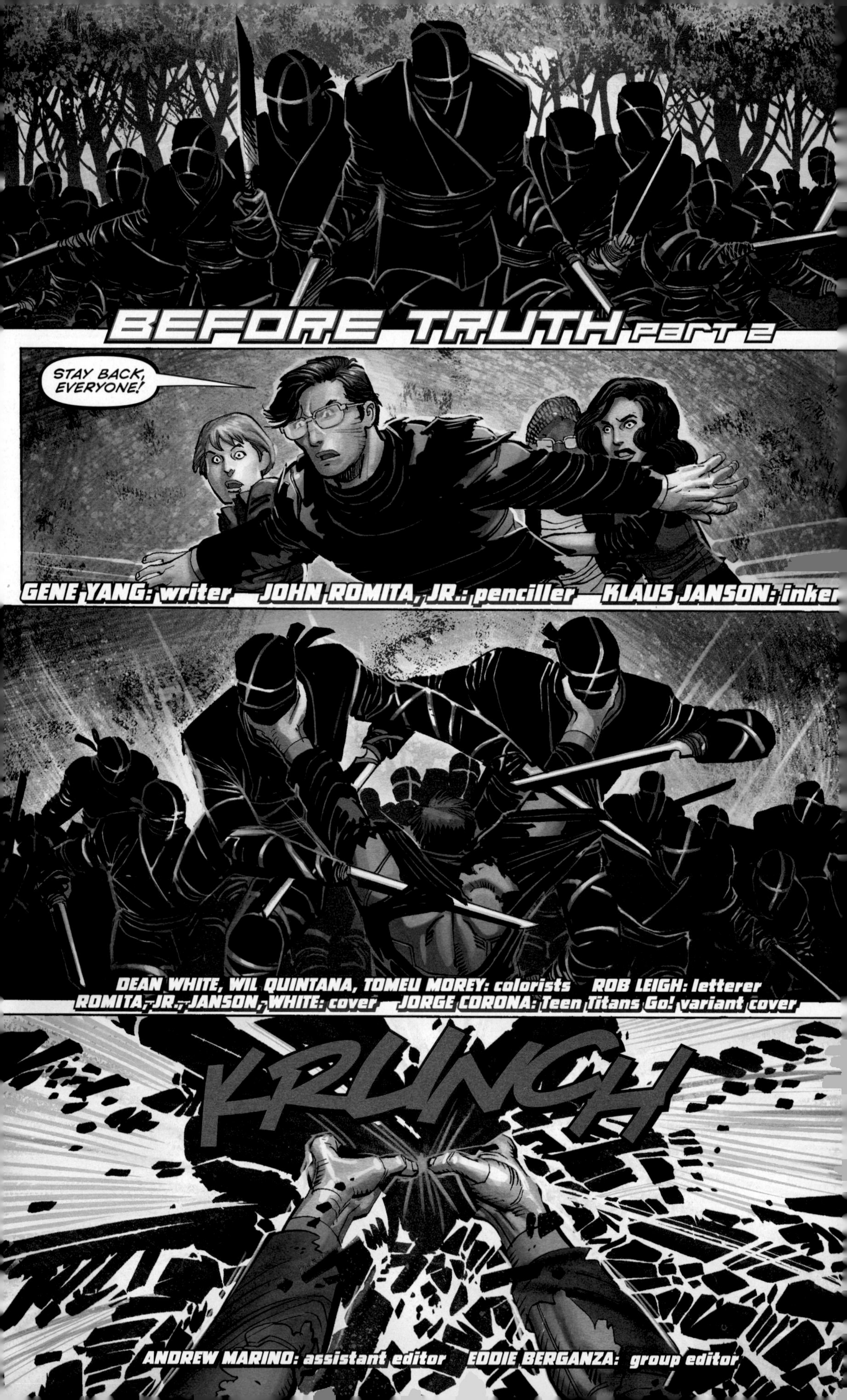
BEFORE TRUTH part 2
STAY BACK, EVERYONE!
GENE YANG: writer JOHN ROMITA, JR.: penciller KLAUS JANSON: inker
DEAN WHITE, WIL QUINTANA, TOMEU MOREY: colorists ROB LEIGH: letterer
ROMITA, JR., JANSON, WHITE: cover JORGE CORONA: Teen Titans Go! variant cover
KRUNCH
ANDREW MARINO: assistant editor EDDIE BERGANZA: group editor

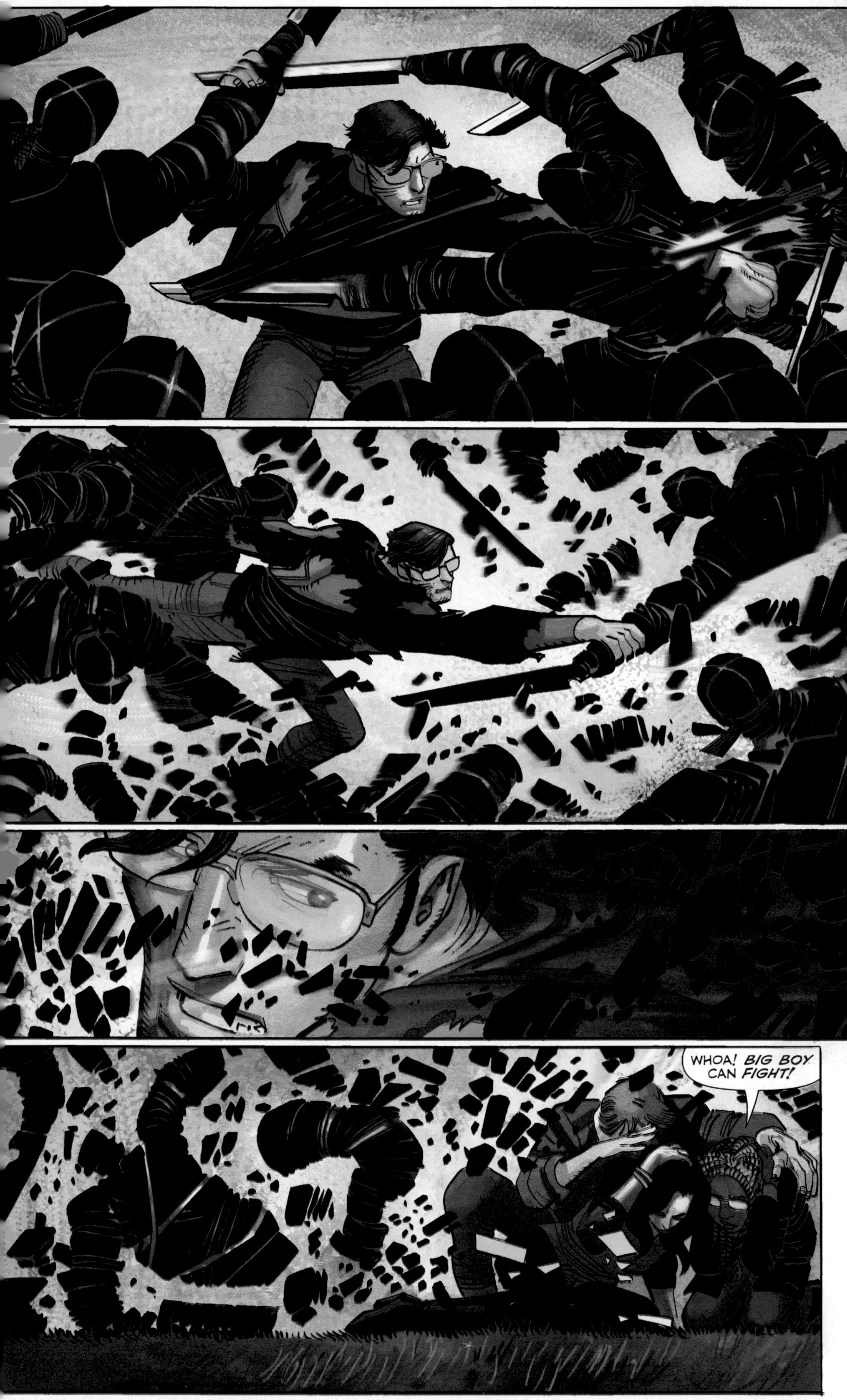
WHOA! *BIG BOY* CAN *FIGHT!*

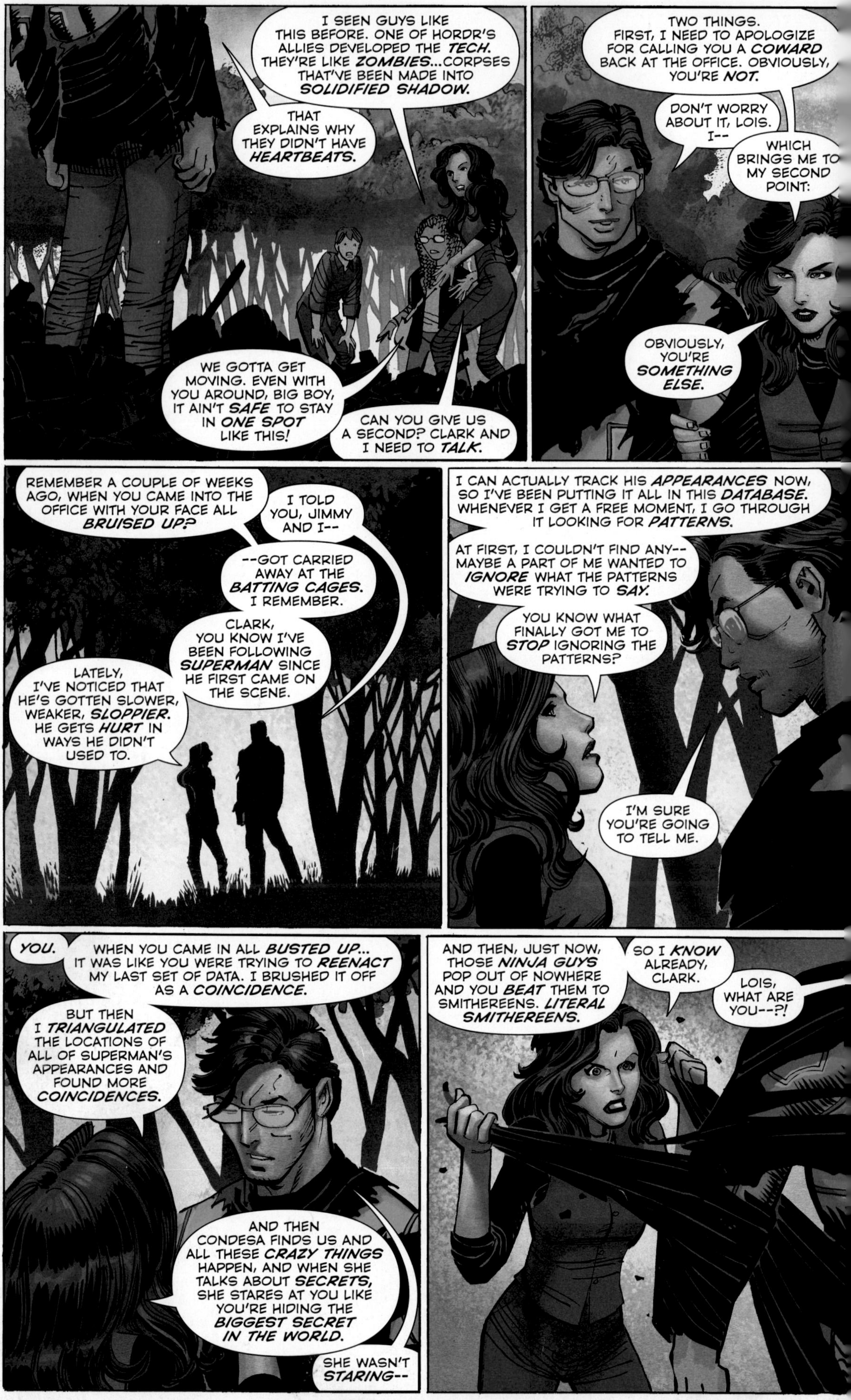
I SEEN GUYS LIKE THIS BEFORE. ONE OF HORDR'S ALLIES DEVELOPED THE *TECH*. THEY'RE LIKE *ZOMBIES*...CORPSES THAT'VE BEEN MADE INTO *SOLIDIFIED SHADOW*.
THAT EXPLAINS WHY THEY DIDN'T HAVE *HEARTBEATS*.
WE GOTTA GET MOVING. EVEN WITH YOU AROUND, BIG BOY, IT AIN'T *SAFE* TO STAY IN *ONE SPOT* LIKE THIS!
CAN YOU GIVE US A SECOND? CLARK AND I NEED TO *TALK*.
TWO THINGS. FIRST, I NEED TO APOLOGIZE FOR CALLING YOU A *COWARD* BACK AT THE OFFICE. OBVIOUSLY, YOU'RE *NOT*.
DON'T WORRY ABOUT IT, LOIS. I--
WHICH BRINGS ME TO MY SECOND POINT:
OBVIOUSLY, YOU'RE *SOMETHING ELSE*.
REMEMBER A COUPLE OF WEEKS AGO, WHEN YOU CAME INTO THE OFFICE WITH YOUR FACE ALL *BRUISED UP*?
I TOLD YOU, JIMMY AND I--
--GOT CARRIED AWAY AT THE *BATTING CAGES*. I REMEMBER.
CLARK, YOU KNOW I'VE BEEN FOLLOWING *SUPERMAN* SINCE HE FIRST CAME ON THE SCENE.
LATELY, I'VE NOTICED THAT HE'S GOTTEN SLOWER, WEAKER, *SLOPPIER*. HE GETS *HURT* IN WAYS HE DIDN'T USED TO.
I CAN ACTUALLY TRACK HIS *APPEARANCES* NOW, SO I'VE BEEN PUTTING IT ALL IN THIS *DATABASE*. WHENEVER I GET A FREE MOMENT, I GO THROUGH IT LOOKING FOR *PATTERNS*.
AT FIRST, I COULDN'T FIND ANY-- MAYBE A PART OF ME WANTED TO *IGNORE* WHAT THE PATTERNS WERE TRYING TO *SAY*.
YOU KNOW WHAT FINALLY GOT ME TO *STOP* IGNORING THE PATTERNS?
I'M SURE YOU'RE GOING TO TELL ME.
*YOU*.
WHEN YOU CAME IN ALL *BUSTED UP*... IT WAS LIKE YOU WERE TRYING TO *REENACT* MY LAST SET OF DATA. I BRUSHED IT OFF AS A *COINCIDENCE*.
BUT THEN I *TRIANGULATED* THE LOCATIONS OF ALL OF SUPERMAN'S APPEARANCES AND FOUND MORE *COINCIDENCES*.
AND THEN CONDESA FINDS US AND ALL THESE *CRAZY THINGS* HAPPEN, AND WHEN SHE TALKS ABOUT *SECRETS*, SHE STARES AT YOU LIKE YOU'RE HIDING THE *BIGGEST SECRET IN THE WORLD*.
SHE WASN'T *STARING*--
AND THEN, JUST NOW, THOSE *NINJA GUYS* POP OUT OF NOWHERE AND YOU *BEAT* THEM TO SMITHEREENS. *LITERAL SMITHEREENS*.
SO I *KNOW* ALREADY, CLARK.
LOIS, WHAT ARE YOU--?!

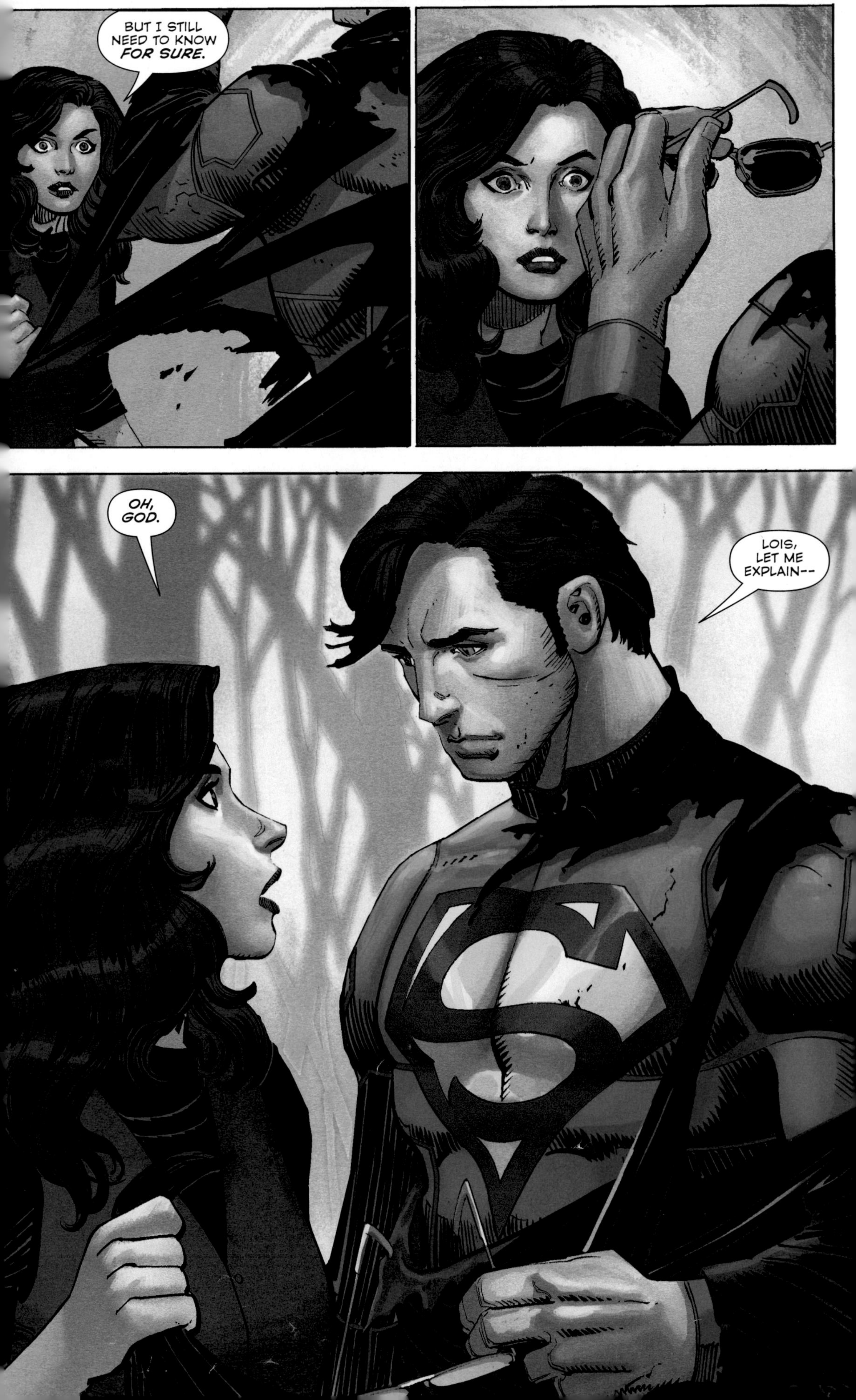
BUT I STILL NEED TO KNOW *FOR SURE.*
*OH, GOD.*
LOIS, LET ME EXPLAIN--

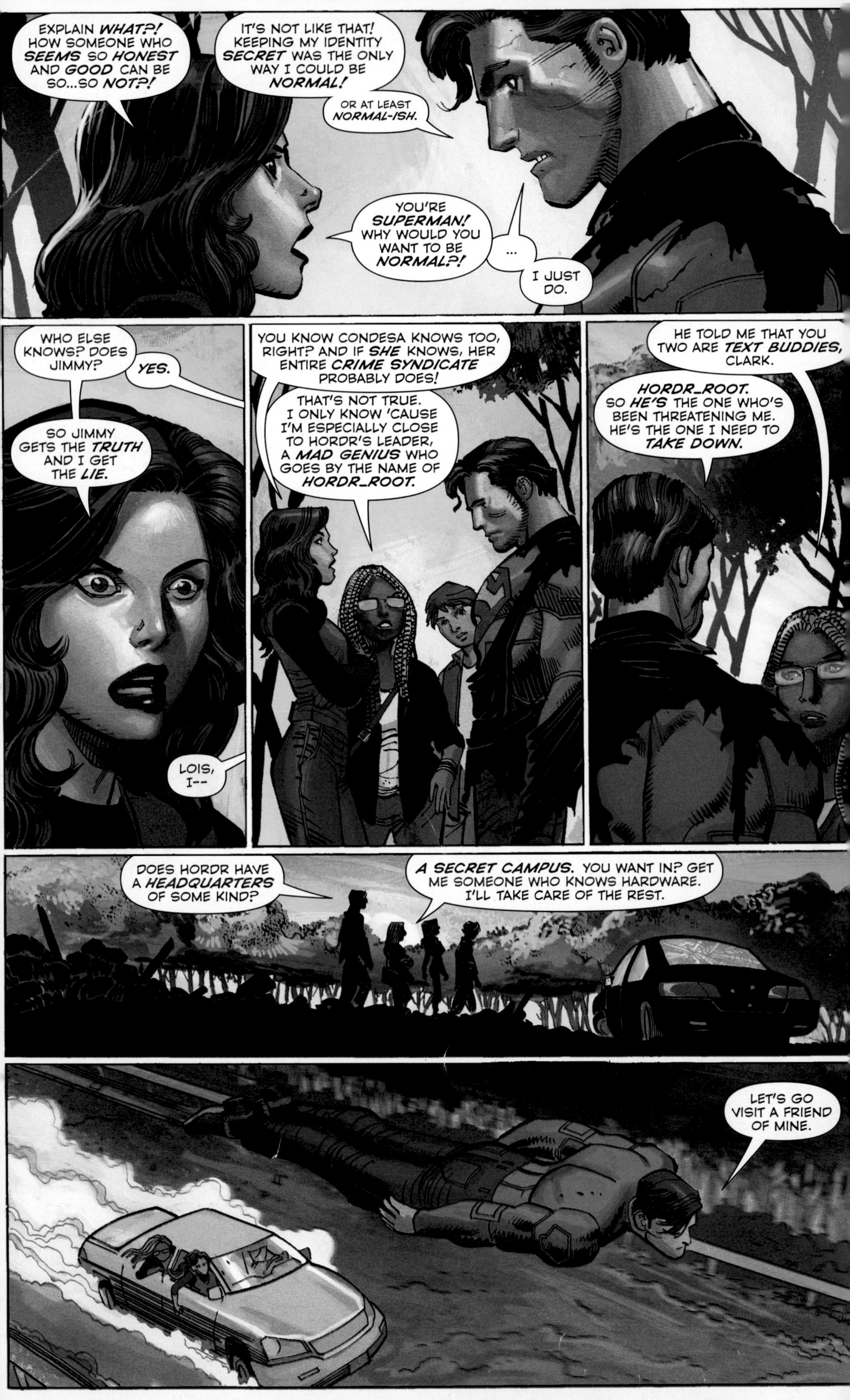
EXPLAIN WHAT?! HOW SOMEONE WHO SEEMS SO HONEST AND GOOD CAN BE SO...SO NOT?!
IT'S NOT LIKE THAT! KEEPING MY IDENTITY SECRET WAS THE ONLY WAY I COULD BE NORMAL!
OR AT LEAST NORMAL-ISH.
YOU'RE SUPERMAN! WHY WOULD YOU WANT TO BE NORMAL?!
...
I JUST DO.
WHO ELSE KNOWS? DOES JIMMY?
YES.
SO JIMMY GETS THE TRUTH AND I GET THE LIE.
LOIS, I--
YOU KNOW CONDESA KNOWS TOO, RIGHT? AND IF SHE KNOWS, HER ENTIRE CRIME SYNDICATE PROBABLY DOES!
THAT'S NOT TRUE. I ONLY KNOW 'CAUSE I'M ESPECIALLY CLOSE TO HORDR'S LEADER, A MAD GENIUS WHO GOES BY THE NAME OF HORDR_ROOT.
HE TOLD ME THAT YOU TWO ARE TEXT BUDDIES, CLARK.
HORDR_ROOT. SO HE'S THE ONE WHO'S BEEN THREATENING ME. HE'S THE ONE I NEED TO TAKE DOWN.
DOES HORDR HAVE A HEADQUARTERS OF SOME KIND?
A SECRET CAMPUS. YOU WANT IN? GET ME SOMEONE WHO KNOWS HARDWARE. I'LL TAKE CARE OF THE REST.
LET'S GO VISIT A FRIEND OF MINE.

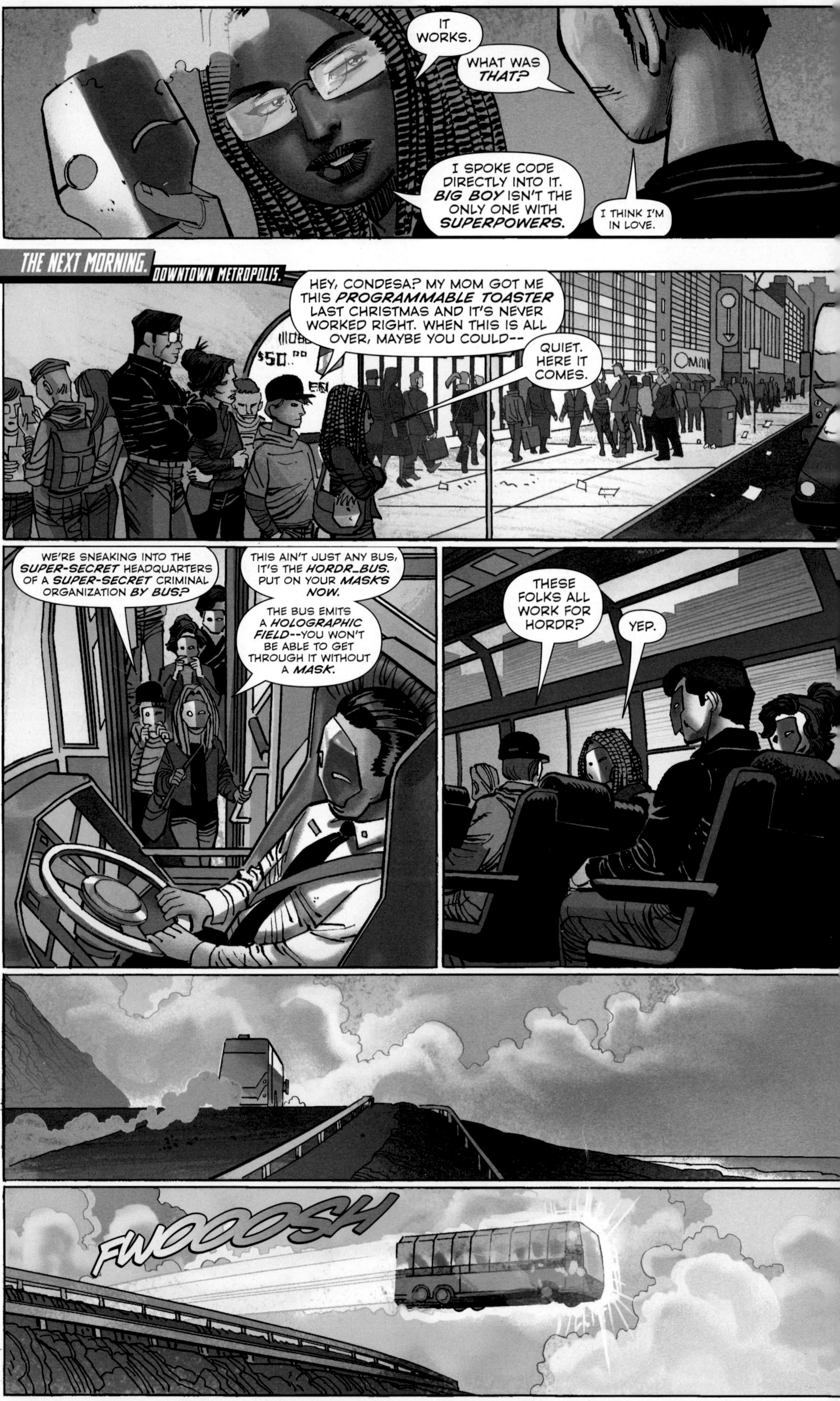
IT WORKS.
WHAT WAS *THAT?*
I SPOKE CODE DIRECTLY INTO IT. *BIG BOY* ISN'T THE ONLY ONE WITH *SUPERPOWERS*.
I THINK I'M IN LOVE.
THE NEXT MORNING.
DOWNTOWN METROPOLIS.
HEY, CONDESA? MY MOM GOT ME THIS *PROGRAMMABLE TOASTER* LAST CHRISTMAS AND IT'S NEVER WORKED RIGHT. WHEN THIS IS ALL OVER, MAYBE YOU COULD--
QUIET. HERE IT COMES.
WE'RE SNEAKING INTO THE *SUPER-SECRET* HEADQUARTERS OF A *SUPER-SECRET* CRIMINAL ORGANIZATION *BY BUS?*
THIS AIN'T JUST ANY BUS, IT'S THE *HORDR_BUS*. PUT ON YOUR *MASKS NOW*.
THE BUS EMITS A *HOLOGRAPHIC FIELD*--YOU WON'T BE ABLE TO GET THROUGH IT WITHOUT A *MASK*.
THESE FOLKS ALL WORK FOR HORDR?
YEP.
FWOOOSH

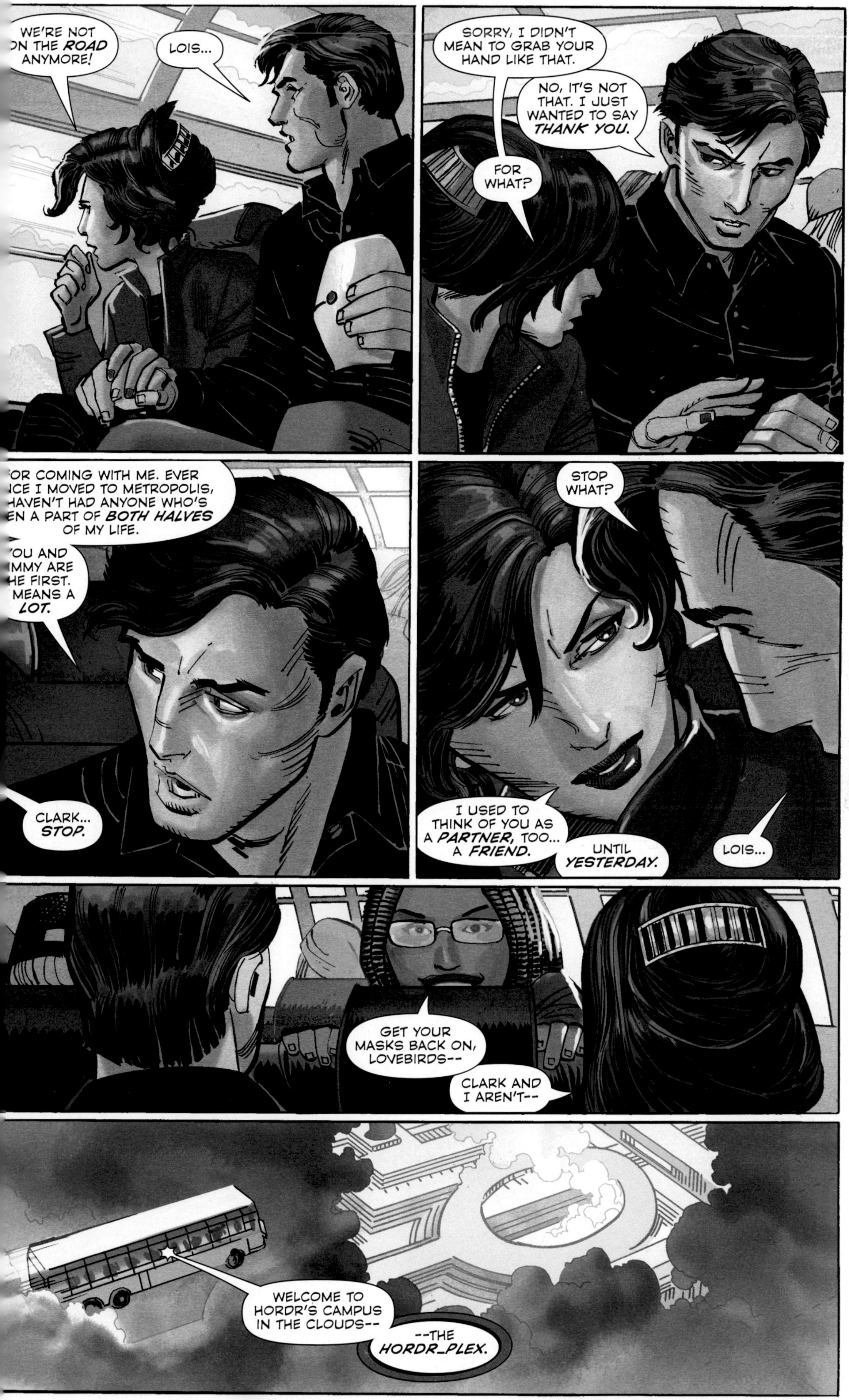

WE'RE NOT
ON THE *ROAD* ANYMORE!
LOIS...
SORRY, I DIDN'T MEAN TO GRAB YOUR HAND LIKE THAT.
NO, IT'S NOT THAT. I JUST WANTED TO SAY *THANK YOU.*
FOR WHAT?
OR COMING WITH ME. EVER ICE I MOVED TO METROPOLIS, HAVEN'T HAD ANYONE WHO'S EN A PART OF *BOTH HALVES* OF MY LIFE.
OU AND IMMY ARE HE FIRST. MEANS A *LOT.*
CLARK... *STOP.*
STOP WHAT?
I USED TO THINK OF YOU AS A *PARTNER,* TOO... A *FRIEND.*
UNTIL *YESTERDAY.*
LOIS...
GET YOUR MASKS BACK ON, LOVEBIRDS--
CLARK AND I AREN'T--
WELCOME TO HORDR'S CAMPUS IN THE CLOUDS--
--THE *HORDR_PLEX.*

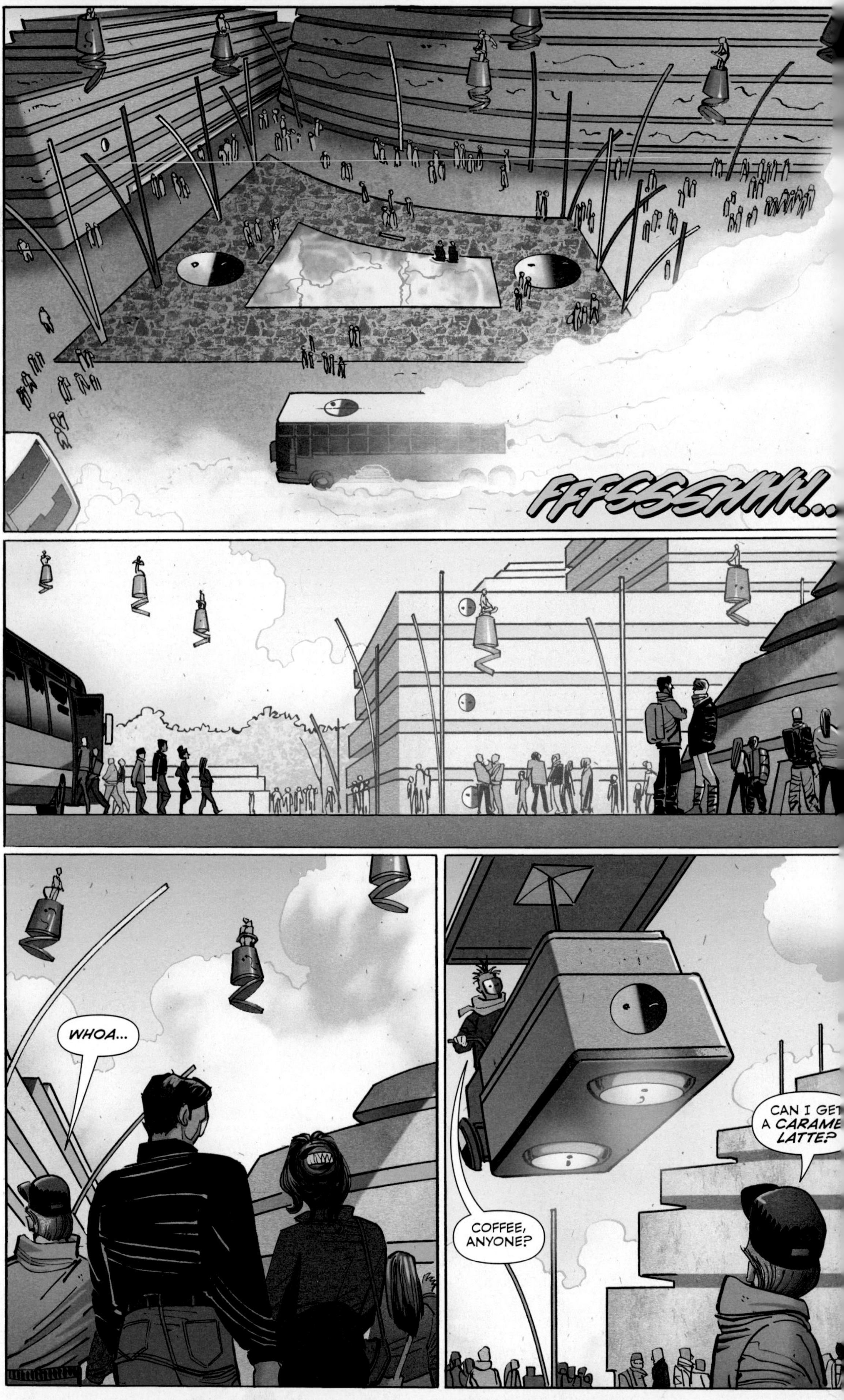
FFFSSSHHH...
WHOA...
COFFEE, ANYONE?
CAN I GET A CARAME LATTE?

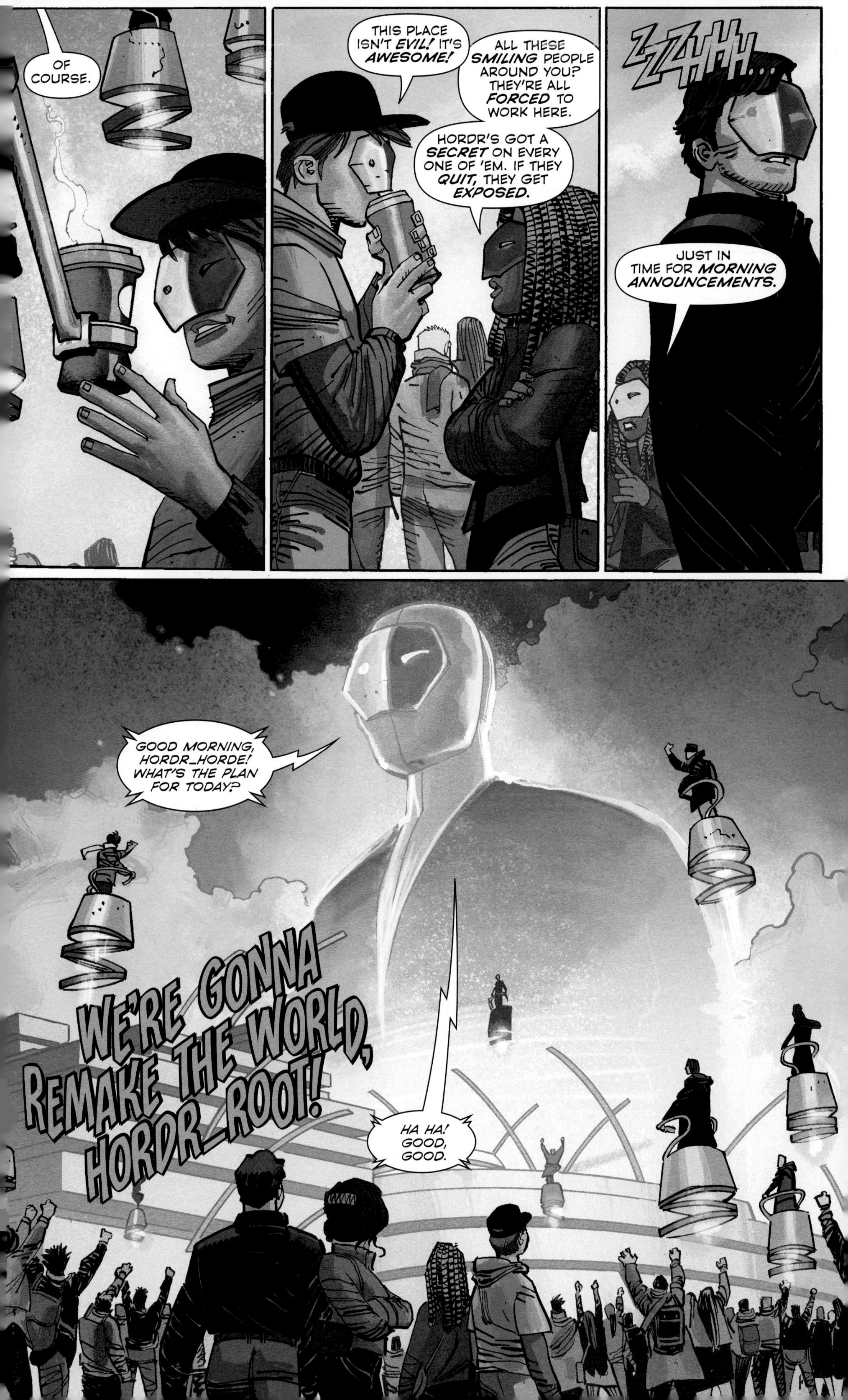
OF COURSE.
THIS PLACE ISN'T *EVIL!* IT'S *AWESOME!*
ALL THESE *SMILING* PEOPLE AROUND YOU? THEY'RE ALL *FORCED* TO WORK HERE.
HORDR'S GOT A *SECRET* ON EVERY ONE OF 'EM. IF THEY *QUIT,* THEY GET *EXPOSED.*
ZZZHHH...
JUST IN TIME FOR *MORNING ANNOUNCEMENTS.*
GOOD MORNING, HORDR_HORDE! WHAT'S THE PLAN FOR TODAY?
WE'RE GONNA REMAKE THE WORLD, HORDR_ROOT!
HA HA! GOOD, GOOD.

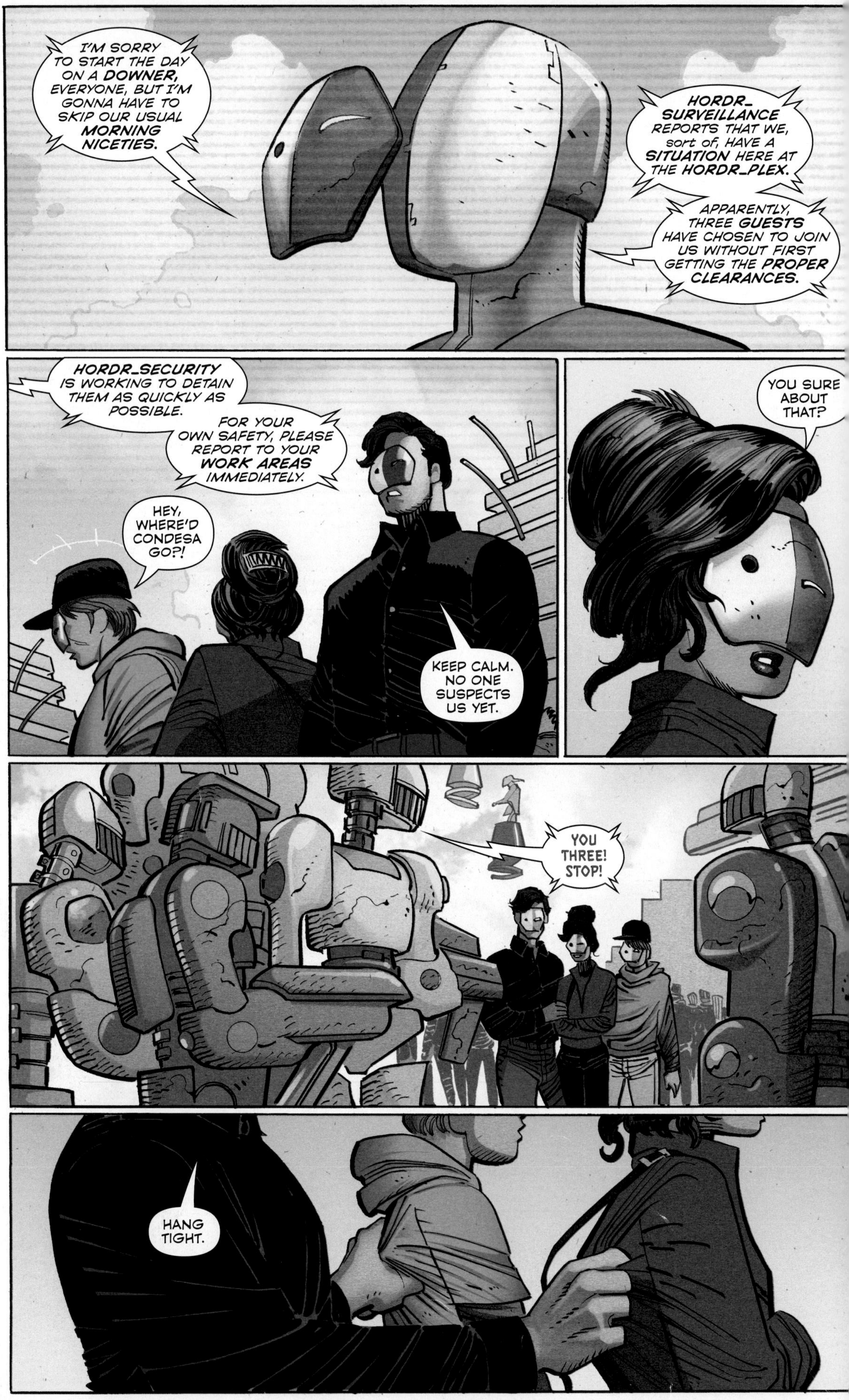
I'M SORRY TO START THE DAY ON A **DOWNER,** EVERYONE, BUT I'M GONNA HAVE TO SKIP OUR USUAL **MORNING NICETIES.**
**HORDR_SURVEILLANCE** REPORTS THAT WE, sort of, HAVE A **SITUATION** HERE AT THE **HORDR_PLEX.**
APPARENTLY, THREE **GUESTS** HAVE CHOSEN TO JOIN US WITHOUT FIRST GETTING THE **PROPER CLEARANCES.**
**HORDR_SECURITY** IS WORKING TO DETAIN THEM AS QUICKLY AS POSSIBLE.
FOR YOUR OWN SAFETY, PLEASE REPORT TO YOUR **WORK AREAS** IMMEDIATELY.
HEY, WHERE'D CONDESA GO?!
KEEP CALM. NO ONE SUSPECTS US YET.
YOU SURE ABOUT THAT?
YOU THREE! STOP!
HANG TIGHT.

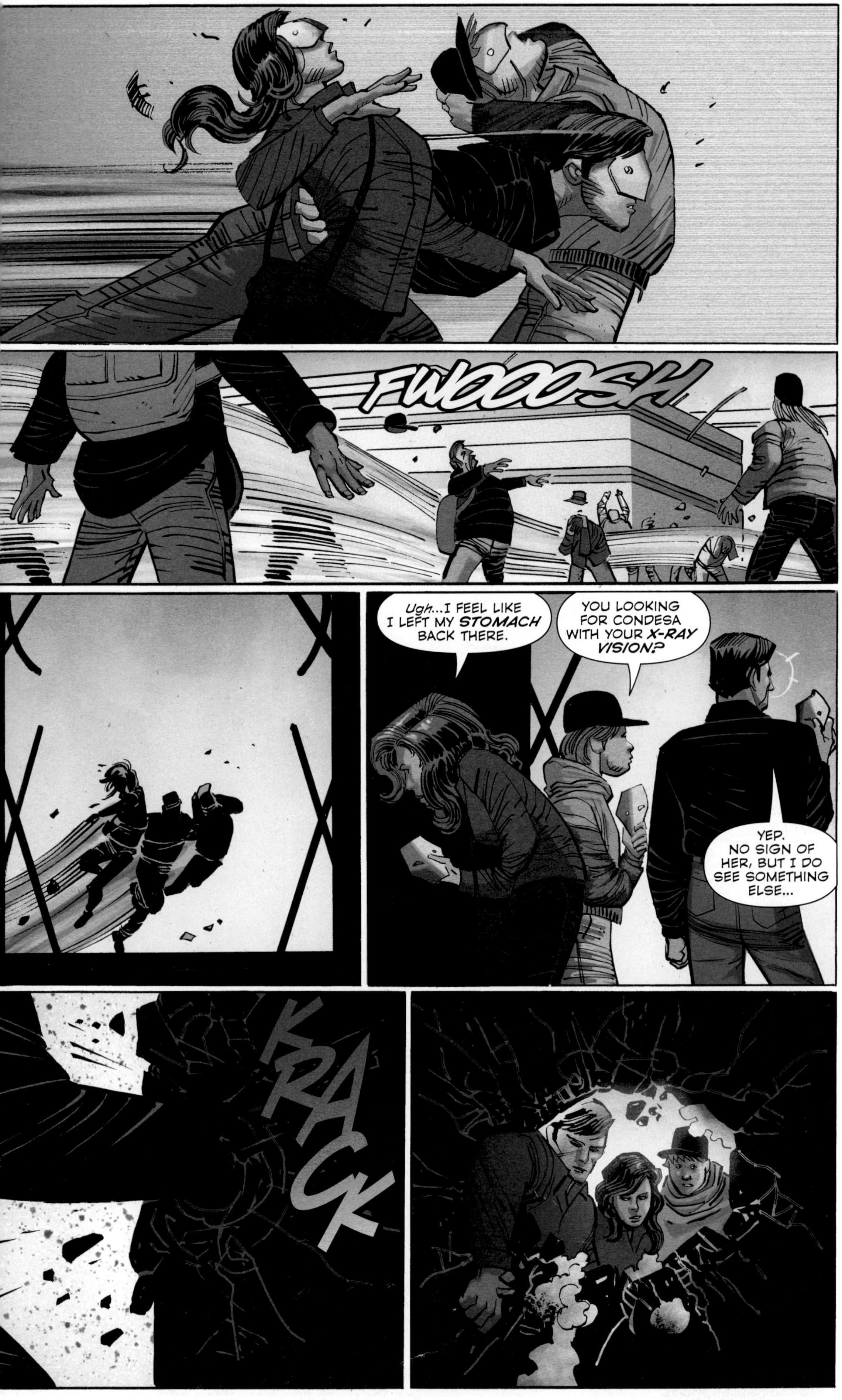
FWOOOSH
Ugh...I FEEL LIKE I LEFT MY STOMACH BACK THERE.
YOU LOOKING FOR CONDESA WITH YOUR X-RAY VISION?
YEP. NO SIGN OF HER, BUT I DO SEE SOMETHING ELSE...
KRACK

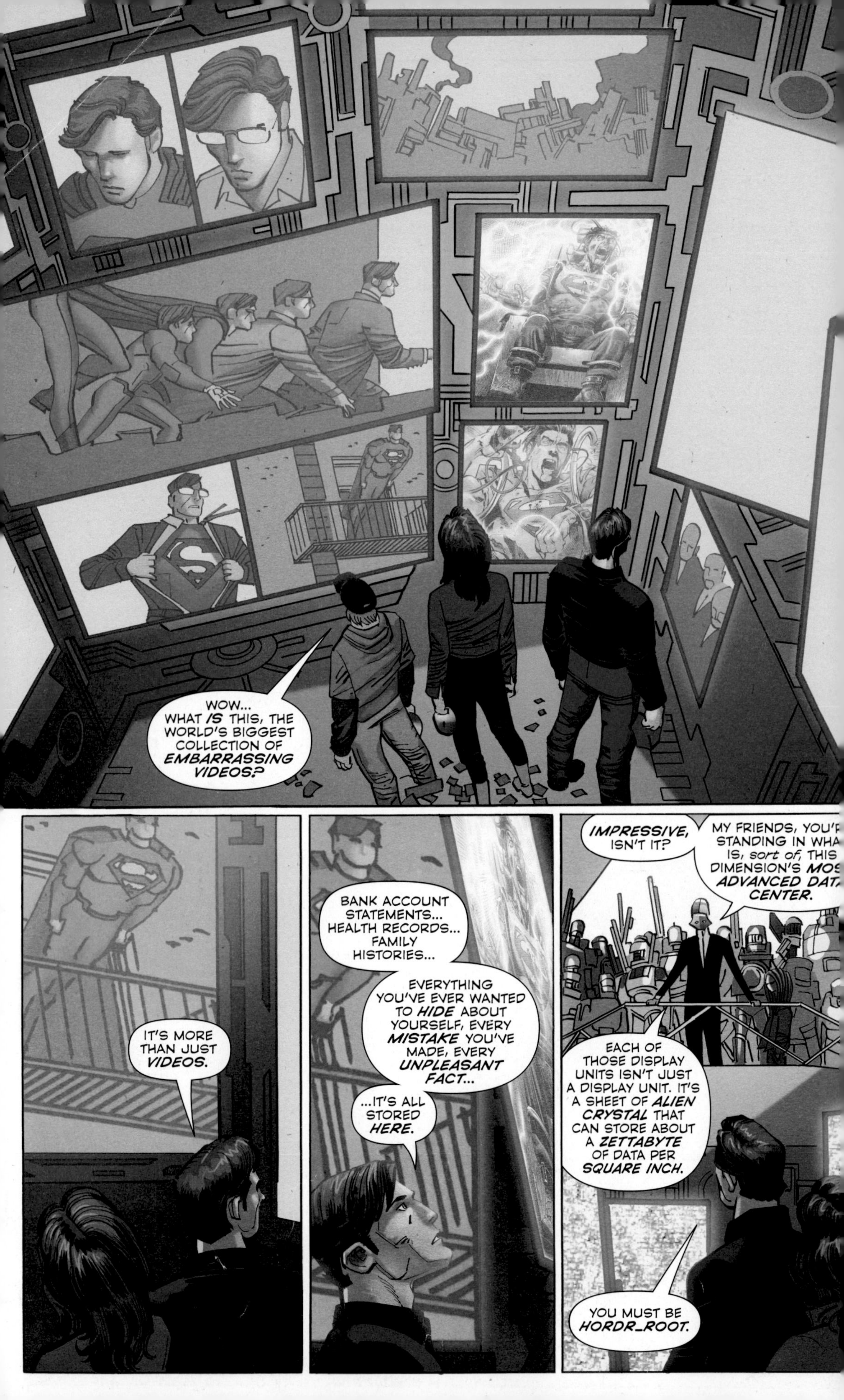
WOW... WHAT *IS* THIS, THE WORLD'S BIGGEST COLLECTION OF ***EMBARRASSING VIDEOS?***
IT'S MORE THAN JUST *VIDEOS.*
BANK ACCOUNT STATEMENTS... HEALTH RECORDS... FAMILY HISTORIES...
EVERYTHING YOU'VE EVER WANTED TO ***HIDE*** ABOUT YOURSELF, EVERY ***MISTAKE*** YOU'VE MADE, EVERY ***UNPLEASANT FACT...***
...IT'S ALL STORED ***HERE.***
***IMPRESSIVE,*** ISN'T IT?
MY FRIENDS, YOU'R STANDING IN WHA IS, *sort of,* THIS DIMENSION'S ***MOS ADVANCED DATA CENTER.***
EACH OF THOSE DISPLAY UNITS ISN'T JUST A DISPLAY UNIT. IT'S A SHEET OF ***ALIEN CRYSTAL*** THAT CAN STORE ABOUT A ***ZETTABYTE*** OF DATA PER ***SQUARE INCH.***
YOU MUST BE ***HORDR_ROOT.***

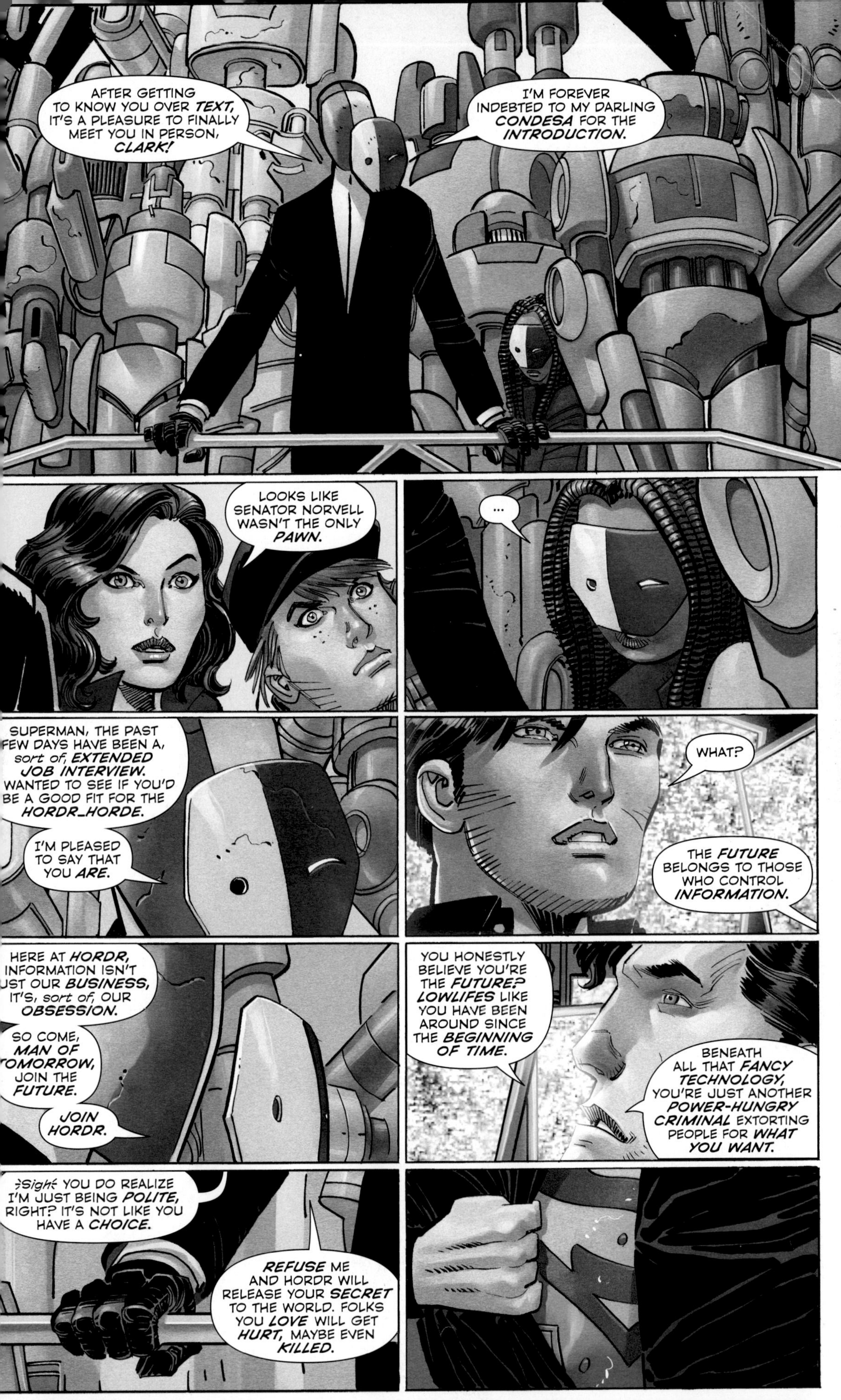
AFTER GETTING TO KNOW YOU OVER *TEXT*, IT'S A PLEASURE TO FINALLY MEET YOU IN PERSON, *CLARK!*
I'M FOREVER INDEBTED TO MY DARLING *CONDESA* FOR THE *INTRODUCTION*.
LOOKS LIKE SENATOR NORVELL WASN'T THE ONLY *PAWN*.
...
SUPERMAN, THE PAST FEW DAYS HAVE BEEN A, *sort of*, *EXTENDED JOB INTERVIEW*. WANTED TO SEE IF YOU'D BE A GOOD FIT FOR THE *HORDR_HORDE*.
I'M PLEASED TO SAY THAT YOU *ARE*.
WHAT?
THE *FUTURE* BELONGS TO THOSE WHO CONTROL *INFORMATION*.
HERE AT *HORDR*, INFORMATION ISN'T JUST OUR *BUSINESS*, IT'S, *sort of*, OUR *OBSESSION*.
SO COME, *MAN OF TOMORROW*, JOIN THE *FUTURE*.
*JOIN HORDR*.
YOU HONESTLY BELIEVE YOU'RE THE *FUTURE? LOWLIFES* LIKE YOU HAVE BEEN AROUND SINCE THE *BEGINNING OF TIME*.
BENEATH ALL THAT *FANCY TECHNOLOGY*, YOU'RE JUST ANOTHER *POWER-HUNGRY CRIMINAL* EXTORTING PEOPLE FOR *WHAT YOU WANT*.
*Sigh* YOU DO REALIZE I'M JUST BEING *POLITE*, RIGHT? IT'S NOT LIKE YOU HAVE A *CHOICE*.
*REFUSE* ME AND HORDR WILL RELEASE YOUR *SECRET* TO THE WORLD. FOLKS YOU *LOVE* WILL GET *HURT*, MAYBE EVEN *KILLED*.

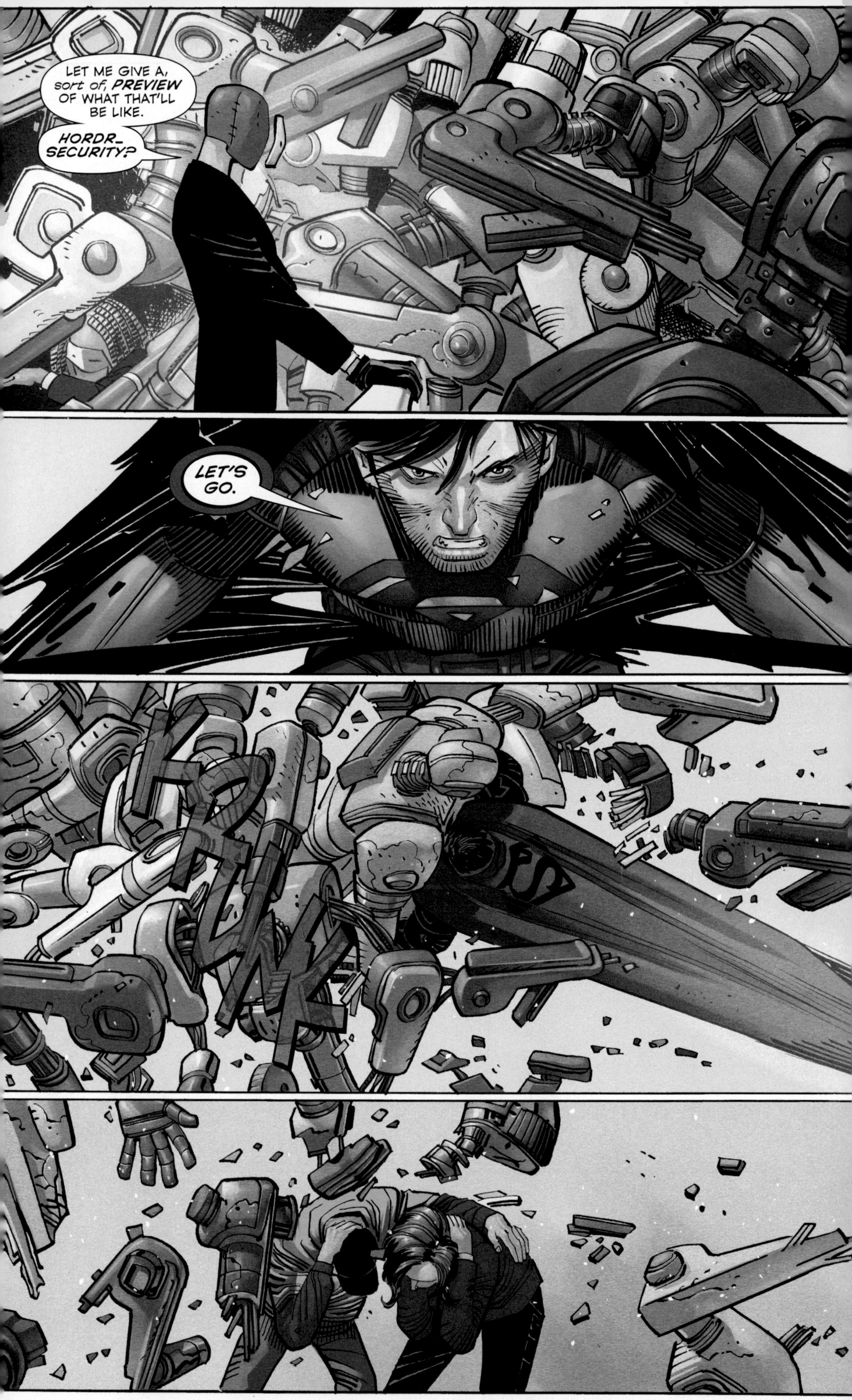
LET ME GIVE A, sort of, PREVIEW OF WHAT THAT'LL BE LIKE.
HORDR-SECURITY?
LET'S GO.
KRUNK

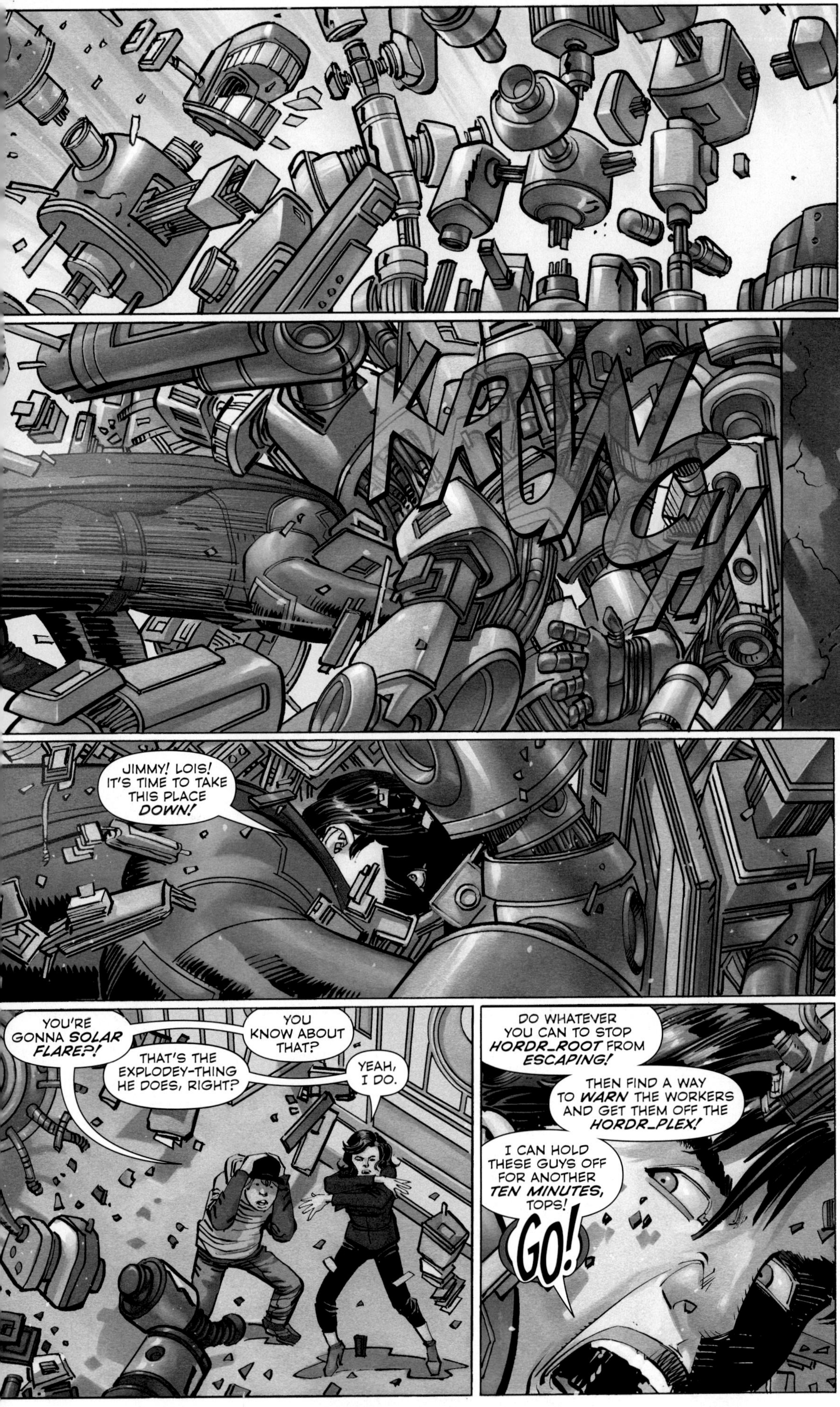
KRUNCH
JIMMY! LOIS! IT'S TIME TO TAKE THIS PLACE DOWN!
YOU'RE GONNA SOLAR FLARE?!
YOU KNOW ABOUT THAT?
THAT'S THE EXPLODEY-THING HE DOES, RIGHT?
YEAH, I DO.
DO WHATEVER YOU CAN TO STOP HORDR_ROOT FROM ESCAPING!
THEN FIND A WAY TO WARN THE WORKERS AND GET THEM OFF THE HORDR_PLEX!
I CAN HOLD THESE GUYS OFF FOR ANOTHER TEN MINUTES, TOPS!
GO!

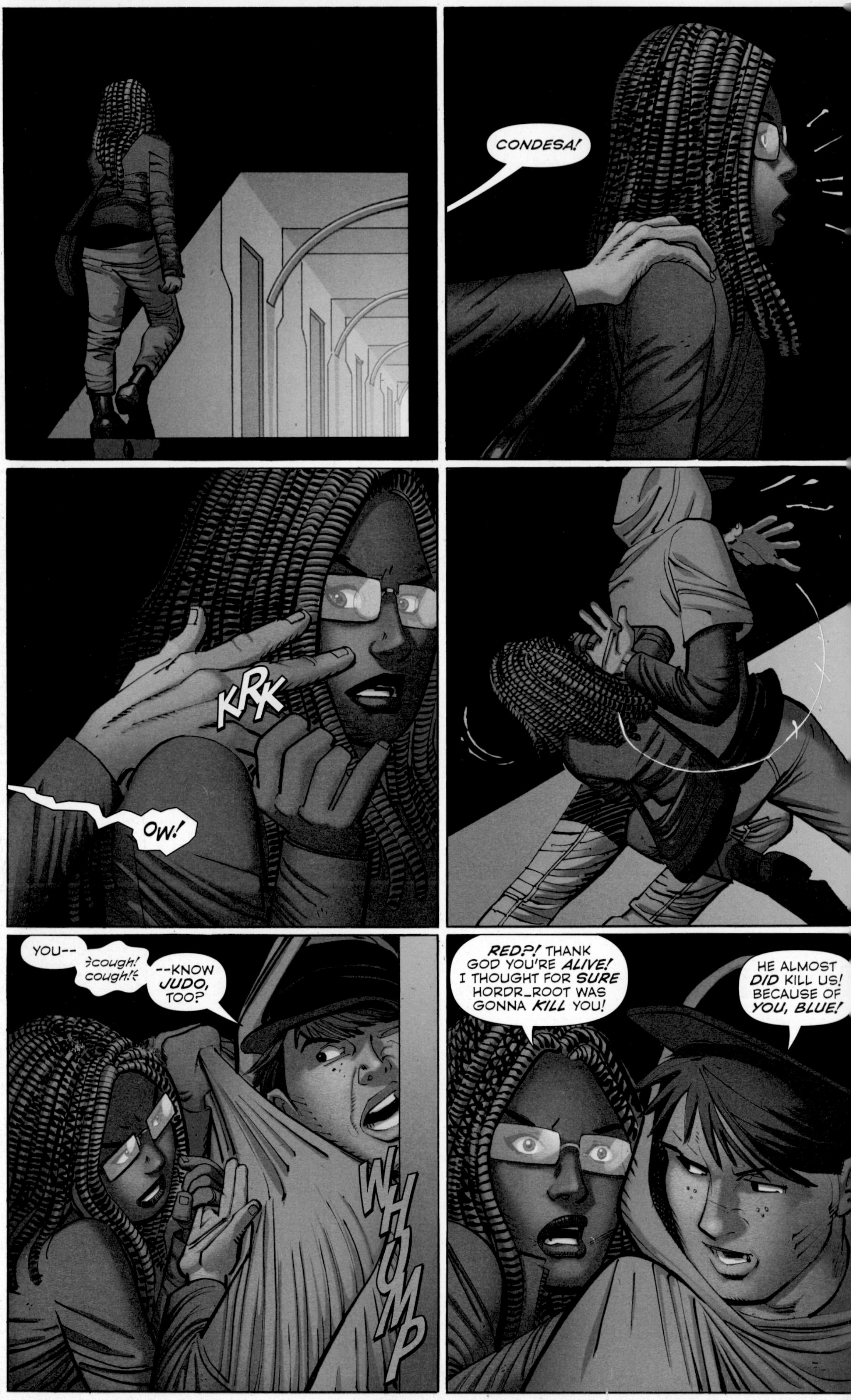
CONDESA!
KRK
OW!
YOU--
cough! cough!
--KNOW JUDO, TOO?
WHUMP
RED?! THANK GOD YOU'RE ALIVE! I THOUGHT FOR SURE HORDR_ROOT WAS GONNA KILL YOU!
HE ALMOST DID KILL US! BECAUSE OF YOU, BLUE!

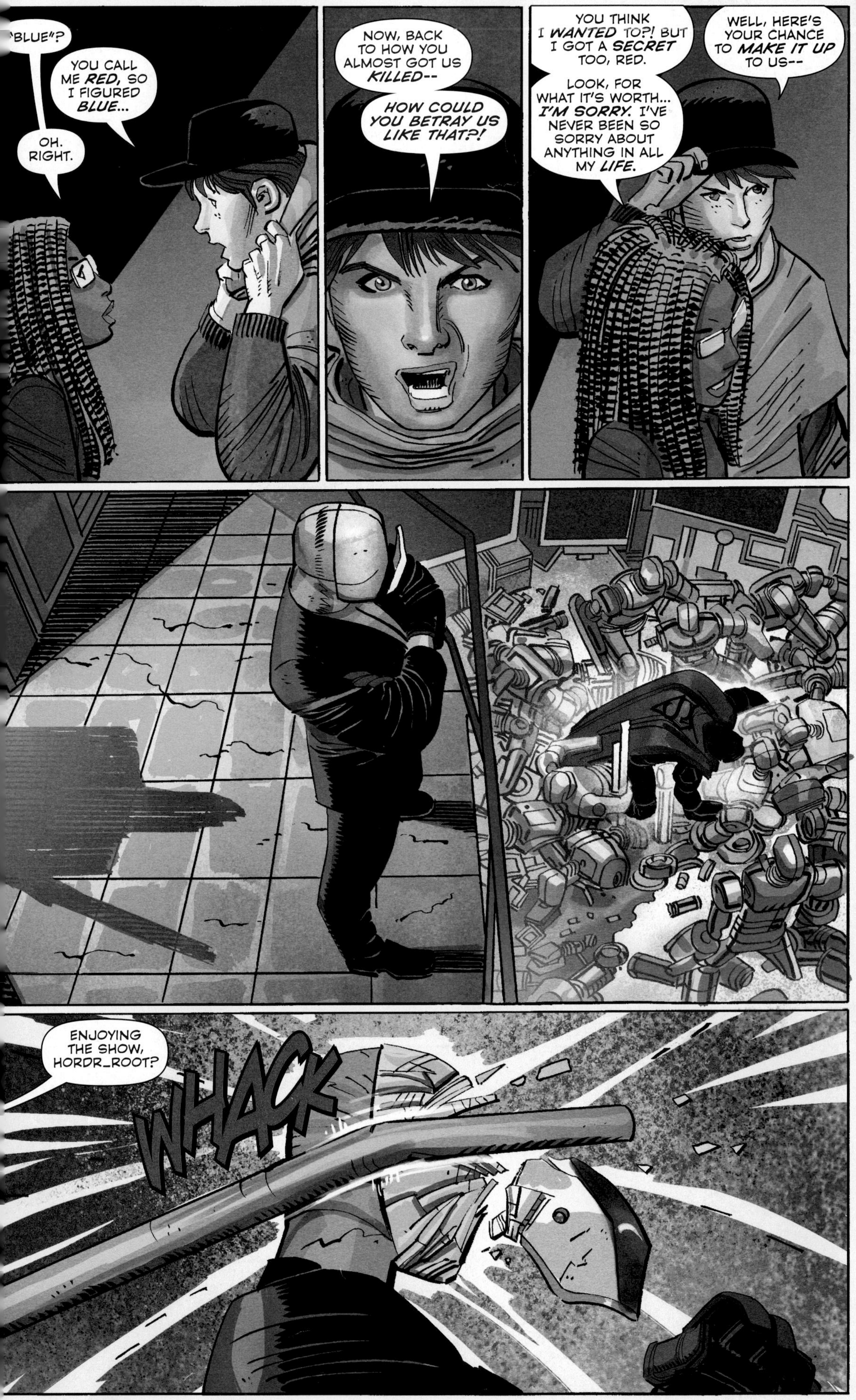
"BLUE"?
YOU CALL ME *RED*, SO I FIGURED *BLUE*...
OH. RIGHT.
NOW, BACK TO HOW YOU ALMOST GOT US *KILLED*--
*HOW COULD YOU BETRAY US LIKE THAT?!*
YOU THINK I *WANTED* TO?! BUT I GOT A *SECRET* TOO, RED.
LOOK, FOR WHAT IT'S WORTH... *I'M SORRY.* I'VE NEVER BEEN SO SORRY ABOUT ANYTHING IN ALL MY *LIFE*.
WELL, HERE'S YOUR CHANCE TO *MAKE IT UP* TO US--
ENJOYING THE SHOW, HORDR_ROOT?
WHACK

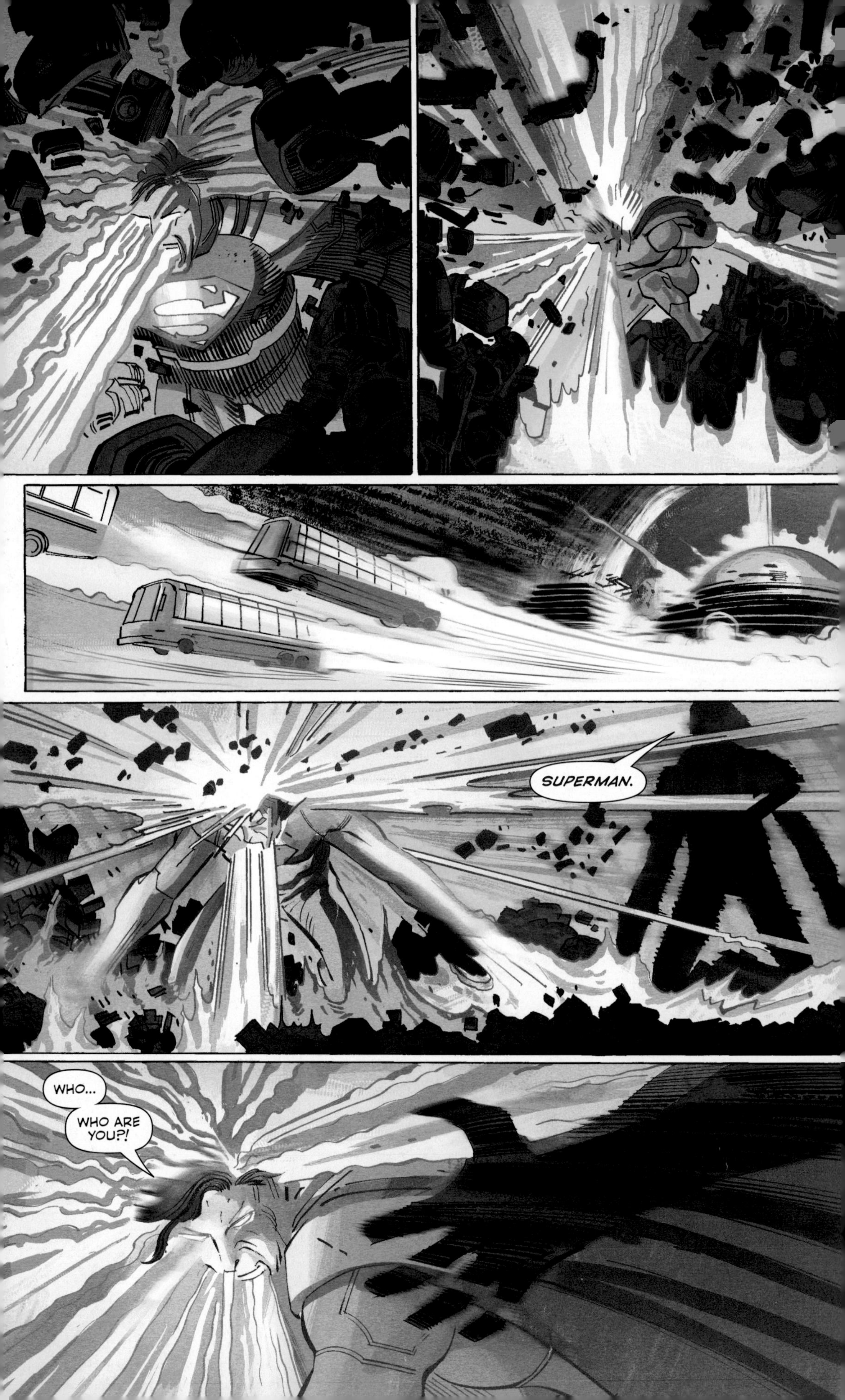
SUPERMAN.
WHO...
WHO ARE YOU?!

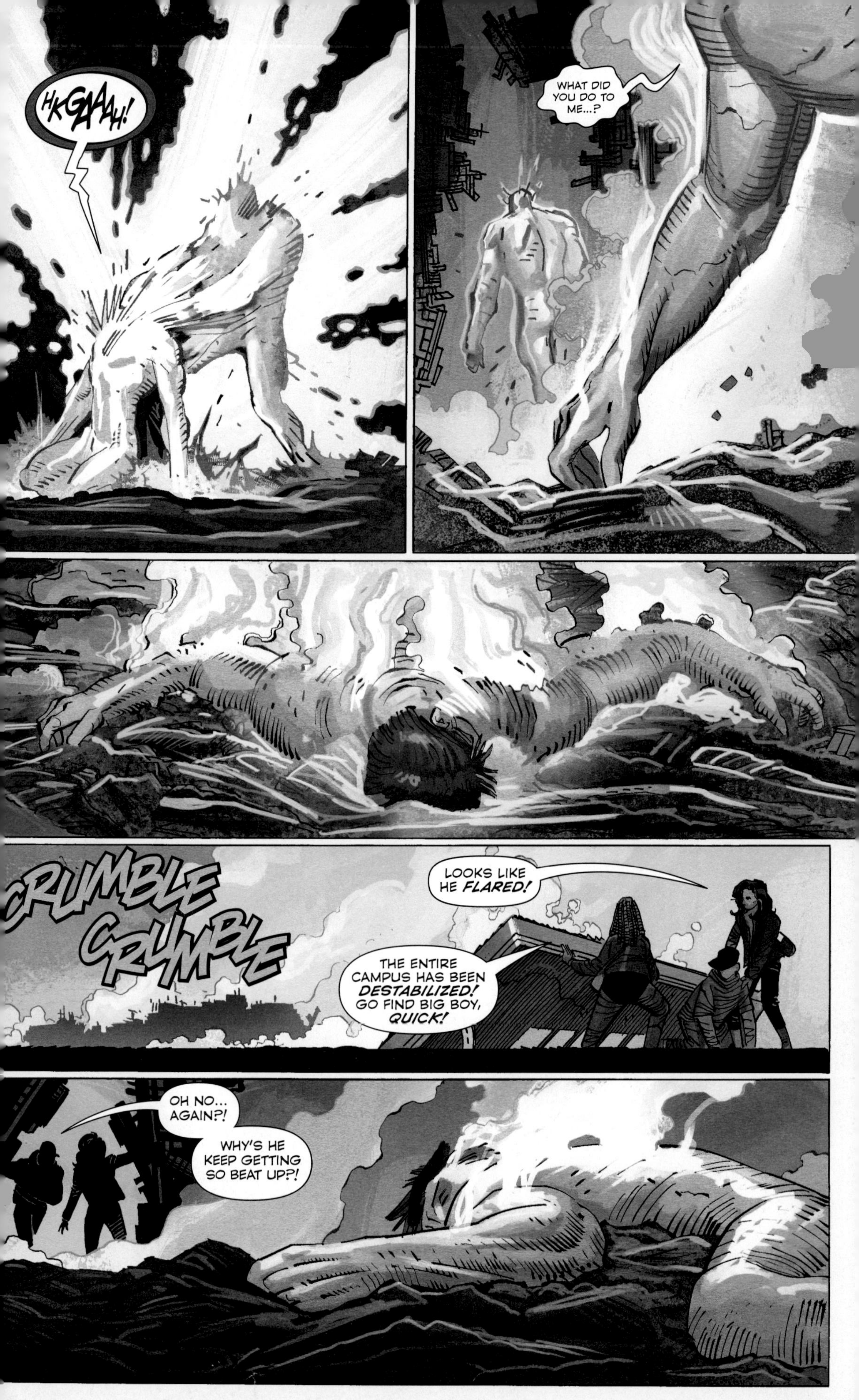
HKGAAAH!
WHAT DID YOU DO TO ME...?
CRUMBLE CRUMBLE
LOOKS LIKE HE *FLARED!*
THE ENTIRE CAMPUS HAS BEEN *DESTABILIZED!* GO FIND BIG BOY, *QUICK!*
OH NO... AGAIN?!
WHY'S HE KEEP GETTING SO BEAT UP?!

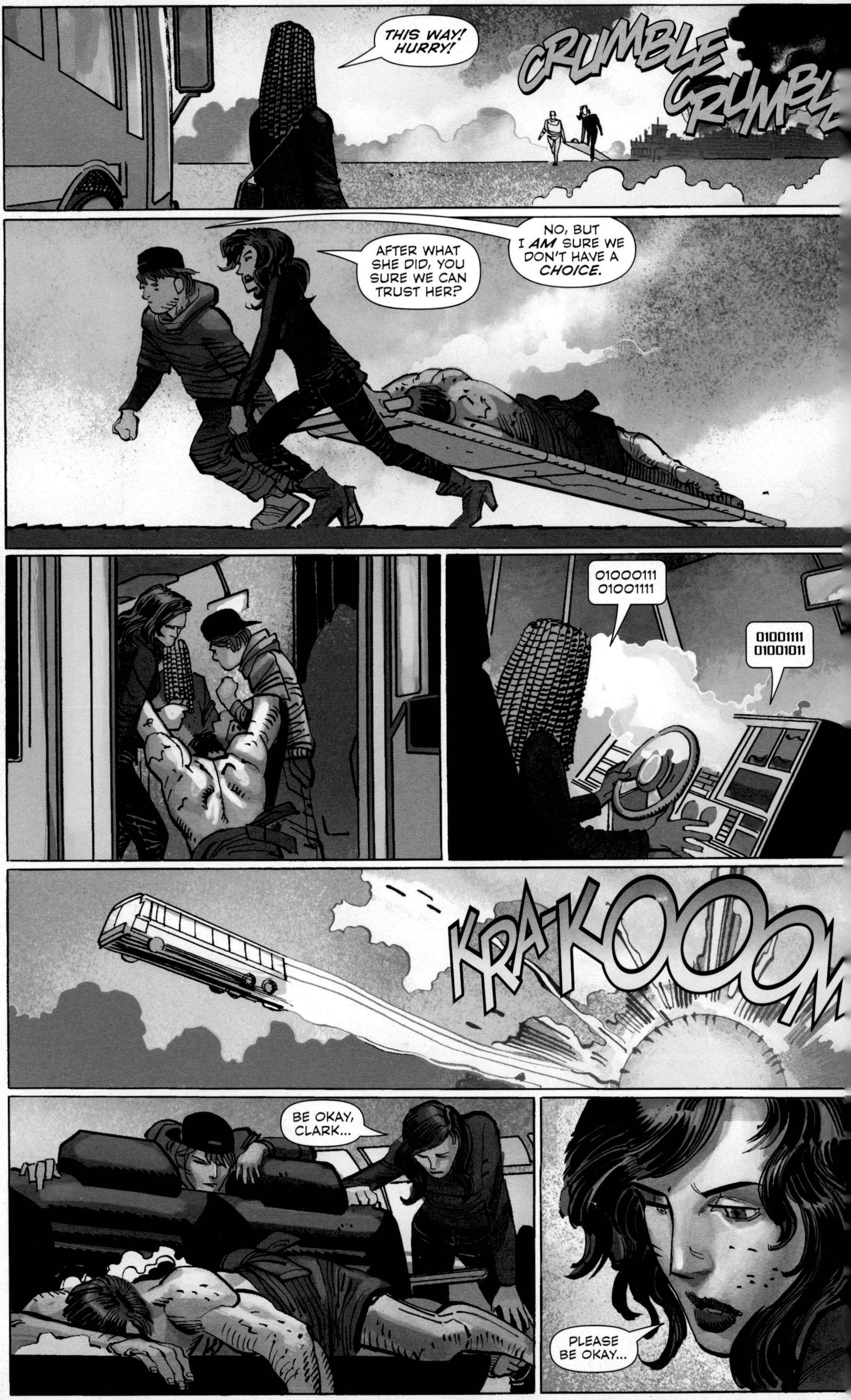
THIS WAY! HURRY!
CRUMBLE
CRUMBLE
AFTER WHAT SHE DID, YOU SURE WE CAN TRUST HER?
NO, BUT I *AM* SURE WE DON'T HAVE A *CHOICE*.
01000111 01001111
01001111 01001011
KRA-KOOOM
BE OKAY, CLARK...
PLEASE BE OKAY...

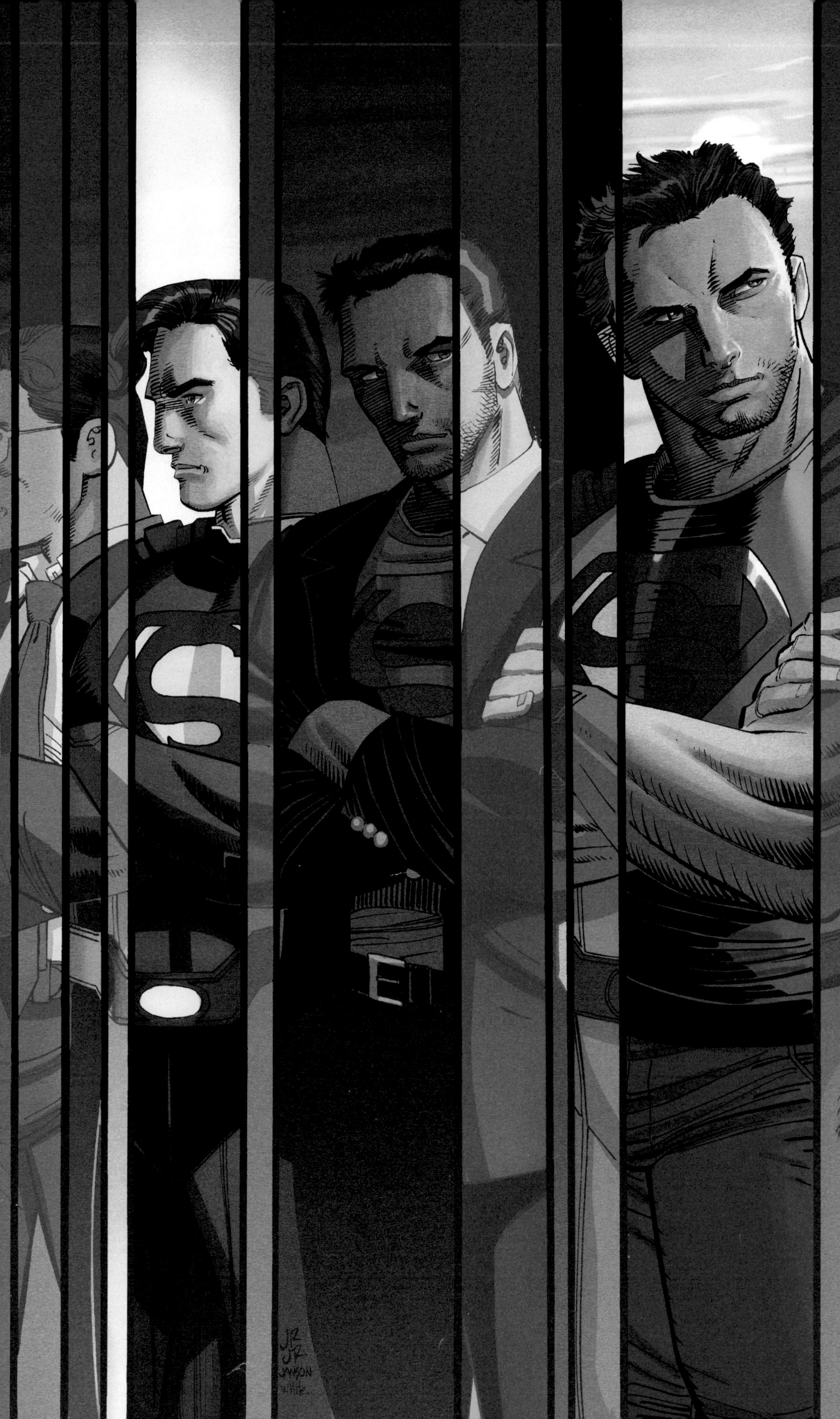
JR JR
JANSON
WHITE

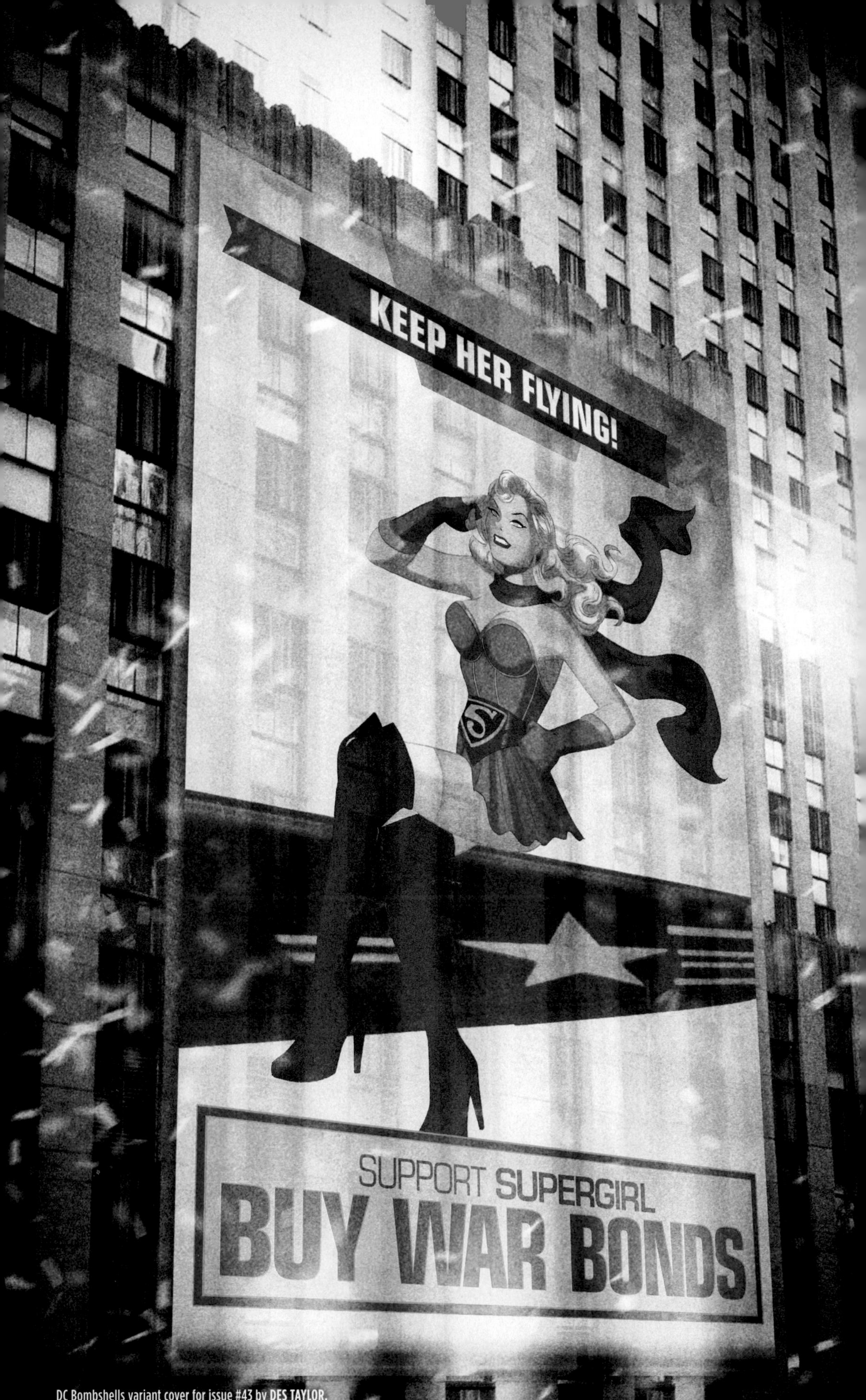
KEEP HER FLYING!
S
SUPPORT SUPERGIRL
BUY WAR BONDS

DC Bombshells variant cover for issue #43 by **DES TAYLOR.**

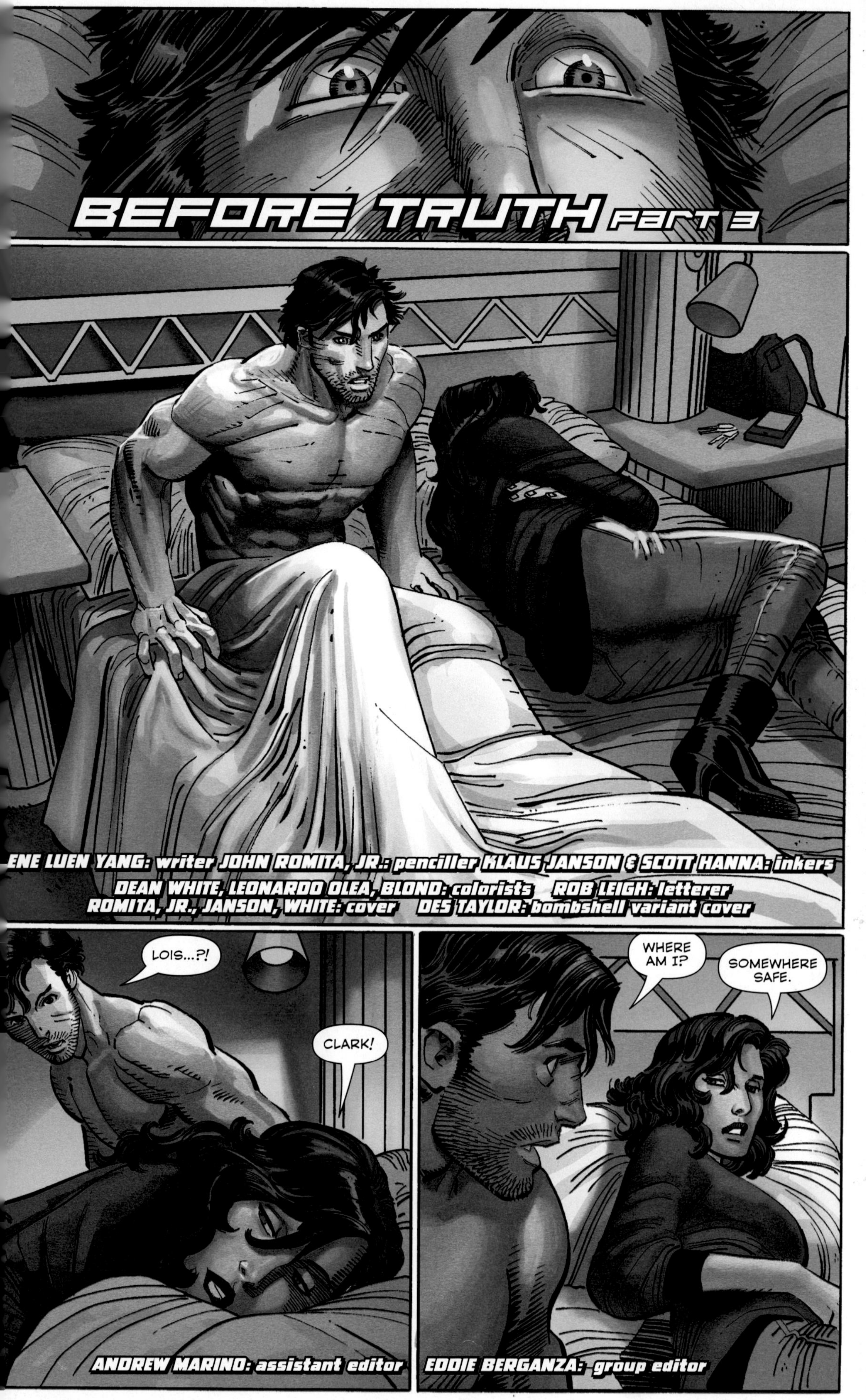
BEFORE TRUTH PART 3
ENE LUEN YANG: writer JOHN ROMITA, JR.: penciller KLAUS JANSON & SCOTT HANNA: inkers
DEAN WHITE, LEONARDO OLEA, BLOND: colorists ROB LEIGH: letterer
ROMITA, JR., JANSON, WHITE: cover DES TAYLOR: bombshell variant cover
LOIS...?!
CLARK!
ANDREW MARINO: assistant editor
WHERE AM I?
SOMEWHERE SAFE.
EDDIE BERGANZA: group editor

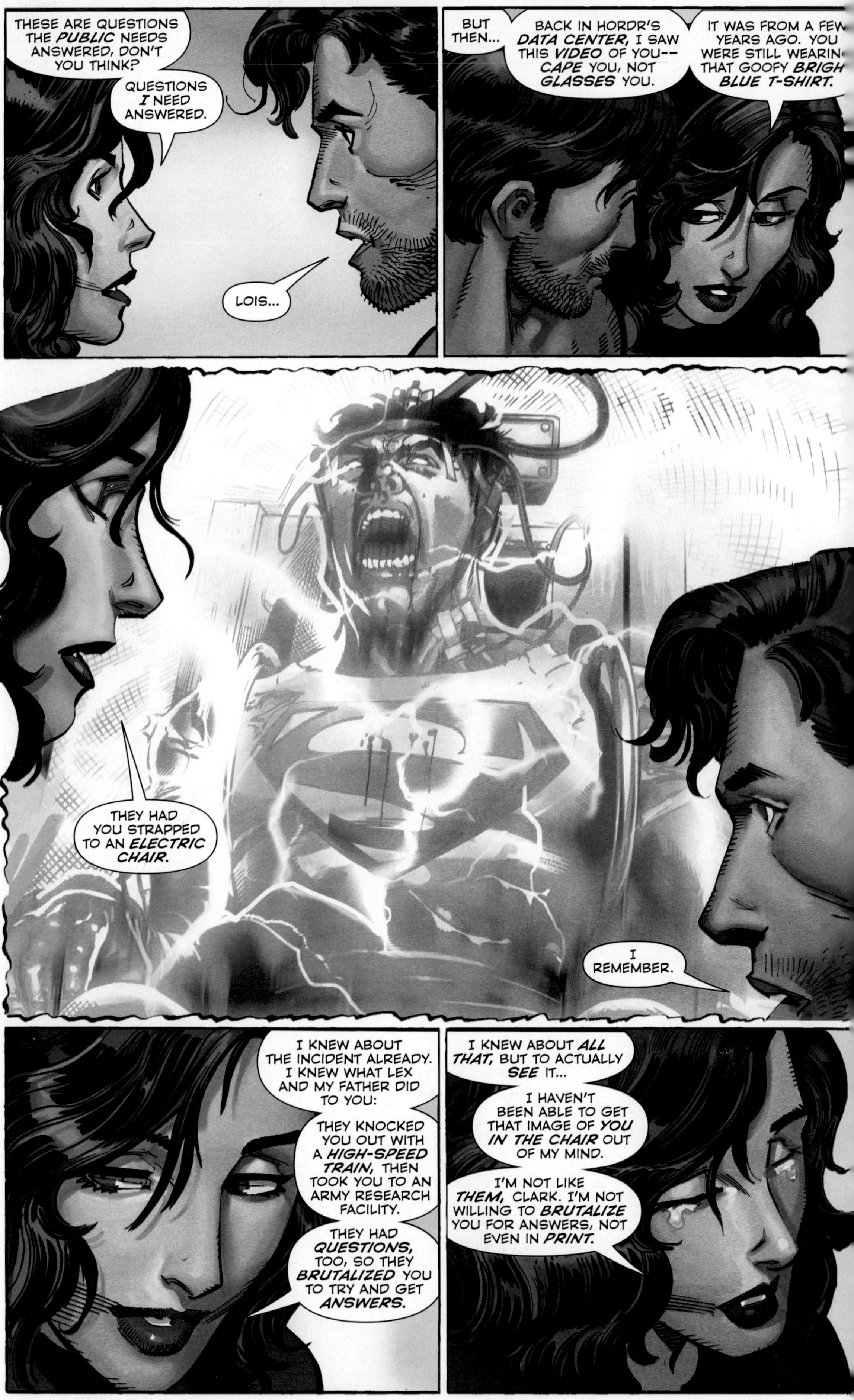
THESE ARE QUESTIONS THE *PUBLIC* NEEDS ANSWERED, DON'T YOU THINK?
QUESTIONS *I* NEED ANSWERED.
LOIS...
BUT THEN...
BACK IN HORDR'S *DATA CENTER,* I SAW THIS *VIDEO* OF YOU-- *CAPE* YOU, NOT *GLASSES* YOU.
IT WAS FROM A FEW YEARS AGO. YOU WERE STILL WEARIN THAT GOOFY *BRIGH* *BLUE T-SHIRT.*
THEY HAD YOU STRAPPED TO AN *ELECTRIC CHAIR.*
I REMEMBER.
I KNEW ABOUT THE INCIDENT ALREADY. I KNEW WHAT LEX AND MY FATHER DID TO YOU:
THEY KNOCKED YOU OUT WITH A *HIGH-SPEED TRAIN,* THEN TOOK YOU TO AN ARMY RESEARCH FACILITY.
THEY HAD *QUESTIONS,* TOO, SO THEY *BRUTALIZED* YOU TO TRY AND GET *ANSWERS.*
I KNEW ABOUT *ALL THAT,* BUT TO ACTUALLY *SEE* IT...
I HAVEN'T BEEN ABLE TO GET THAT IMAGE OF *YOU IN THE CHAIR* OUT OF MY MIND.
I'M NOT LIKE *THEM,* CLARK. I'M NOT WILLING TO *BRUTALIZE* YOU FOR ANSWERS, NOT EVEN IN *PRINT.*

I'VE DECIDED TO KEEP YOUR *SECRET.*
*THANK YOU.* I CAN'T TELL YOU HOW MUCH THAT MEANS TO ME.
BESIDES, MAYBE I ALREADY *HAVE* MY ANSWERS. YOU MAY BE *SUPERMAN,* BUT YOU'RE STILL *CLARK KENT.*
AND I *KNOW* CLARK KENT. I KNOW THE GUY I ALMOST *FELL IN LOVE* WITH.
LOIS...!
I-I'M WITH SOMEONE ALREADY, SOMEONE WHO'S *MORE* THAN JUST A GIRLFRIEND. SHE'S A *TRUE--*
OH, RELAX. I'VE GOT SOMEONE NOW, TOO.
AND BESIDES, I KNOW I'M NOT *MYTHOLOGICAL* ENOUGH FOR YOUR TASTES.
BUT BEING *FRIENDS*...THAT'S SOMETHING, TOO, RIGHT?
LOIS, CAN YOU DO ME A FAVOR?
*ANYTHING.*
*STAB ME.*

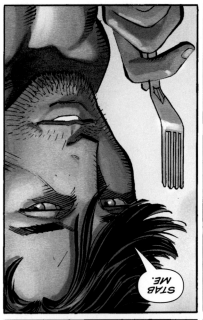

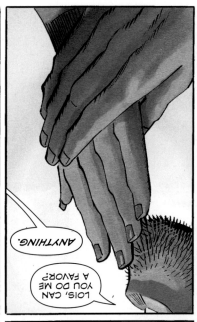

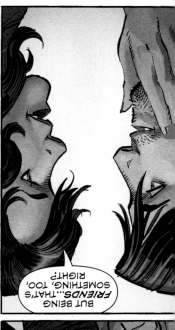

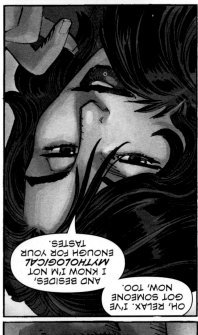

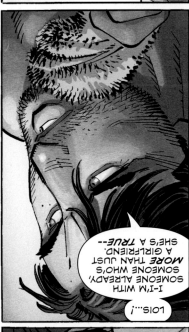

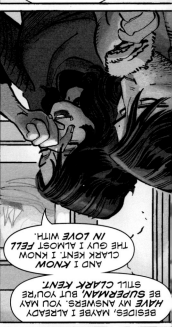

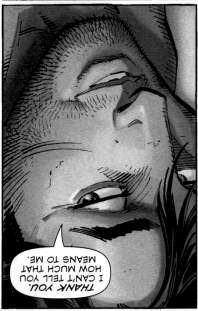

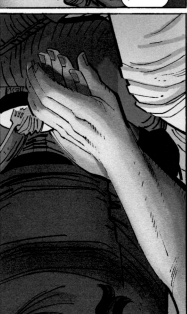

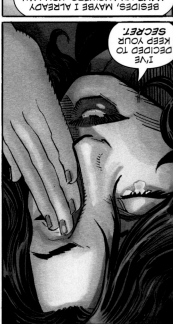

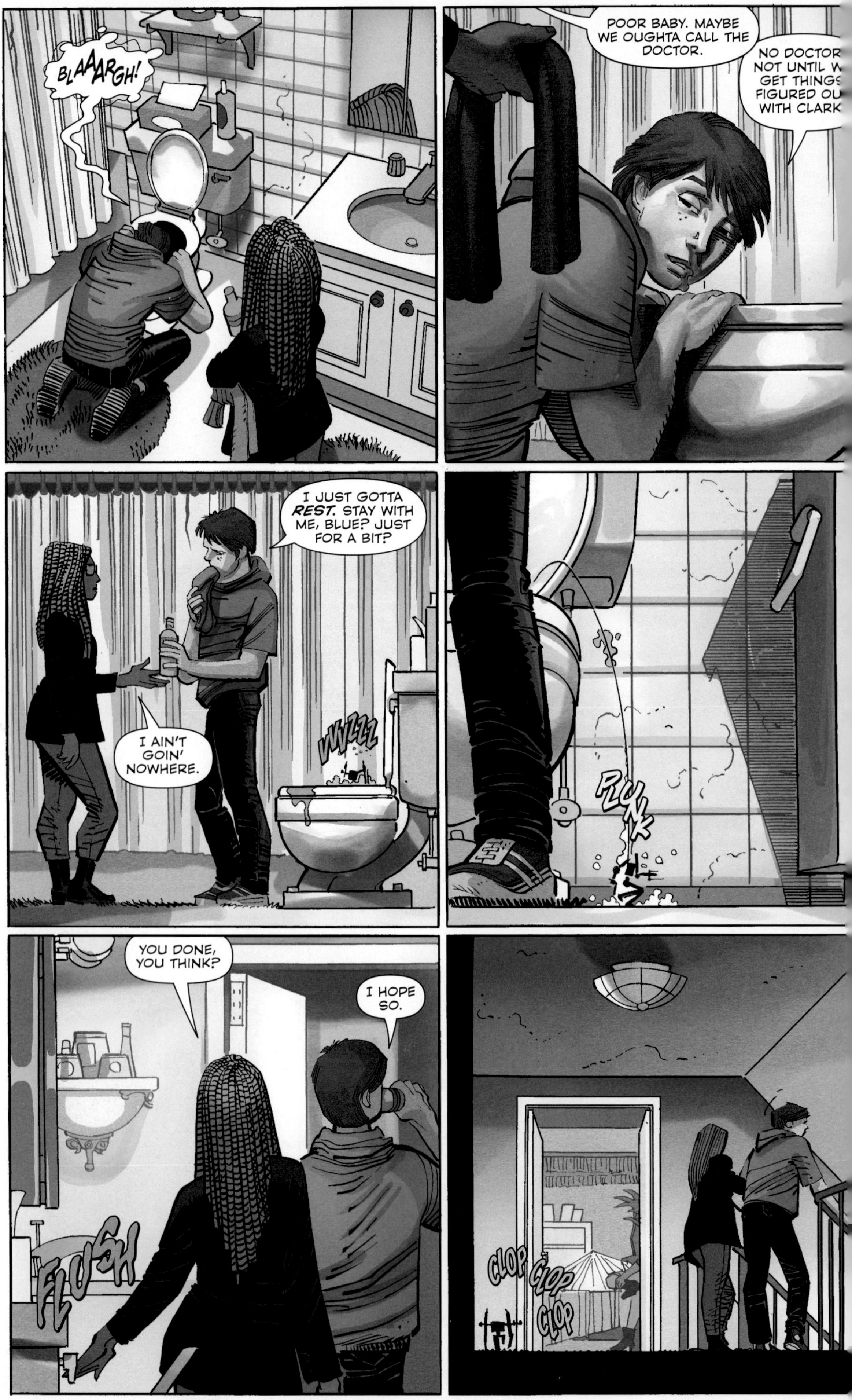
BLAAARGH!
POOR BABY. MAYBE WE OUGHTA CALL THE DOCTOR.
NO DOCTOR
I JUST GOTTA *REST.* STAY WITH ME, BLUE? JUST FOR A BIT?
I AIN'T GOIN' NOWHERE.
VVVZZZZ
PLUNK
YOU DONE, YOU THINK?
I HOPE SO.
FLUSH
CLOP CLOP CLOP

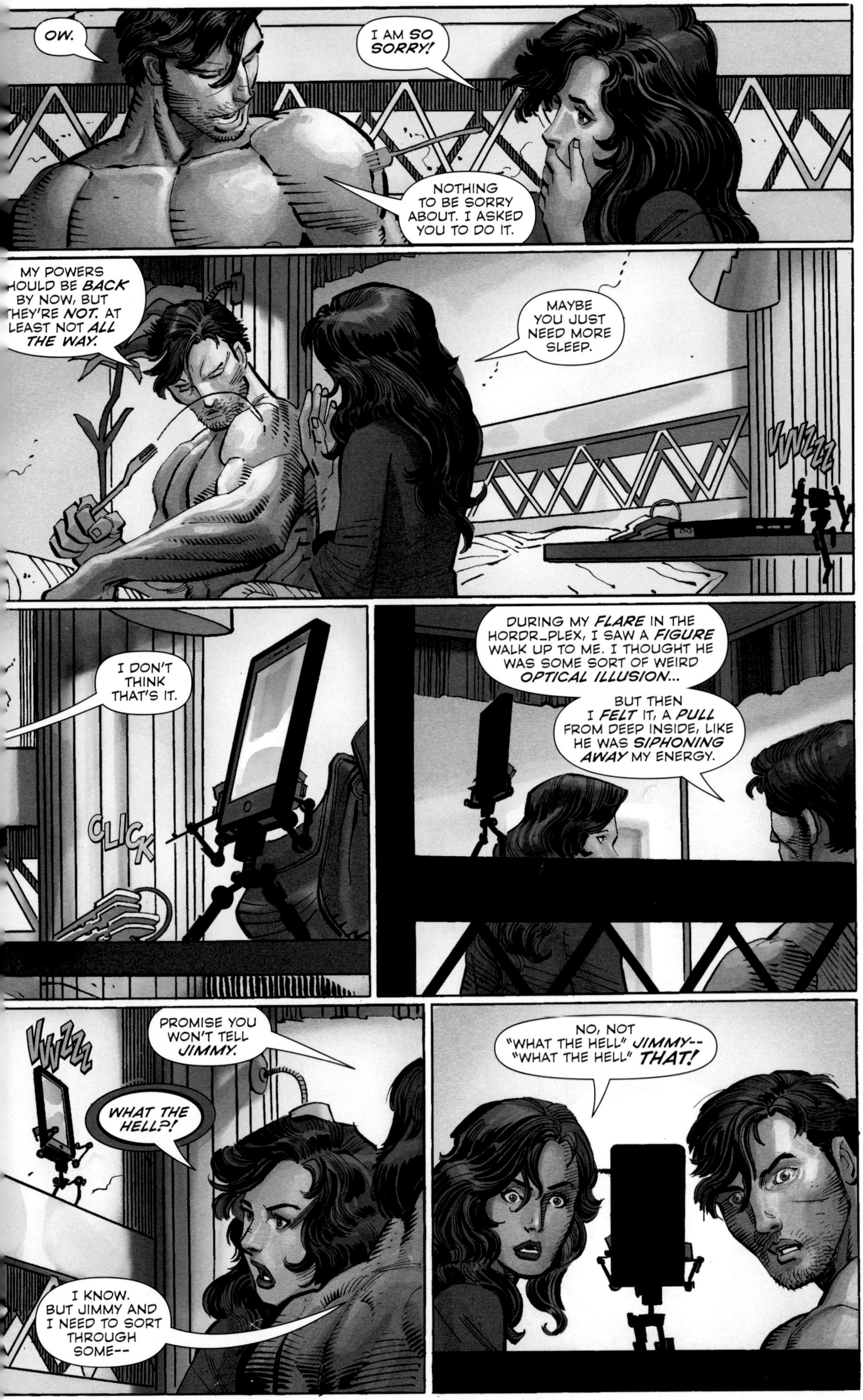
OW.
I AM SO SORRY!
NOTHING TO BE SORRY ABOUT. I ASKED YOU TO DO IT.
MY POWERS HOULD BE BACK BY NOW, BUT THEY'RE NOT. AT LEAST NOT ALL THE WAY.
MAYBE YOU JUST NEED MORE SLEEP.
VVVZZZ
I DON'T THINK THAT'S IT.
CLICK
DURING MY FLARE IN THE HORDR_PLEX, I SAW A FIGURE WALK UP TO ME. I THOUGHT HE WAS SOME SORT OF WEIRD OPTICAL ILLUSION...
BUT THEN I FELT IT, A PULL FROM DEEP INSIDE, LIKE HE WAS SIPHONING AWAY MY ENERGY.
VVVZZZ
PROMISE YOU WON'T TELL JIMMY.
I KNOW. BUT JIMMY AND I NEED TO SORT THROUGH SOME--
WHAT THE HELL?!
NO, NOT "WHAT THE HELL" JIMMY-- "WHAT THE HELL" THAT!

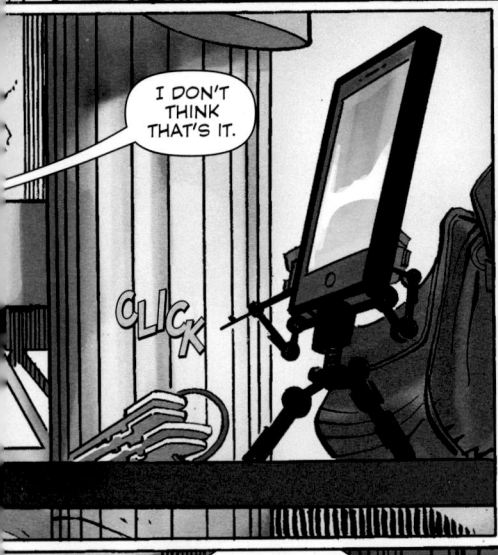

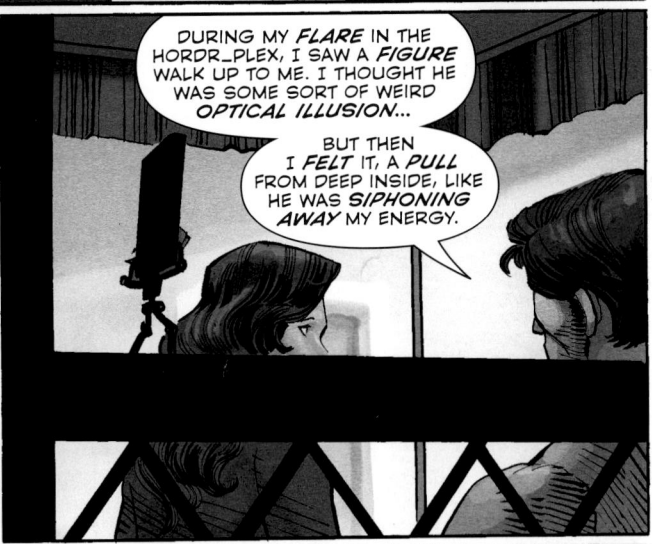

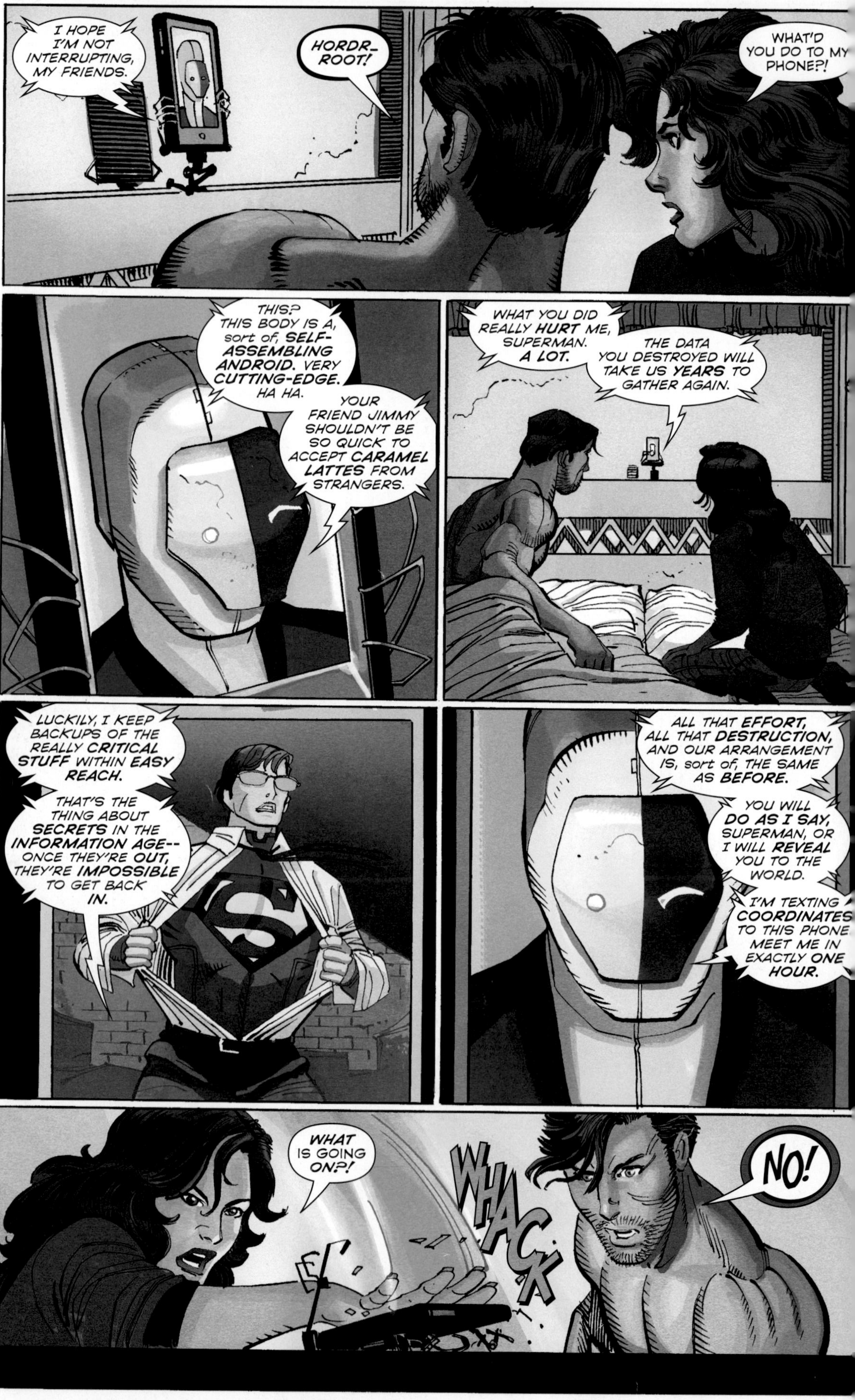
I HOPE I'M NOT INTERRUPTING, MY FRIENDS.
HORDR-ROOT!
WHAT'D YOU DO TO MY PHONE?!
THIS? THIS BODY IS A, sort of, SELF-ASSEMBLING ANDROID. VERY CUTTING-EDGE. HA HA.
YOUR FRIEND JIMMY SHOULDN'T BE SO QUICK TO ACCEPT CARAMEL LATTES FROM STRANGERS.
WHAT YOU DID REALLY HURT ME, SUPERMAN. A LOT.
THE DATA YOU DESTROYED WILL TAKE US YEARS TO GATHER AGAIN.
LUCKILY, I KEEP BACKUPS OF THE REALLY CRITICAL STUFF WITHIN EASY REACH.
THAT'S THE THING ABOUT SECRETS IN THE INFORMATION AGE-- ONCE THEY'RE OUT, THEY'RE IMPOSSIBLE TO GET BACK IN.
ALL THAT EFFORT, ALL THAT DESTRUCTION, AND OUR ARRANGEMENT IS, sort of, THE SAME AS BEFORE.
YOU WILL DO AS I SAY, SUPERMAN, OR I WILL REVEAL YOU TO THE WORLD.
I'M TEXTING COORDINATES TO THIS PHONE MEET ME IN EXACTLY ONE HOUR.
WHAT IS GOING ON?!
WHACK
NO!

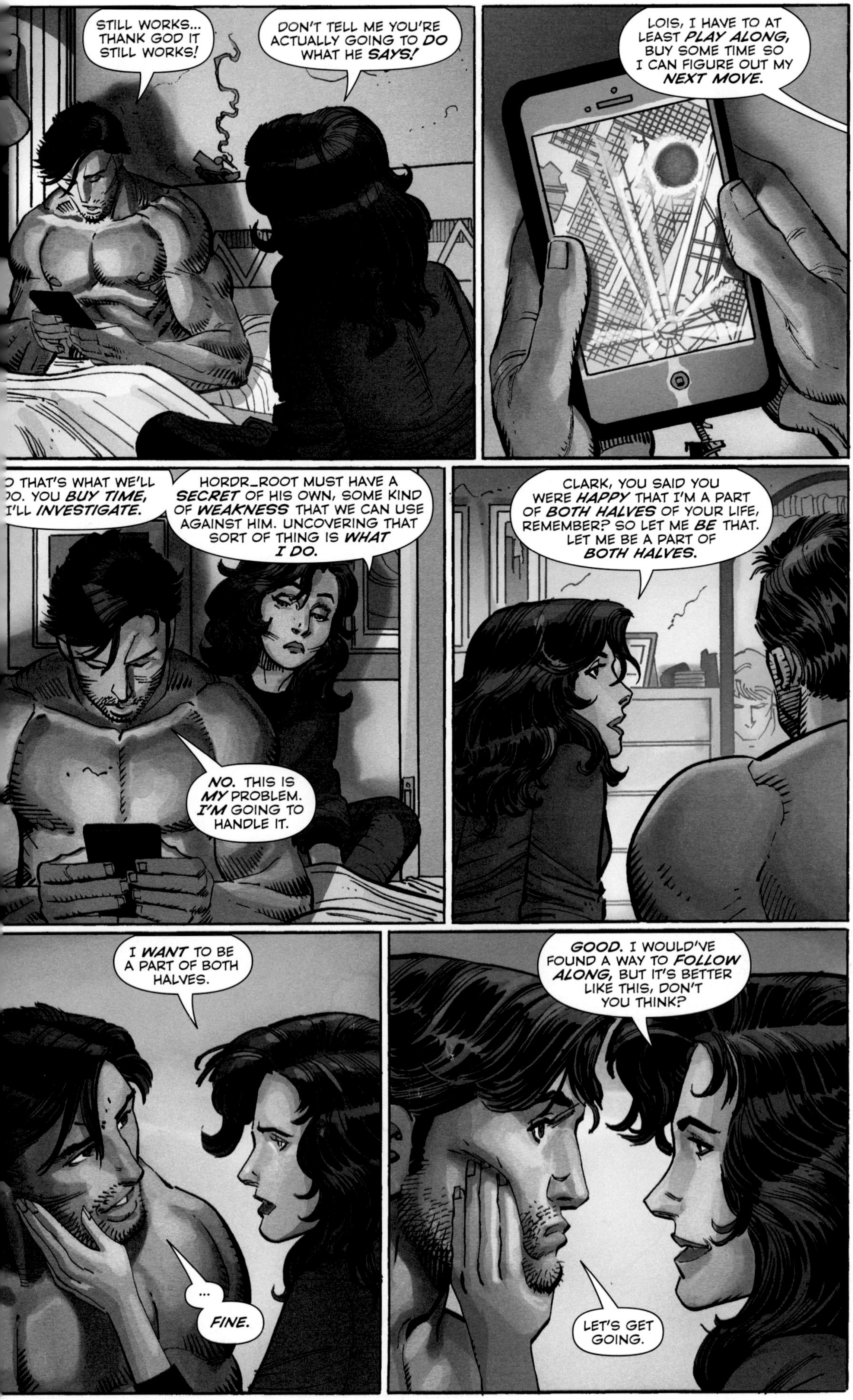
STILL WORKS... THANK GOD IT STILL WORKS!
DON'T TELL ME YOU'RE ACTUALLY GOING TO *DO* WHAT HE *SAYS!*
LOIS, I HAVE TO AT LEAST *PLAY ALONG,* BUY SOME TIME SO I CAN FIGURE OUT MY *NEXT MOVE.*
O THAT'S WHAT WE'LL DO. YOU *BUY TIME,* I'LL *INVESTIGATE.*
HORDR_ROOT MUST HAVE A *SECRET* OF HIS OWN, SOME KIND OF *WEAKNESS* THAT WE CAN USE AGAINST HIM. UNCOVERING THAT SORT OF THING IS *WHAT I DO.*
*NO.* THIS IS *MY* PROBLEM. *I'M* GOING TO HANDLE IT.
CLARK, YOU SAID YOU WERE *HAPPY* THAT I'M A PART OF *BOTH HALVES* OF YOUR LIFE, REMEMBER? SO LET ME *BE* THAT. LET ME BE A PART OF *BOTH HALVES.*
I *WANT* TO BE A PART OF BOTH HALVES.
...
*FINE.*
*GOOD.* I WOULD'VE FOUND A WAY TO *FOLLOW ALONG,* BUT IT'S BETTER LIKE THIS, DON'T YOU THINK?
LET'S GET GOING.

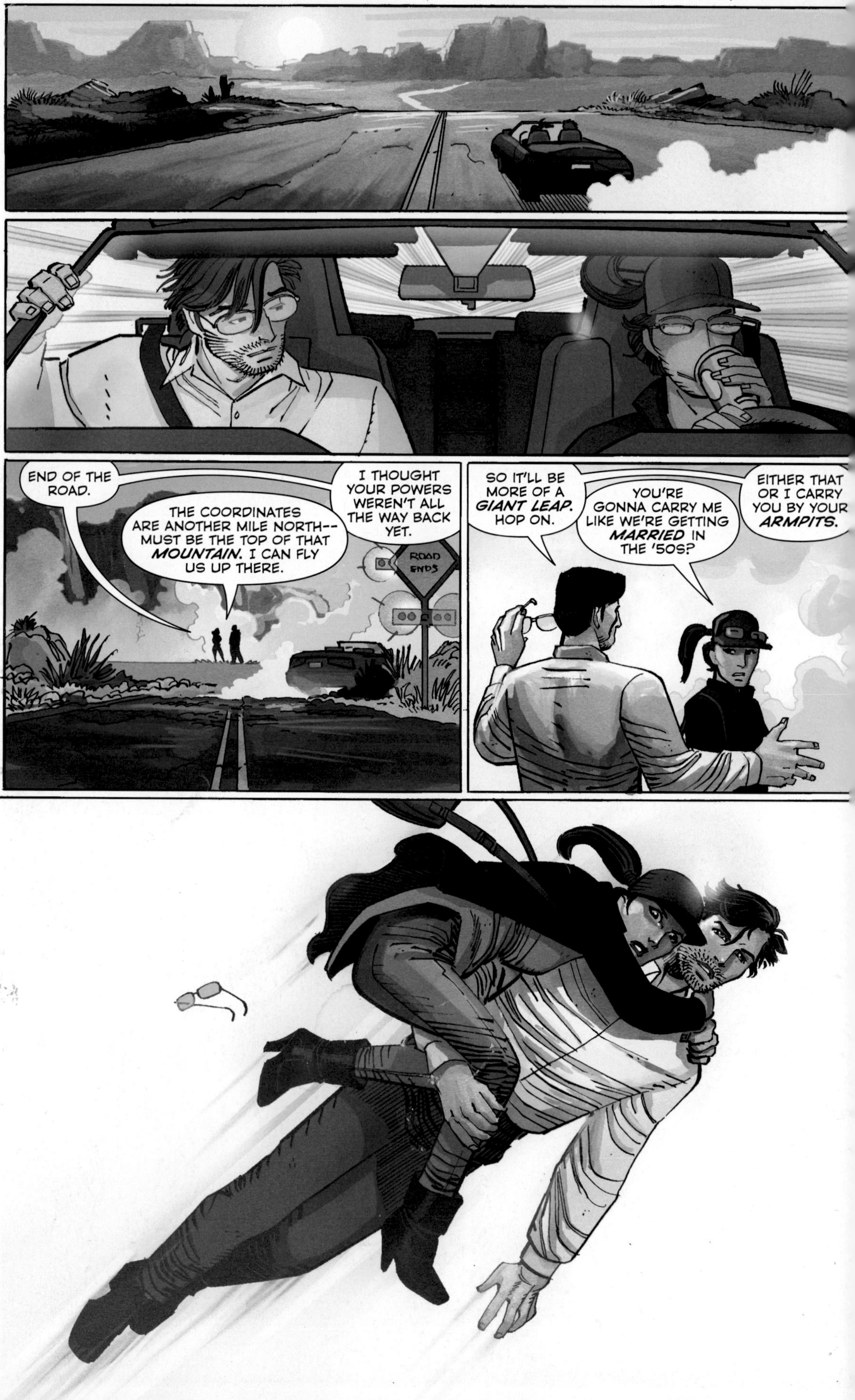
END OF THE ROAD.
THE COORDINATES ARE ANOTHER MILE NORTH-- MUST BE THE TOP OF THAT ***MOUNTAIN.*** I CAN FLY US UP THERE.
I THOUGHT YOUR POWERS WEREN'T ALL THE WAY BACK YET.
ROAD ENDS
SO IT'LL BE MORE OF A ***GIANT LEAP.*** HOP ON.
YOU'RE GONNA CARRY ME LIKE WE'RE GETTING ***MARRIED*** IN THE '50S?
EITHER THAT OR I CARRY YOU BY YOUR ***ARMPITS.***

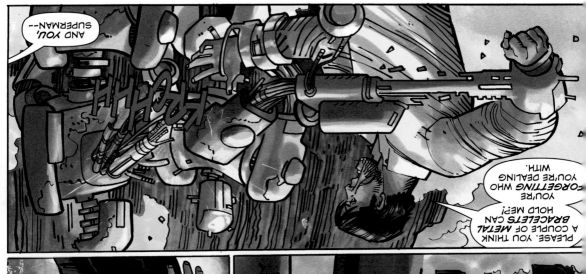

AND YOU, SUPERMAN--

YOU'RE *FORGETTING* WHO YOU'RE DEALING WITH.

PLEASE. YOU THINK A COUPLE OF *METAL BRACELETS* CAN HOLD ME?

SHNK

SUPERMAN. WE'VE BEEN EXPECTING YOU.

LET'S GET THIS OVER WITH. WHERE IS HE?

YOU DON'T NEED ME TO HOLD YOUR HAND. YOU'LL BE OKAY.

THAT'S NOT WHAT I *MEANT*--

I KNOW WHAT YOU MEANT, CLARK. I APPRECIATE THE *CONCERN,* BUT LIKE I SAID, THIS IS *WHAT I DO.* I'LL FIGURE IT OUT.

NOW GO.

THEY'RE WAITING FOR YOU. GO.

I DON'T FEEL RIGHT LEAVING YOU HERE.

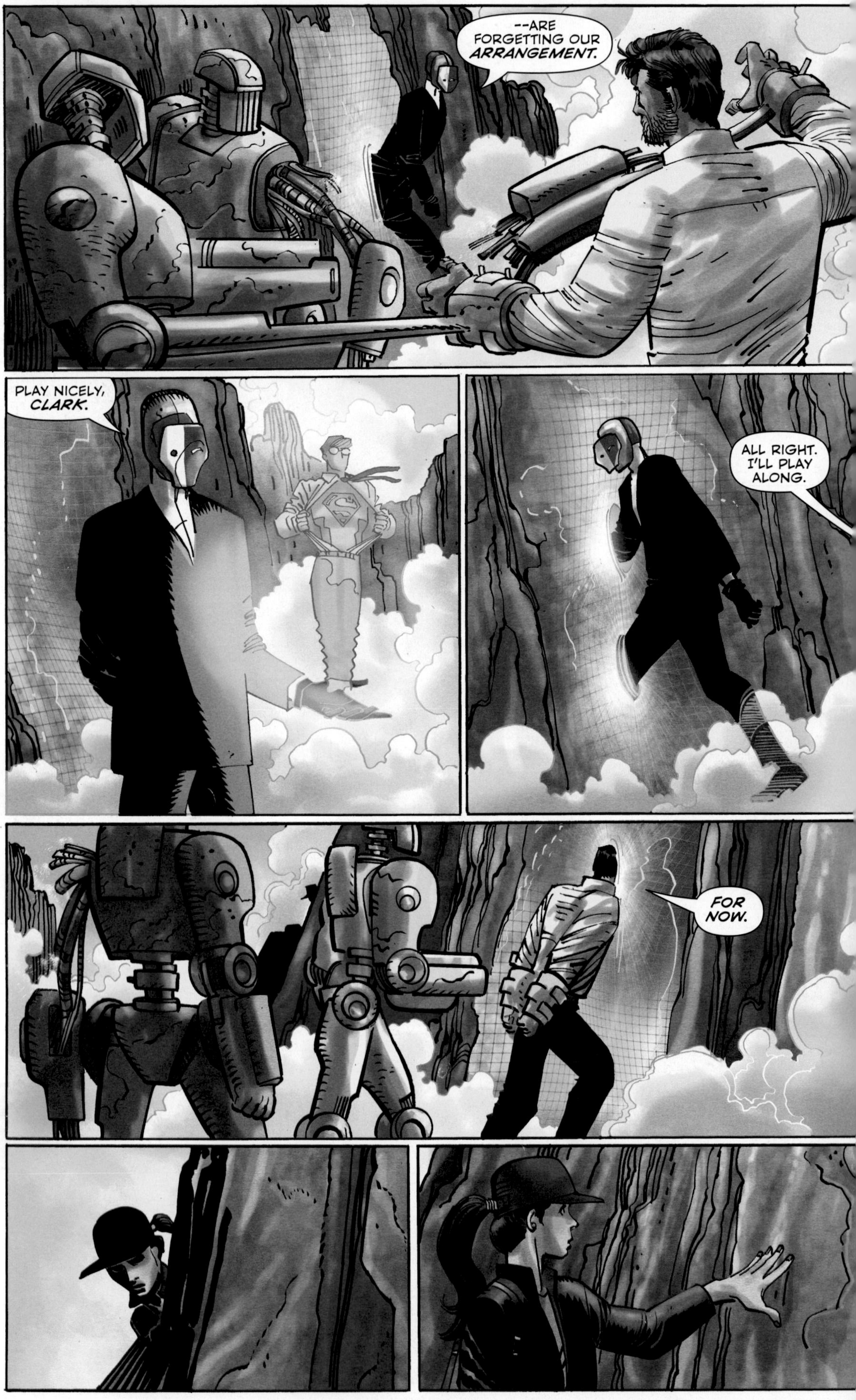
--ARE FORGETTING OUR *ARRANGEMENT*.
PLAY NICELY, *CLARK*.
ALL RIGHT. I'LL PLAY ALONG.
*FOR NOW.*

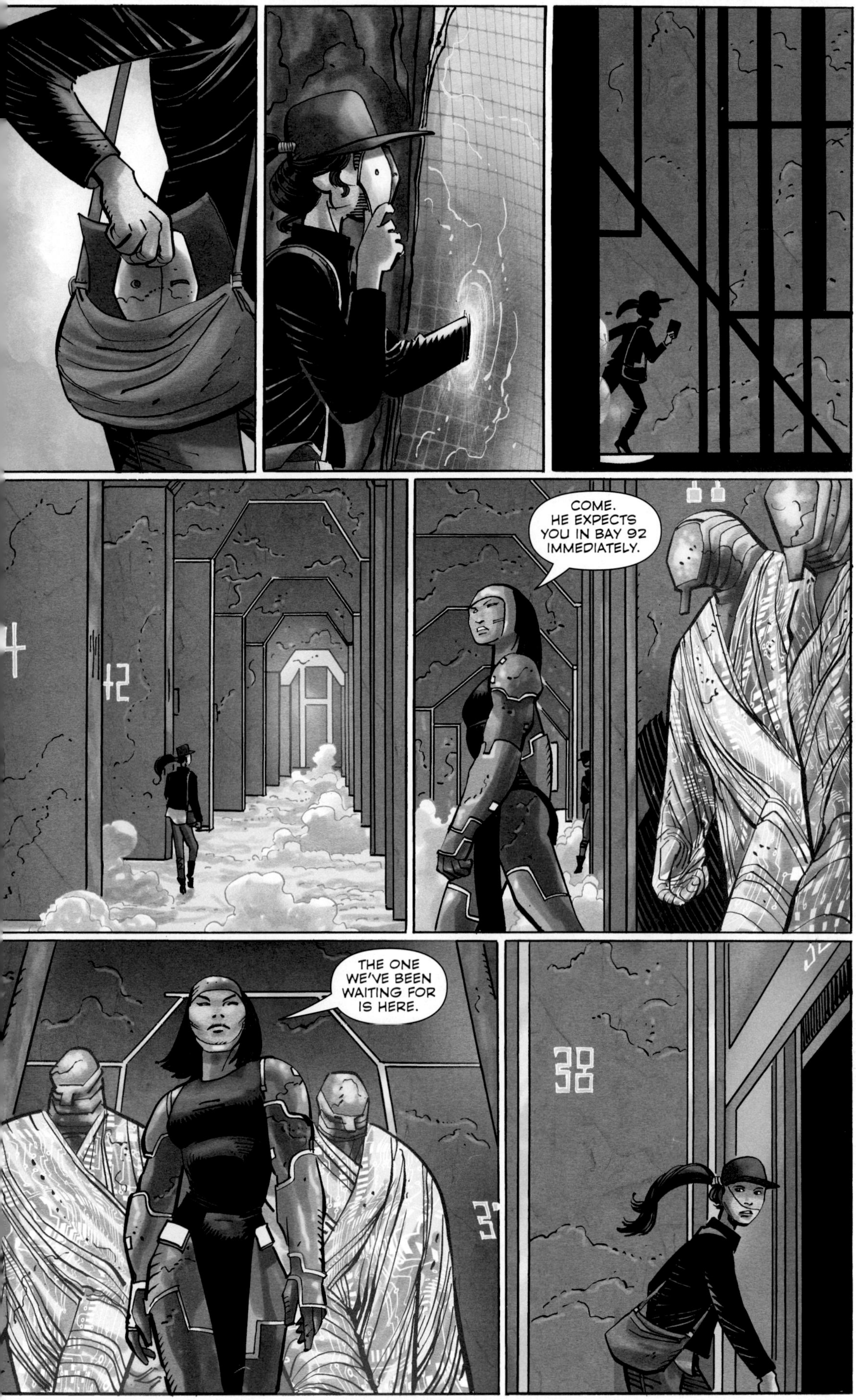
42
COME.
HE EXPECTS
YOU IN BAY 92
IMMEDIATELY.
THE ONE
WE'VE BEEN
WAITING FOR
IS HERE.
38

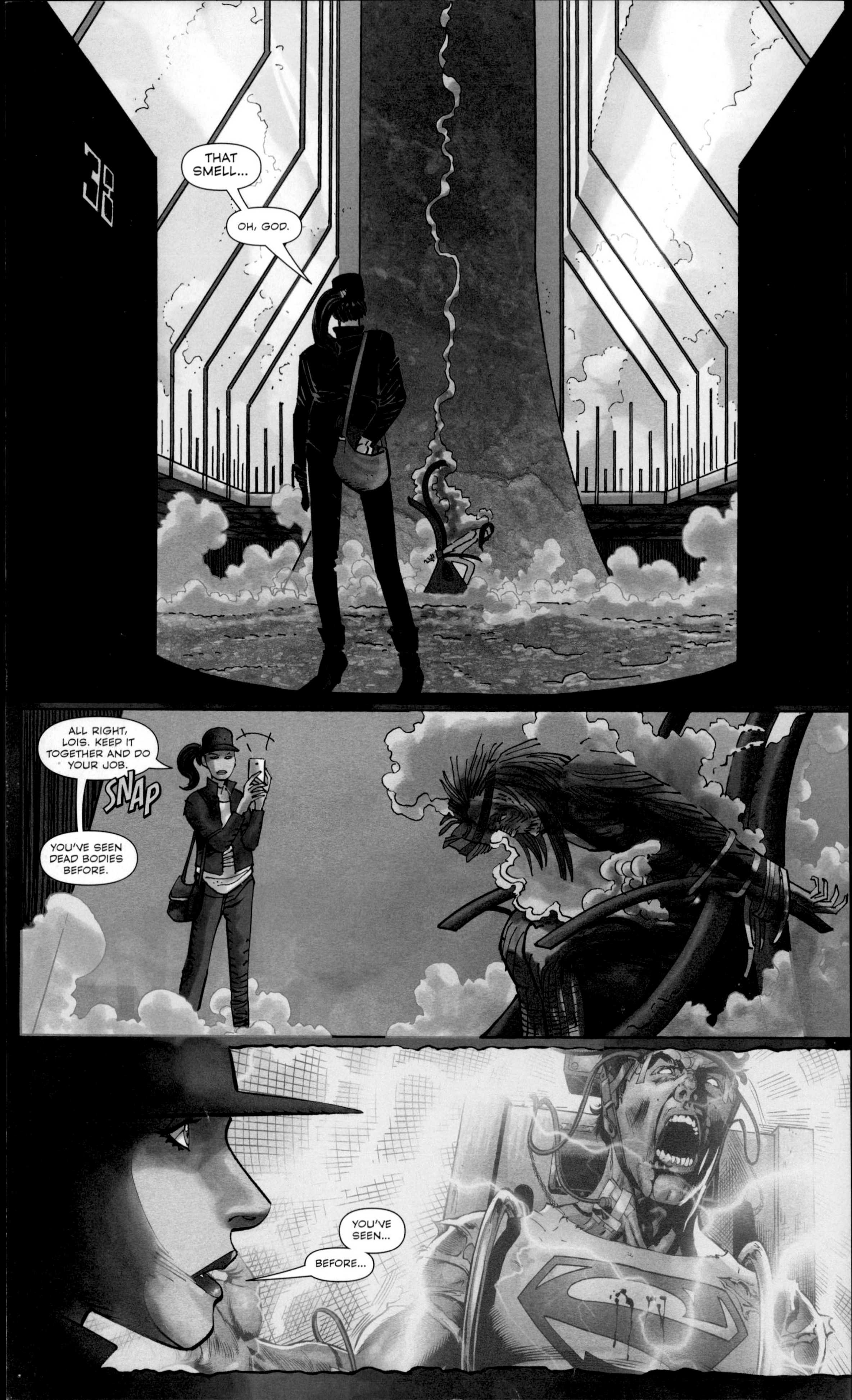
38
THAT SMELL...
OH, GOD.
ALL RIGHT, LOIS. KEEP IT TOGETHER AND DO YOUR JOB.
SNAP
YOU'VE SEEN DEAD BODIES BEFORE.
YOU'VE SEEN...
BEFORE...

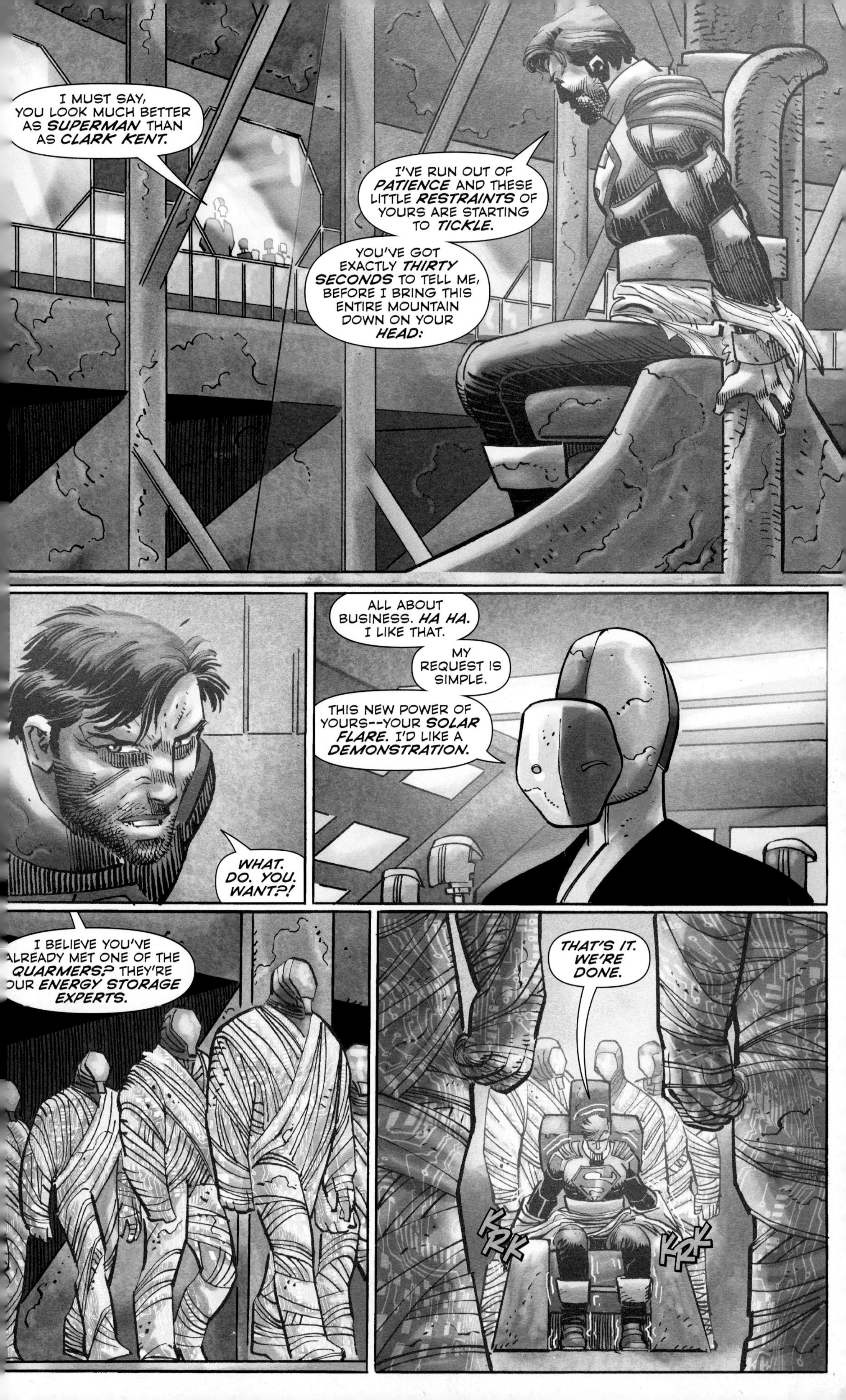
I MUST SAY, YOU LOOK MUCH BETTER AS *SUPERMAN* THAN AS *CLARK KENT.*
I'VE RUN OUT OF *PATIENCE* AND THESE LITTLE *RESTRAINTS* OF YOURS ARE STARTING TO *TICKLE*.
YOU'VE GOT EXACTLY *THIRTY SECONDS* TO TELL ME, BEFORE I BRING THIS ENTIRE MOUNTAIN DOWN ON YOUR *HEAD:*
*WHAT. DO. YOU. WANT?!*
ALL ABOUT BUSINESS. *HA HA*. I LIKE THAT.
MY REQUEST IS SIMPLE.
THIS NEW POWER OF YOURS--YOUR *SOLAR FLARE*. I'D LIKE A *DEMONSTRATION.*
I BELIEVE YOU'VE ALREADY MET ONE OF THE *QUARMERS?* THEY'RE OUR *ENERGY STORAGE EXPERTS.*
*THAT'S IT. WE'RE DONE.*
KRK
KRK

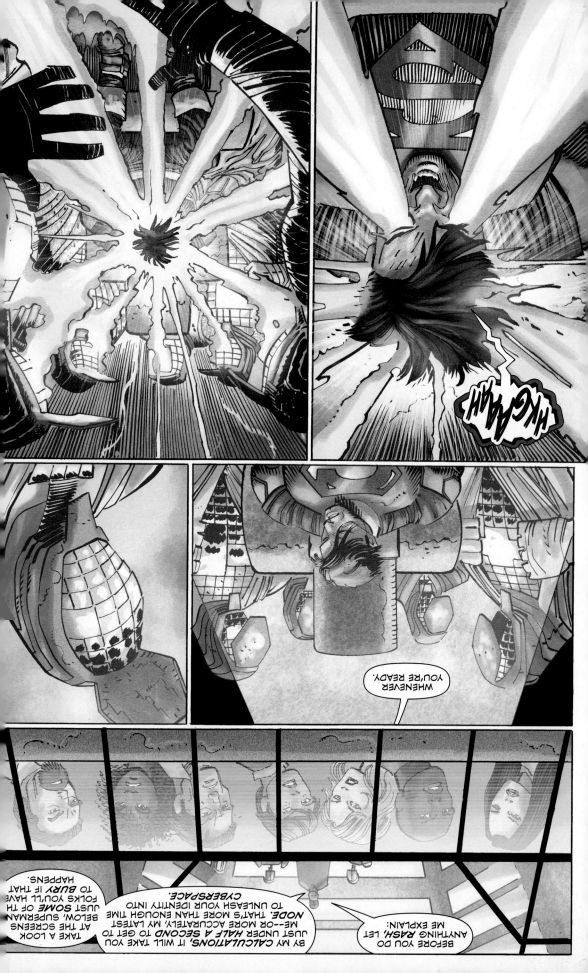

HKG-AAAH

WHENEVER YOU'RE READY.

BEFORE YOU DO ANYTHING *RASH*, LET ME EXPLAIN:

BY MY *CALCULATIONS*, IT WILL TAKE YOU JUST UNDER HALF A *SECOND* TO GET TO ME--OR MORE ACCURATELY, MY LATEST *NODE*. THAT'S MORE THAN ENOUGH TIME TO UNLEASH YOUR IDENTITY INTO *CYBERSPACE*.

TAKE A LOOK AT THE *SCREENS* BELOW, SUPERMAN. JUST *SOME* OF TH FOLKS YOU'LL HAVE TO *BURY* IF THAT HAPPENS.

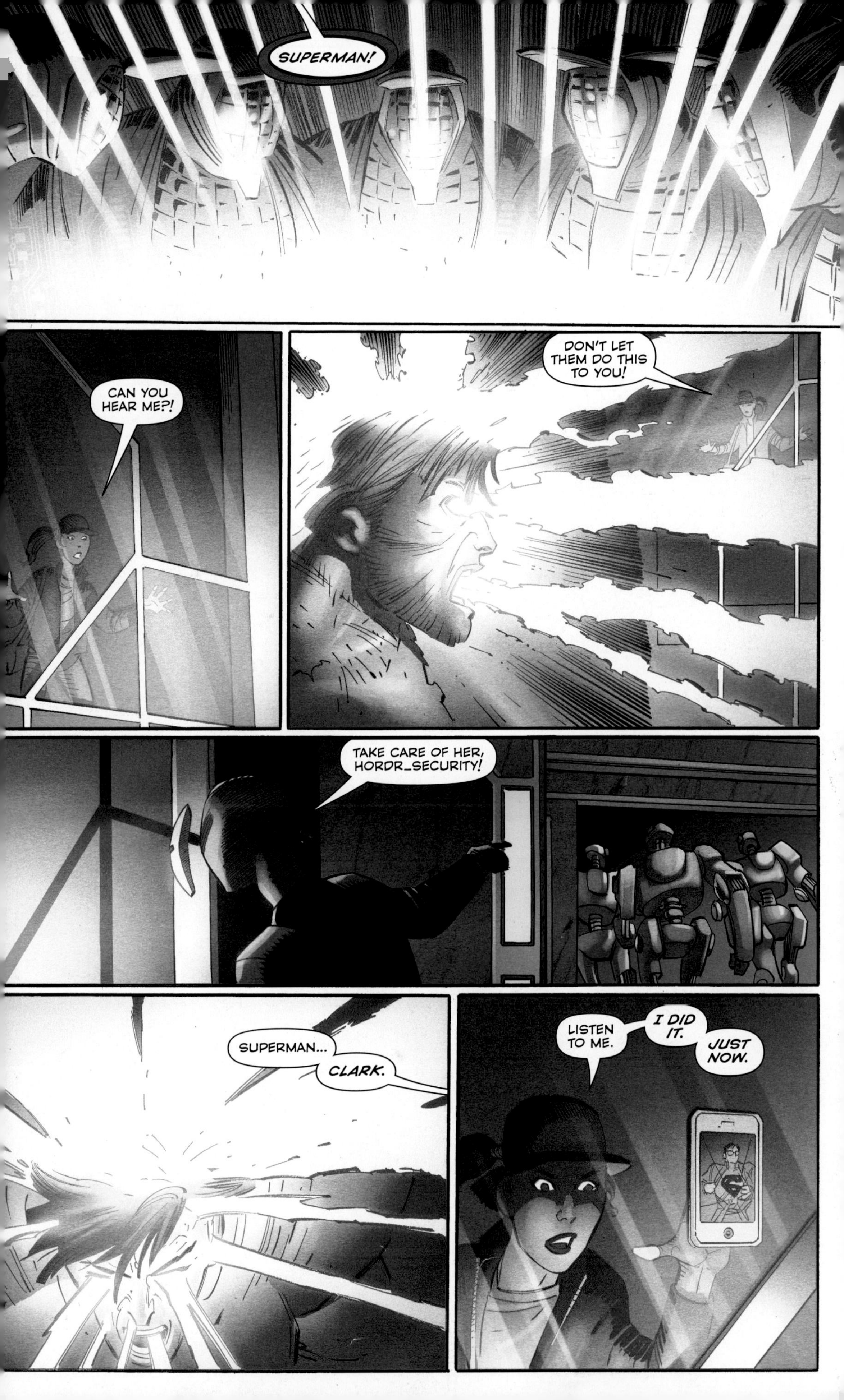
SUPERMAN!
CAN YOU HEAR ME?!
DON'T LET THEM DO THIS TO YOU!
TAKE CARE OF HER, HORDR_SECURITY!
SUPERMAN...
CLARK.
LISTEN TO ME.
I DID IT.
JUST NOW.

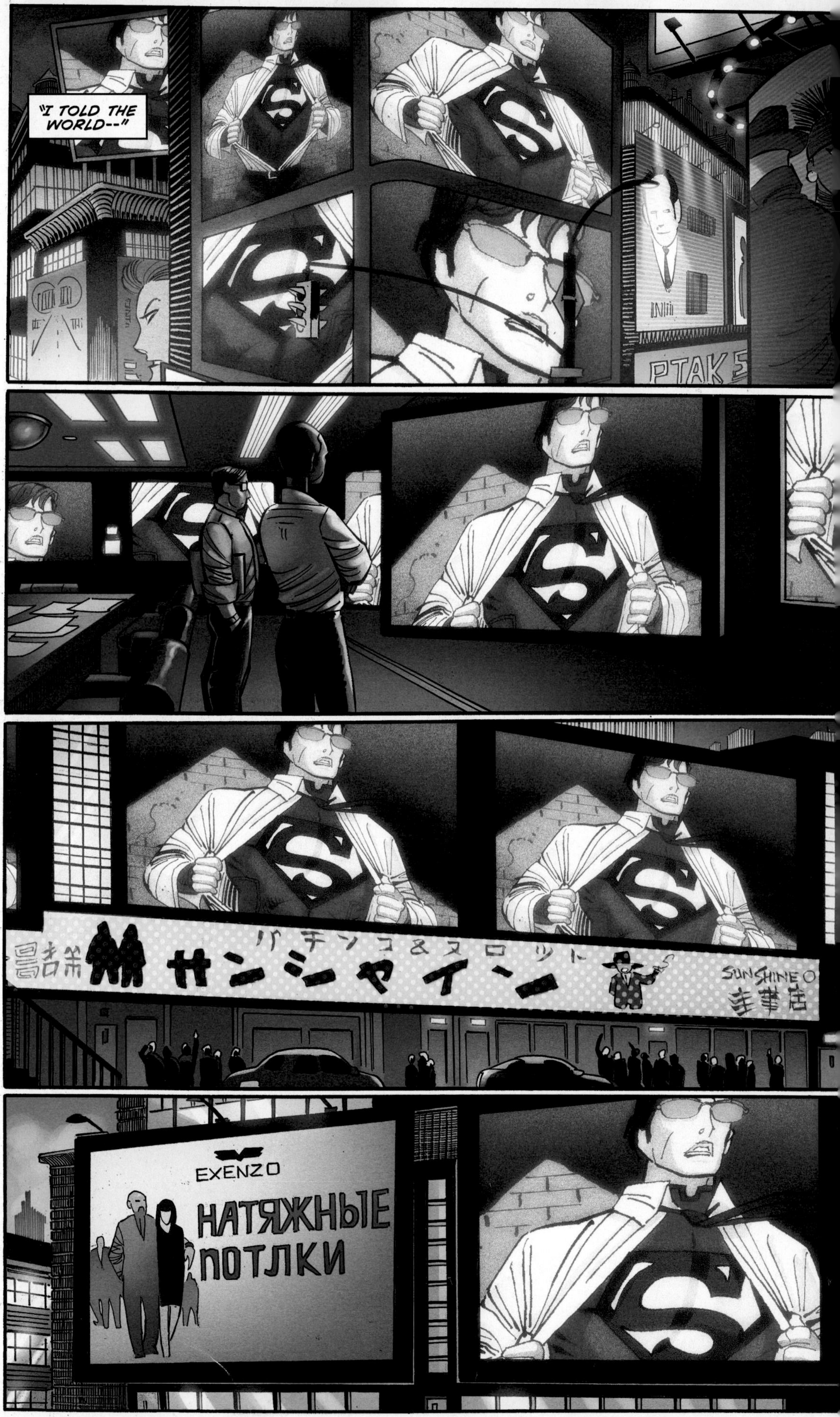
"I TOLD THE WORLD--"
PTAK
SUNSHINE
EXENZO
НАТЯЖНЫЕ
ПОТЛКИ

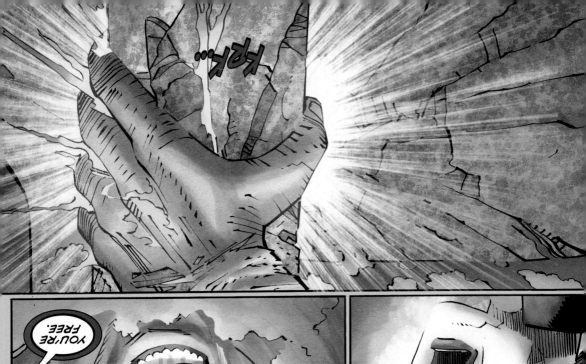

YOU'RE FREE.

THEY DON'T HAVE ANYTHING ON YOU ANYMORE.

HFN.

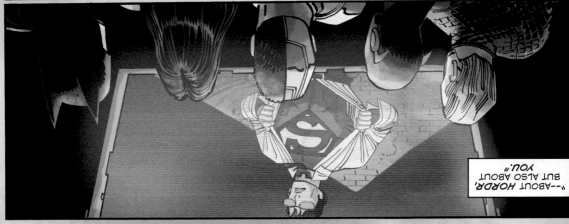

"--ABOUT HORDR, BUT ALSO ABOUT YOU."

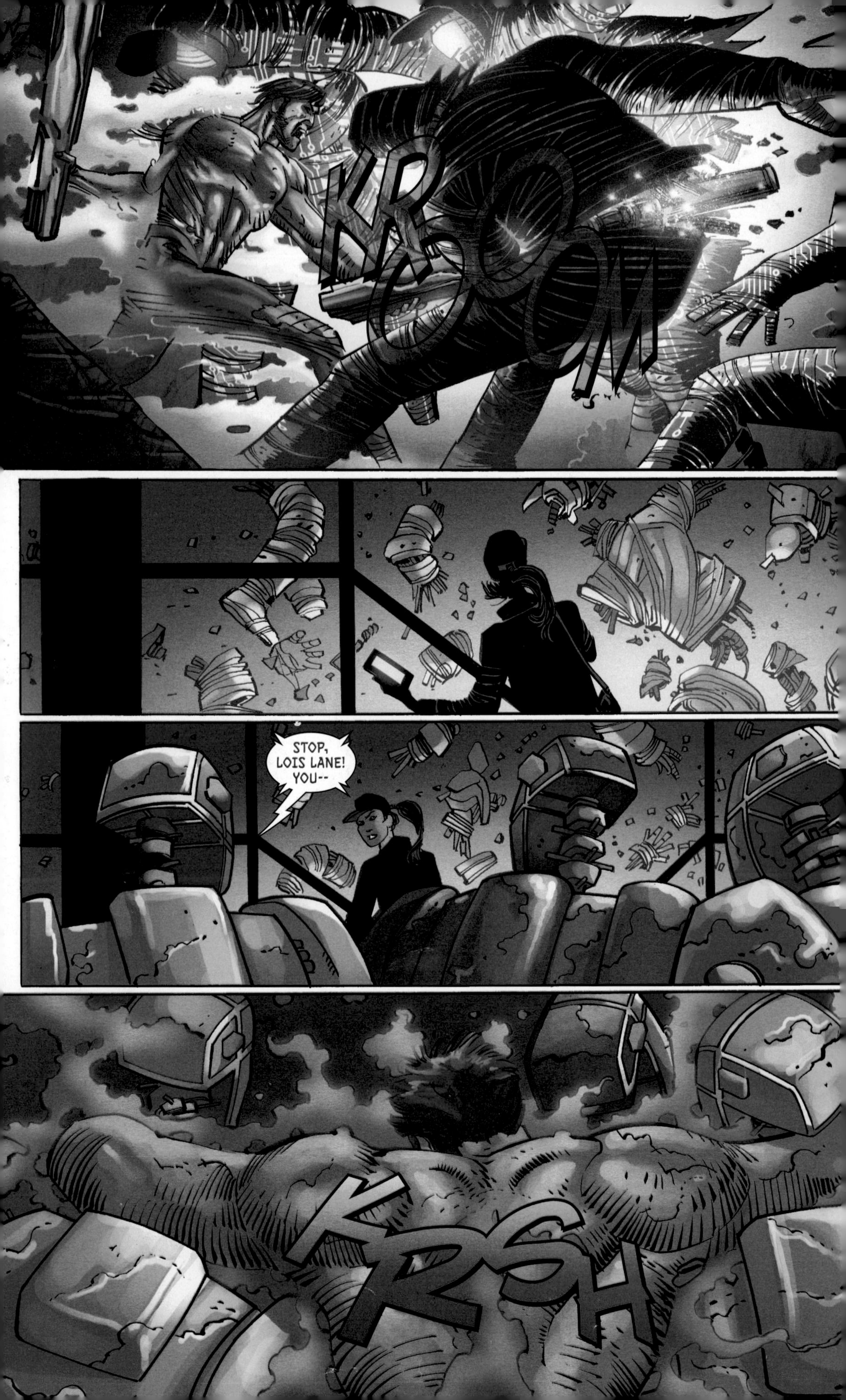
KRBOOM
STOP, LOIS LANE! YOU--
KRSH

KRUNK
CLARK... YOU'RE OKAY!
WHY, LOIS?!
*Sigh*
YOU HAD NO RIGHT! I WOULD'VE FIGURED IT OUT!
EVERYTHING'S GONNA BE OKAY, YOU HEAR ME?! WE'LL GET THROUGH THIS TOGETHER!

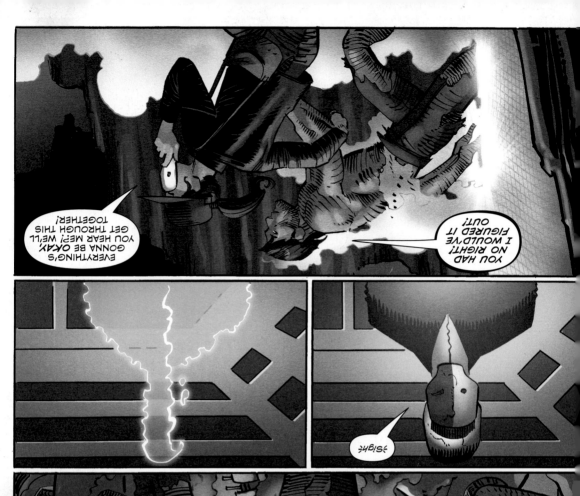

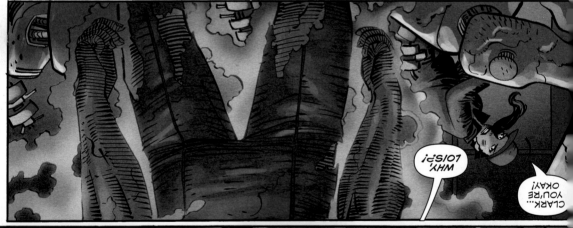

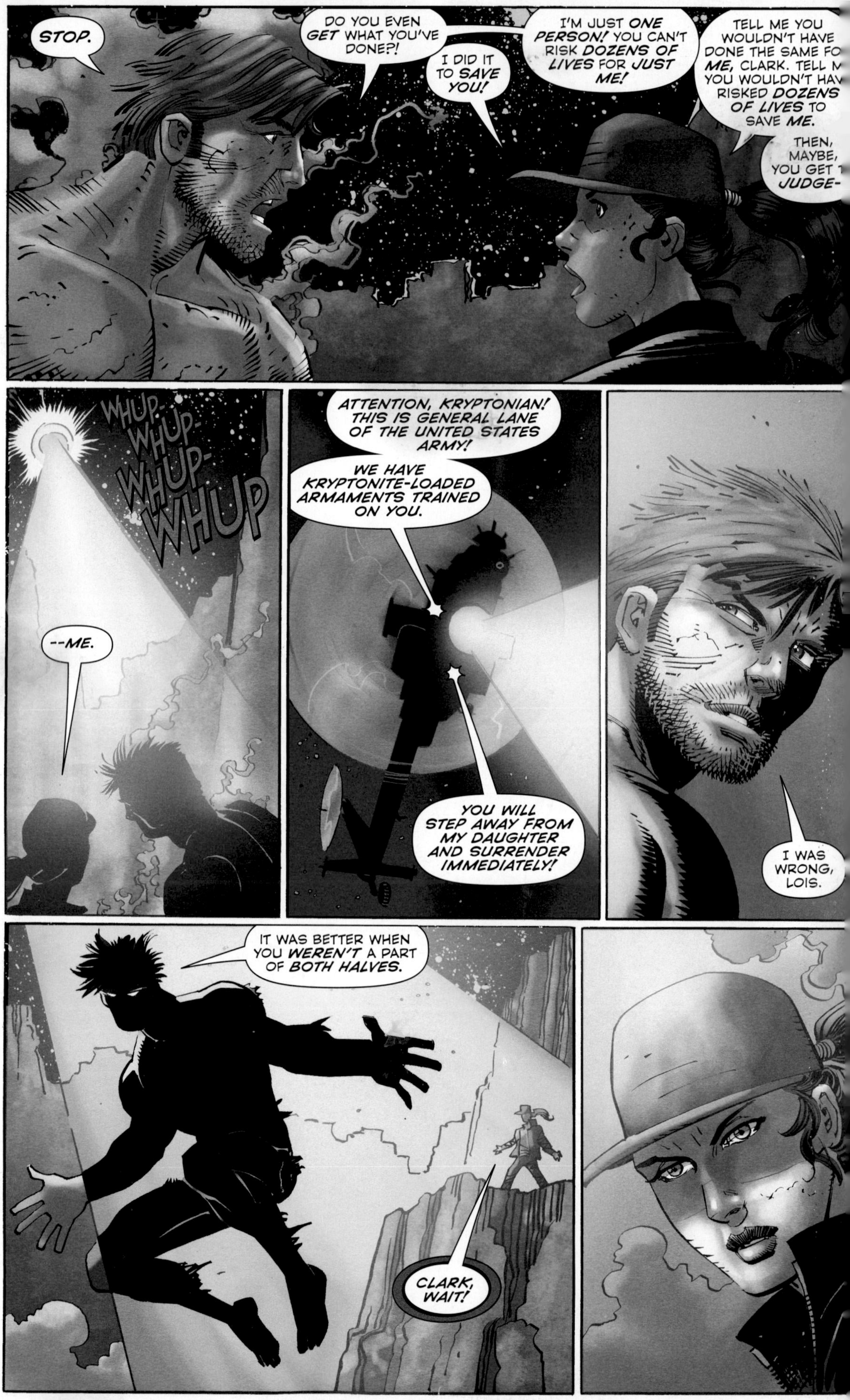
STOP.
DO YOU EVEN GET WHAT YOU'VE DONE?!
I DID IT TO SAVE YOU!
I'M JUST ONE PERSON! YOU CAN'T RISK DOZENS OF LIVES FOR JUST ME!
TELL ME YOU WOULDN'T HAVE DONE THE SAME FO ME, CLARK. TELL M YOU WOULDN'T HAV RISKED DOZENS OF LIVES TO SAVE ME.
THEN, MAYBE, YOU GET JUDGE-
WHUP-WHUP-WHUP-WHUP
--ME.
ATTENTION, KRYPTONIAN! THIS IS GENERAL LANE OF THE UNITED STATES ARMY!
WE HAVE KRYPTONITE-LOADED ARMAMENTS TRAINED ON YOU.
YOU WILL STEP AWAY FROM MY DAUGHTER AND SURRENDER IMMEDIATELY!
I WAS WRONG, LOIS.
IT WAS BETTER WHEN YOU WEREN'T A PART OF BOTH HALVES.
CLARK, WAIT!

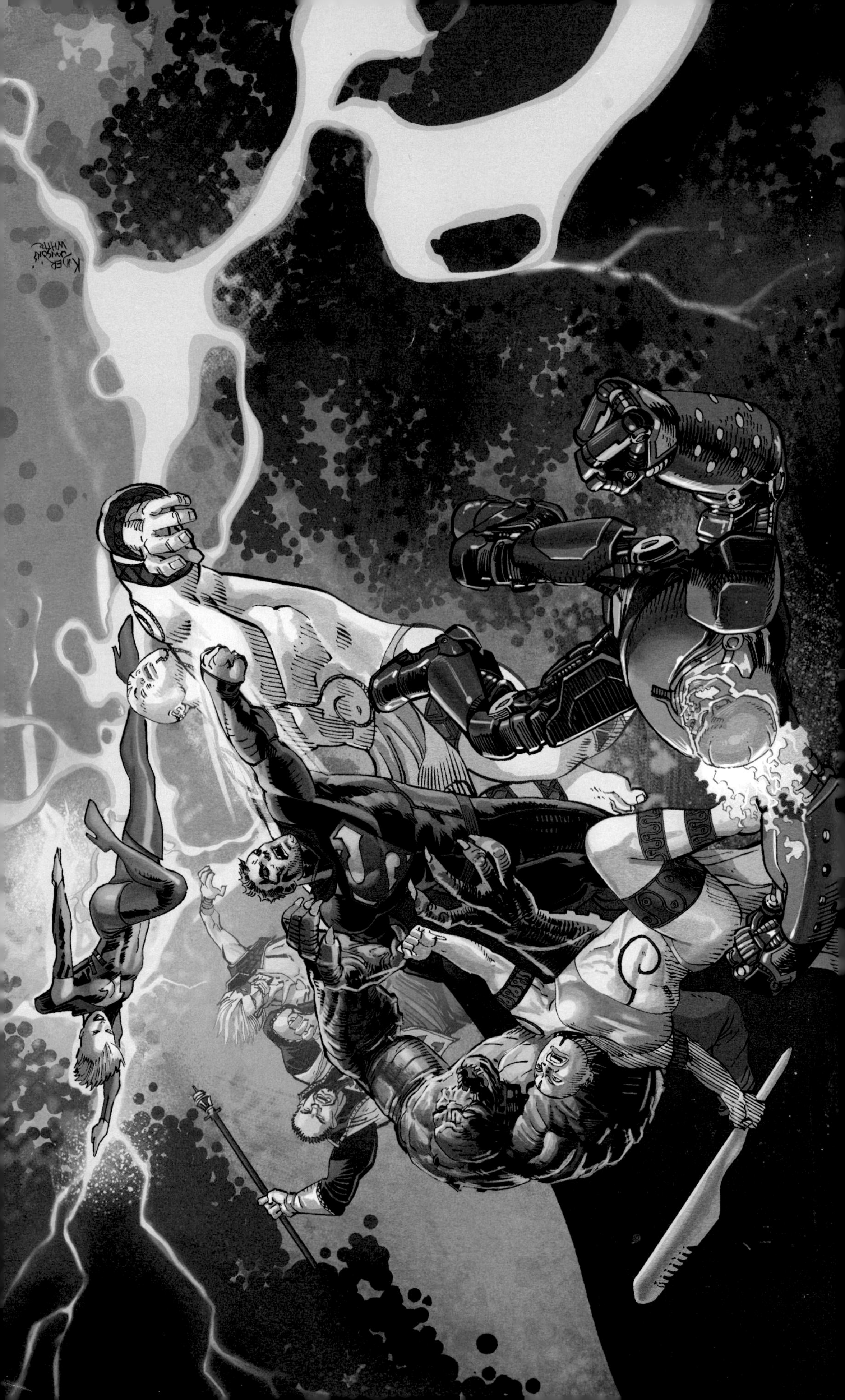

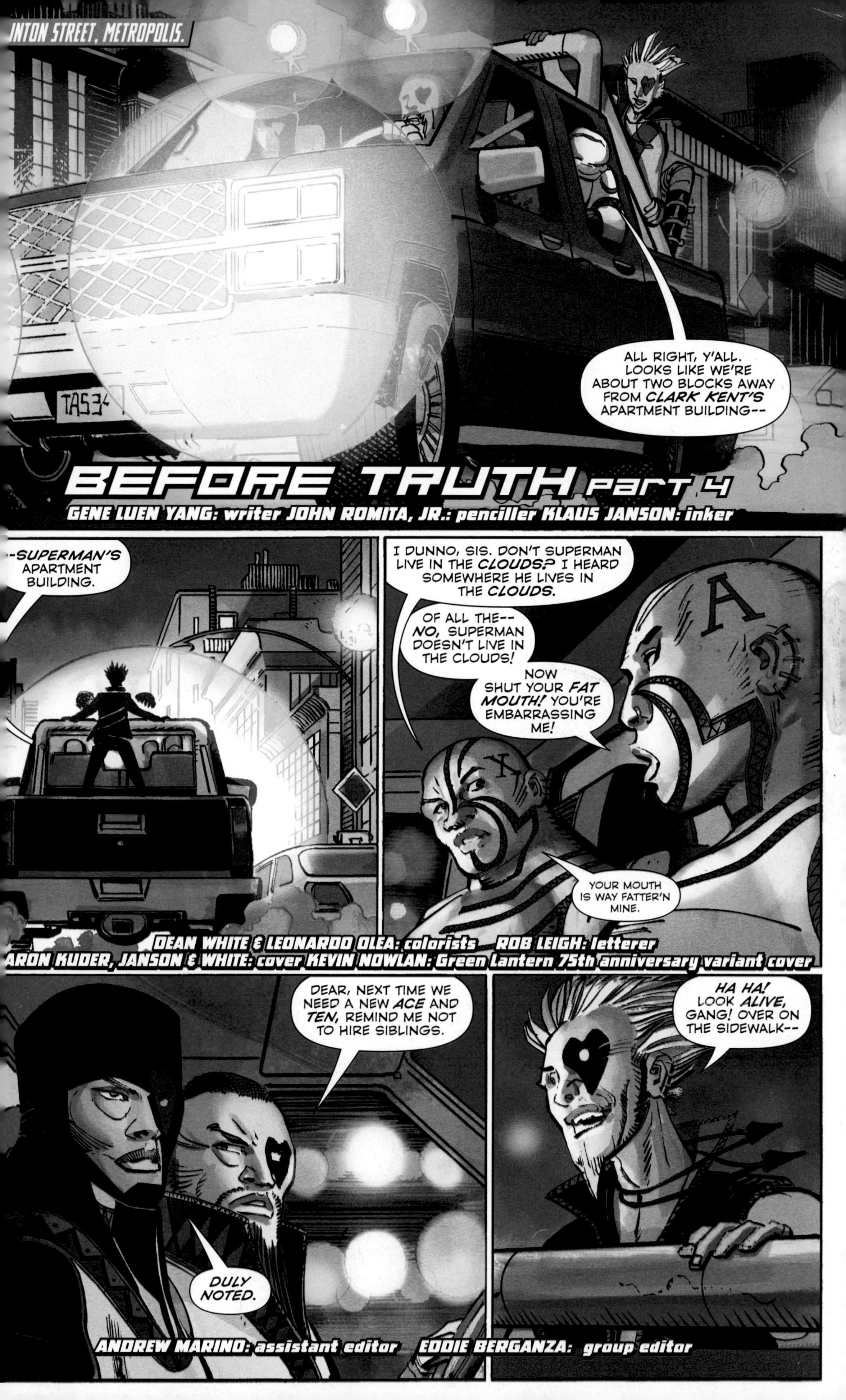

INTON STREET, METROPOLIS.
ALL RIGHT, Y'ALL. LOOKS LIKE WE'RE ABOUT TWO BLOCKS AWAY FROM CLARK KENT'S APARTMENT BUILDING--
BEFORE TRUTH part 4
GENE LUEN YANG: writer JOHN ROMITA, JR.: penciller KLAUS JANSON: inker
--SUPERMAN'S APARTMENT BUILDING.
I DUNNO, SIS. DON'T SUPERMAN LIVE IN THE CLOUDS? I HEARD SOMEWHERE HE LIVES IN THE CLOUDS.
OF ALL THE-- NO, SUPERMAN DOESN'T LIVE IN THE CLOUDS!
NOW SHUT YOUR FAT MOUTH! YOU'RE EMBARRASSING ME!
YOUR MOUTH IS WAY FATTER'N MINE.
DEAN WHITE & LEONARDO OLEA: colorists ROB LEIGH: letterer
ARON KUDER, JANSON & WHITE: cover KEVIN NOWLAN: Green Lantern 75th anniversary variant cover
DEAR, NEXT TIME WE NEED A NEW ACE AND TEN, REMIND ME NOT TO HIRE SIBLINGS.
DULY NOTED.
HA HA! LOOK ALIVE, GANG! OVER ON THE SIDEWALK--
ANDREW MARINO: assistant editor EDDIE BERGANZA: group editor

GOOD EVENING, MR. KENT.

WHO---?!

SORRY, BUDDY, MY BUILDING'S GOT A NO SOLICITORS POLICY.

YOU LIVE NOT TOO FAR FROM HERE, NO? THE ROYAL FLUSH GANG WOULD LOVE TO COME OVER FOR A VISIT.

I'VE HEARD IT SAID THAT ONCE UPON A TIME, YOU HAD THE ABILITY TO CRUSH COAL INTO DIAMONDS.

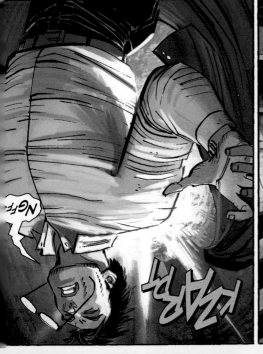

NGH!

ZARR!

JACKPOT!

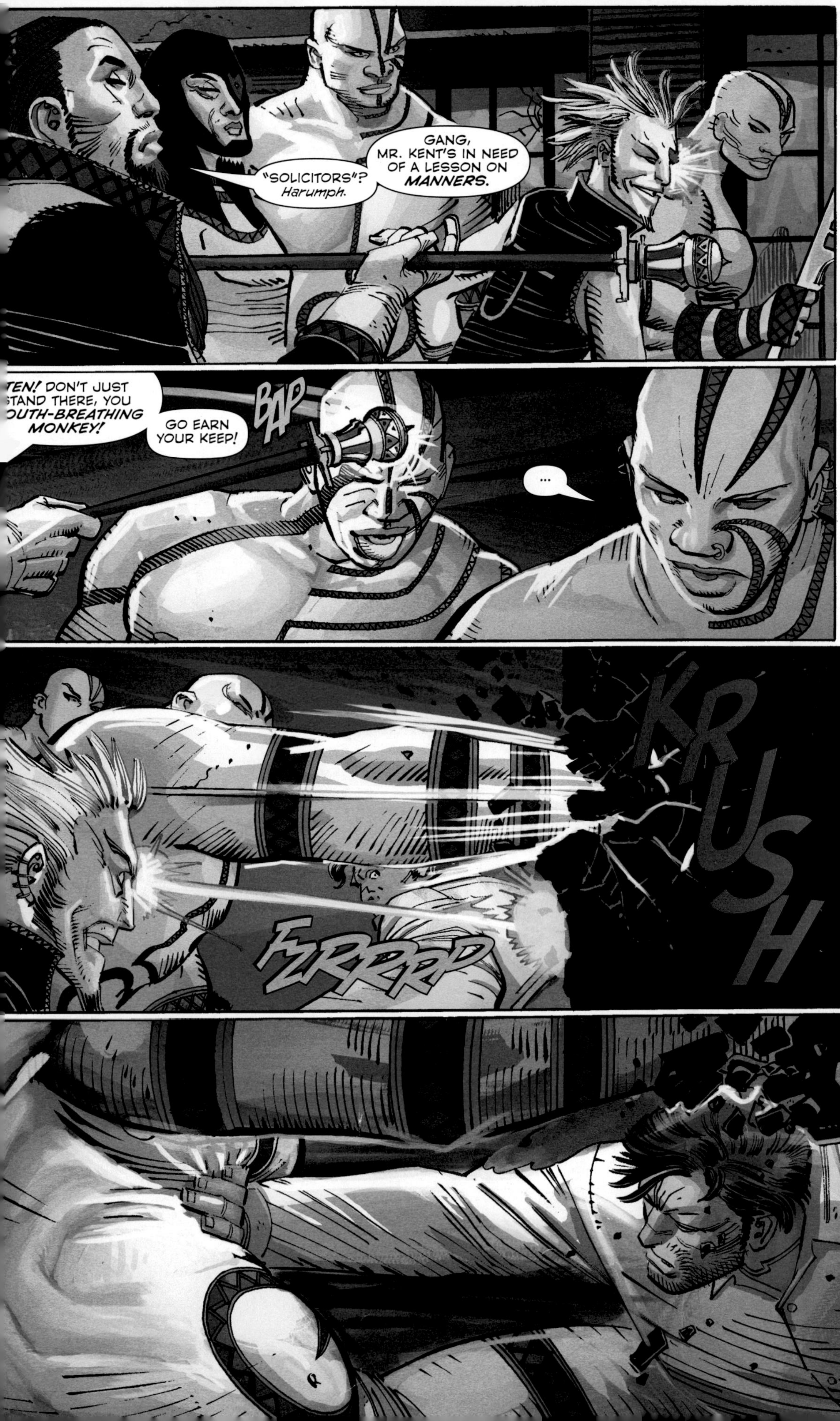
"SOLICITORS"? Harumph.
GANG, MR. KENT'S IN NEED OF A LESSON ON **MANNERS.**
*TEN!* DON'T JUST STAND THERE, YOU *OUTH-BREATHING MONKEY!*
GO EARN YOUR KEEP!
BAP
...
KRUSH
FZRRRP

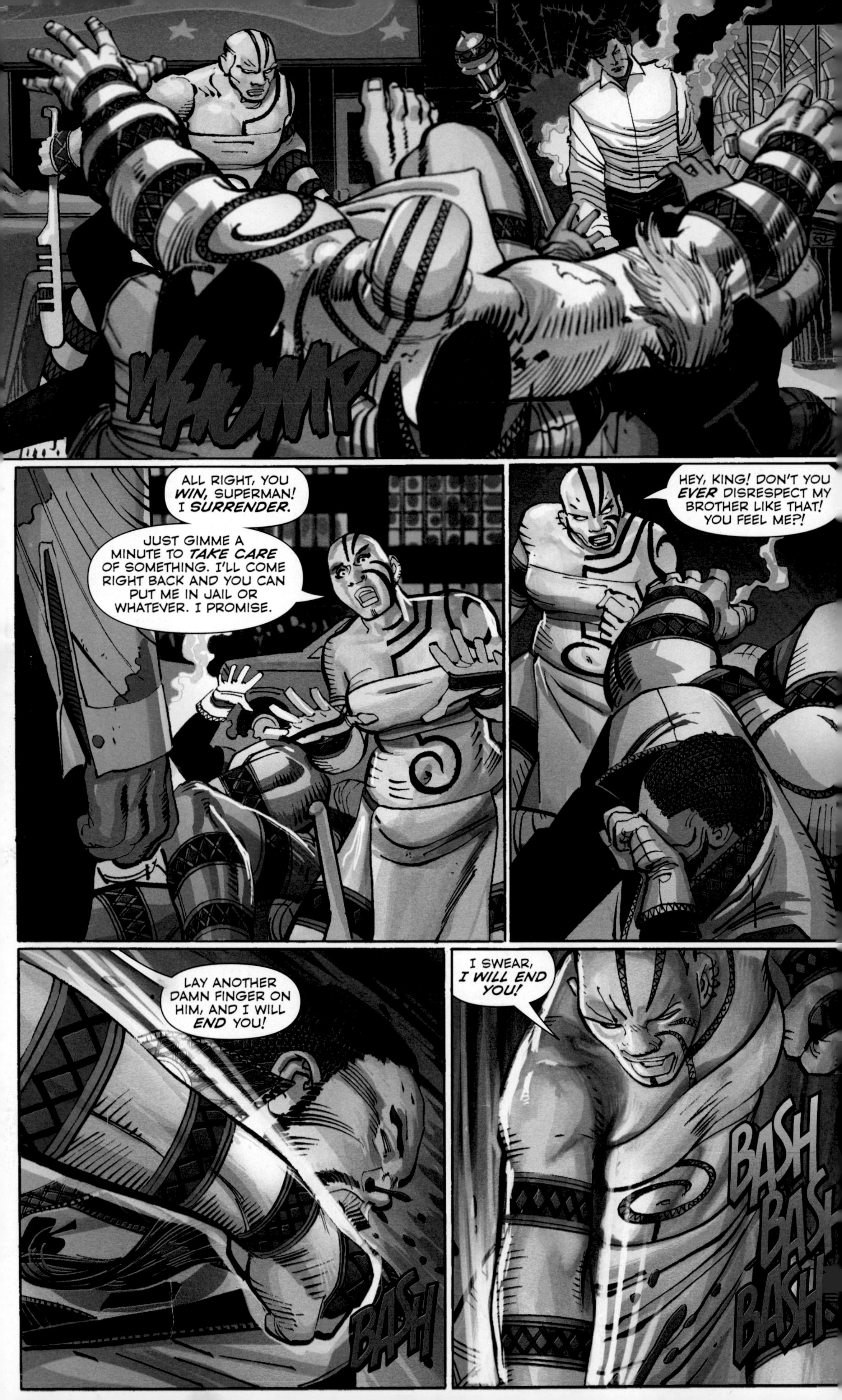
WHUMP
ALL RIGHT, YOU *WIN,* SUPERMAN! I *SURRENDER.*
JUST GIMME A MINUTE TO *TAKE CARE* OF SOMETHING. I'LL COME RIGHT BACK AND YOU CAN PUT ME IN JAIL OR WHATEVER. I PROMISE.
HEY, KING! DON'T YOU *EVER* DISRESPECT MY BROTHER LIKE THAT! YOU FEEL ME?!
LAY ANOTHER DAMN FINGER ON HIM, AND I WILL *END* YOU!
BASH
I SWEAR, *I WILL END YOU!*
BASH BASH BASH

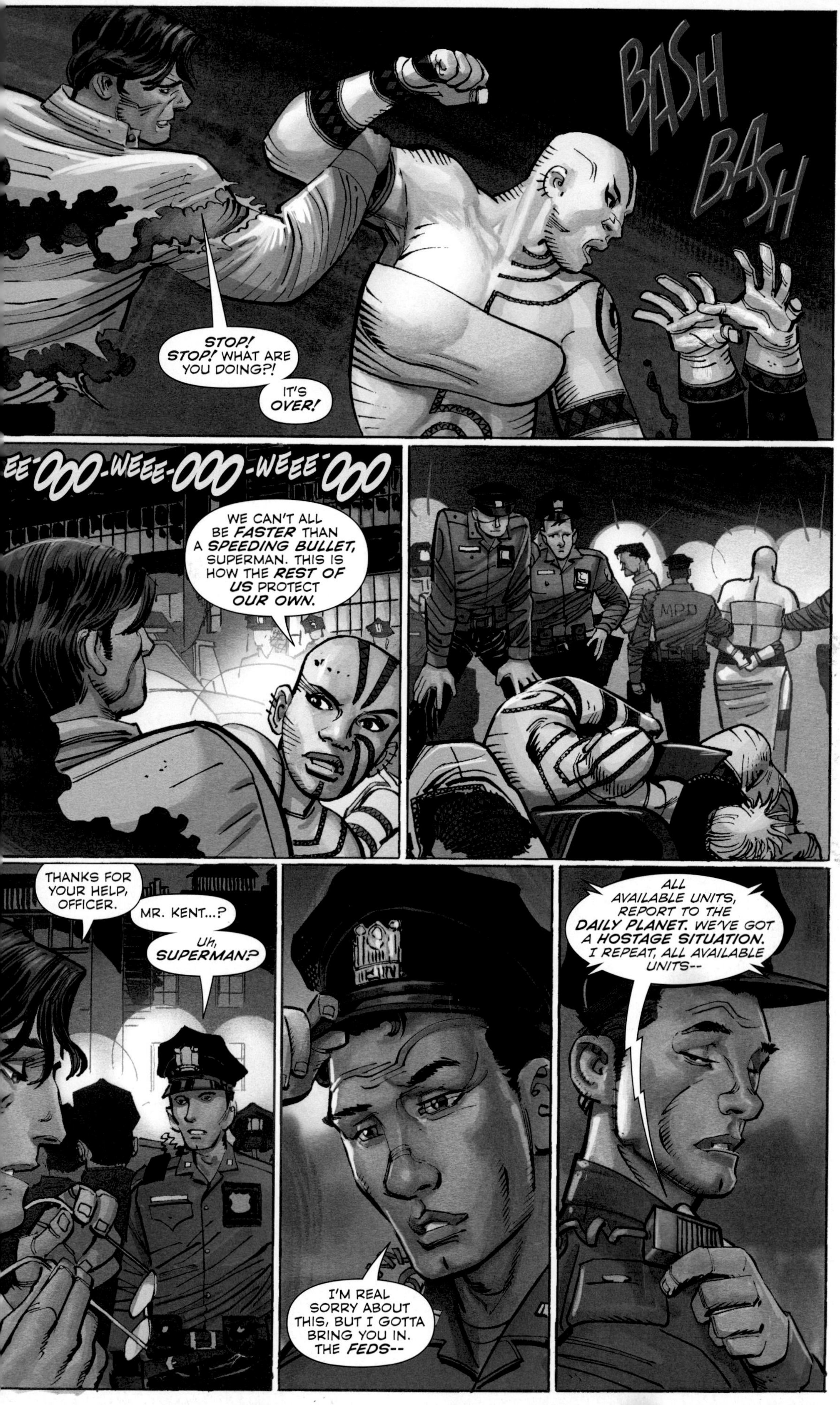
BASH
BASH
STOP! STOP! WHAT ARE YOU DOING?!
IT'S OVER!
EE-OOO-WEEE-OOO-WEEE-OOO
WE CAN'T ALL BE FASTER THAN A SPEEDING BULLET, SUPERMAN. THIS IS HOW THE REST OF US PROTECT OUR OWN.
MPD
THANKS FOR YOUR HELP, OFFICER.
MR. KENT...?
Uh, SUPERMAN?
I'M REAL SORRY ABOUT THIS, BUT I GOTTA BRING YOU IN. THE FEDS--
ALL AVAILABLE UNITS, REPORT TO THE DAILY PLANET. WE'VE GOT A HOSTAGE SITUATION. I REPEAT, ALL AVAILABLE UNITS--

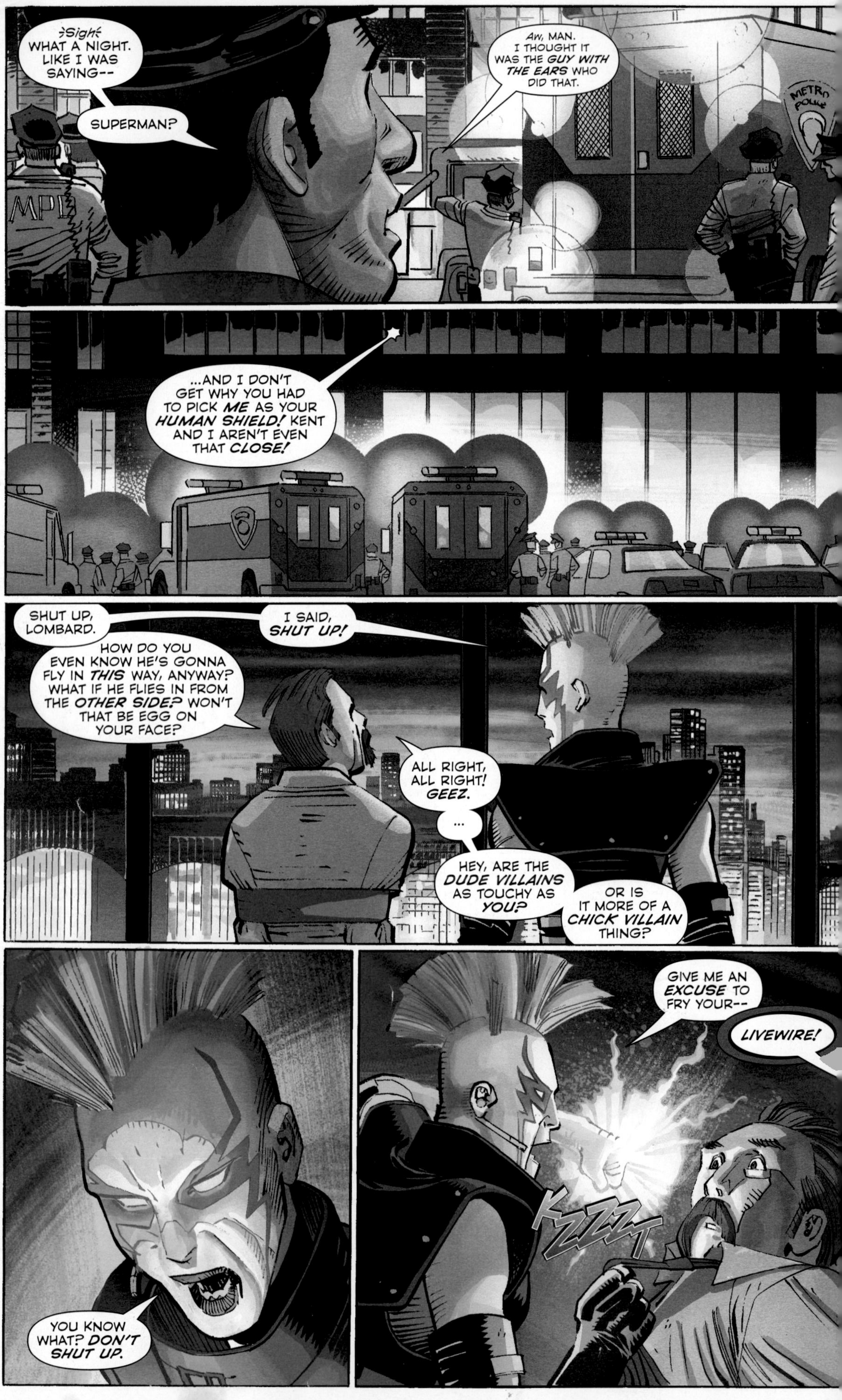
*Sigh*
WHAT A NIGHT. LIKE I WAS SAYING--
SUPERMAN?
AW, MAN. I THOUGHT IT WAS THE ***GUY WITH THE EARS*** WHO DID THAT.
METRO POLICE
MPD
...AND I DON'T GET WHY YOU HAD TO PICK ***ME*** AS YOUR ***HUMAN SHIELD!*** KENT AND I AREN'T EVEN THAT ***CLOSE!***
SHUT UP, LOMBARD.
HOW DO YOU EVEN KNOW HE'S GONNA FLY IN ***THIS*** WAY, ANYWAY? WHAT IF HE FLIES IN FROM THE ***OTHER SIDE?*** WON'T THAT BE EGG ON YOUR FACE?
I SAID, ***SHUT UP!***
ALL RIGHT, ALL RIGHT! ***GEEZ.***
...
HEY, ARE THE ***DUDE VILLAINS*** AS TOUCHY AS ***YOU?***
OR IS IT MORE OF A ***CHICK VILLAIN*** THING?
YOU KNOW WHAT? ***DON'T SHUT UP.***
GIVE ME AN ***EXCUSE*** TO FRY YOUR--
***LIVEWIRE!***
KZZZT

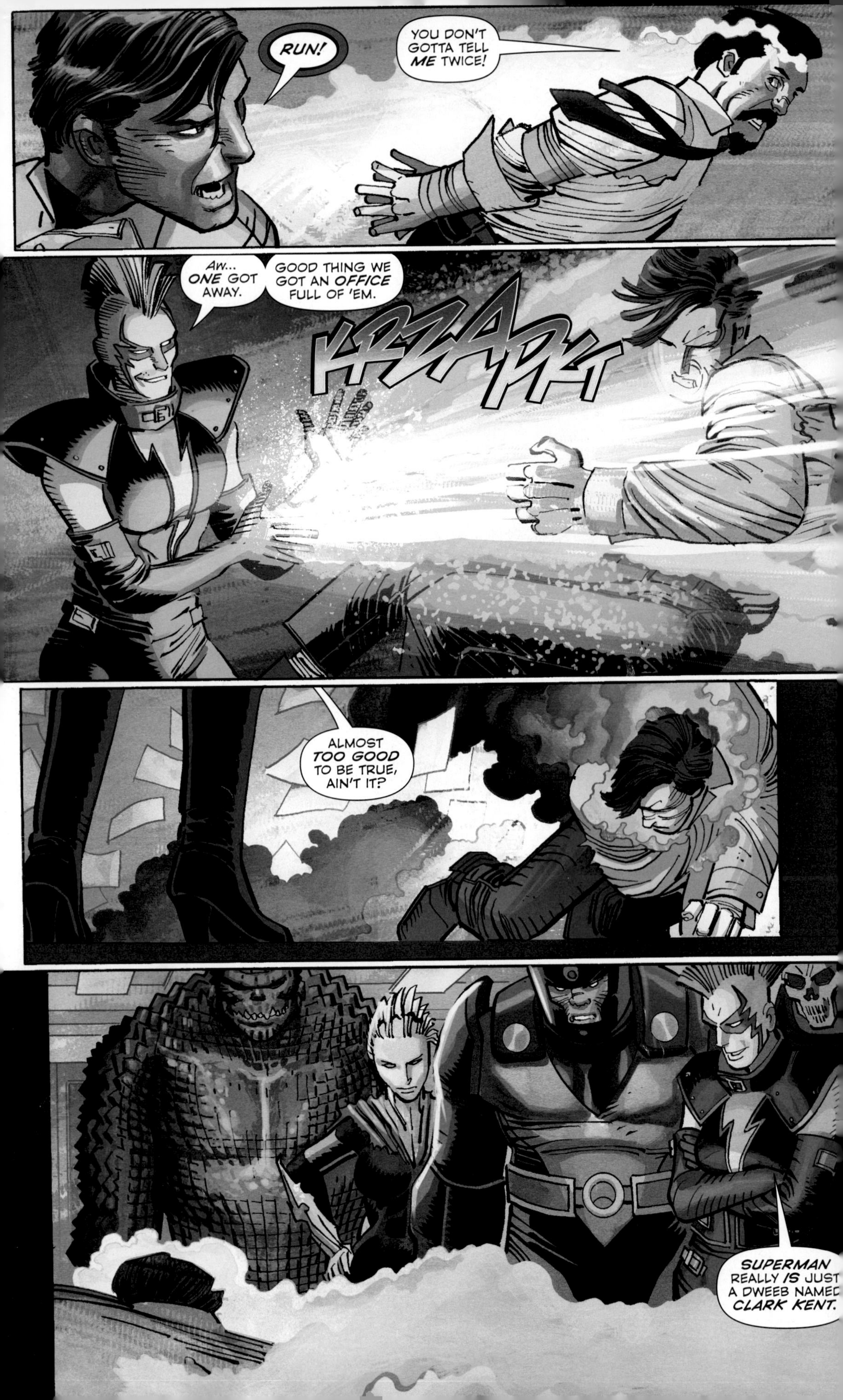

RUN!
YOU DON'T GOTTA TELL *ME* TWICE!
AW... *ONE* GOT AWAY.
GOOD THING WE GOT AN *OFFICE* FULL OF 'EM.
KRZAPKT
ALMOST *TOO GOOD* TO BE TRUE, AIN'T IT?
*SUPERMAN* REALLY *IS* JUST A DWEEB NAMED *CLARK KENT.*

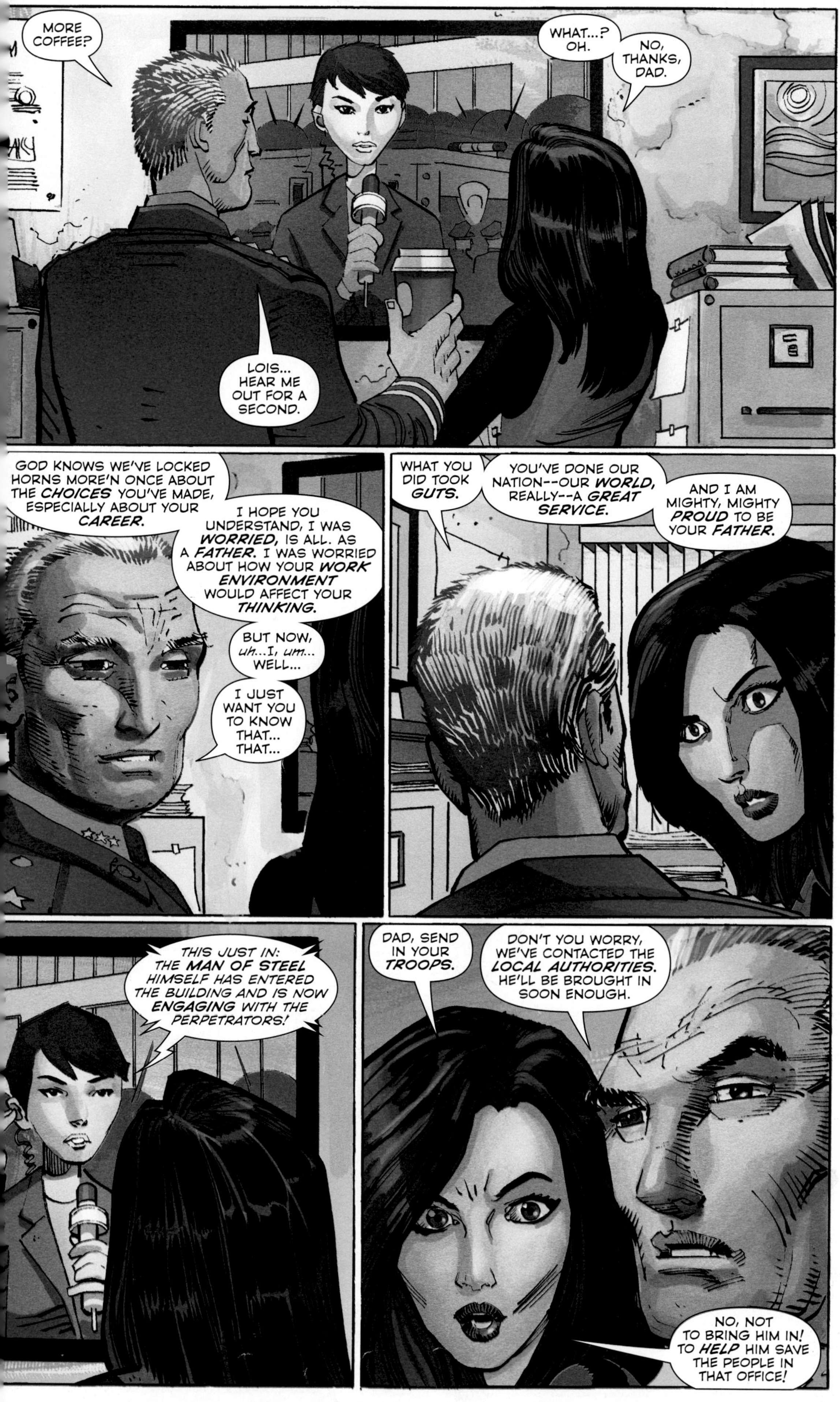
MORE COFFEE?
WHAT...? OH.
NO, THANKS, DAD.
LOIS... HEAR ME OUT FOR A SECOND.
GOD KNOWS WE'VE LOCKED HORNS MORE'N ONCE ABOUT THE *CHOICES* YOU'VE MADE, ESPECIALLY ABOUT YOUR *CAREER*.
I HOPE YOU UNDERSTAND, I WAS *WORRIED*, IS ALL. AS A *FATHER*. I WAS WORRIED ABOUT HOW YOUR *WORK ENVIRONMENT* WOULD AFFECT YOUR *THINKING*.
BUT NOW, *uh*...I, *um*... WELL...
I JUST WANT YOU TO KNOW THAT... THAT...
WHAT YOU DID TOOK *GUTS*.
YOU'VE DONE OUR NATION--OUR *WORLD*, REALLY--A *GREAT SERVICE*.
AND I AM MIGHTY, MIGHTY *PROUD* TO BE YOUR *FATHER*.
*THIS JUST IN: THE MAN OF STEEL HIMSELF HAS ENTERED THE BUILDING AND IS NOW ENGAGING WITH THE PERPETRATORS!*
DAD, SEND IN YOUR *TROOPS*.
DON'T YOU WORRY, WE'VE CONTACTED THE *LOCAL AUTHORITIES*. HE'LL BE BROUGHT IN SOON ENOUGH.
NO, NOT TO BRING HIM IN! TO *HELP* HIM SAVE THE PEOPLE IN THAT OFFICE!

DAD, HE DOESN'T HAVE A MOMENT!

GIVE ME A MOMENT.

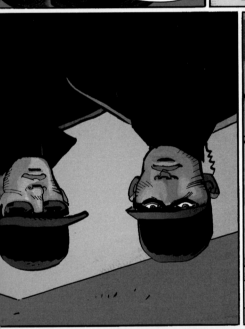

FORGIVE THE INTERRUPTION, GENERAL LANE, BUT THESE MEN INSISTED ON SEEING YOU RIGHT AWAY.

HE'S IMPORTANT TO ME AS A FRIEND.

PLEASE, DAD, HE'S IMPORTANT TO ME.

NO, NOT AS A NEWS STORY.

OF COURSE, HE'S THE MOST IMPORTANT NEWS STORY OF THE DECADE! THE FOREIGN POLICY IMPLICATIONS ALONE--

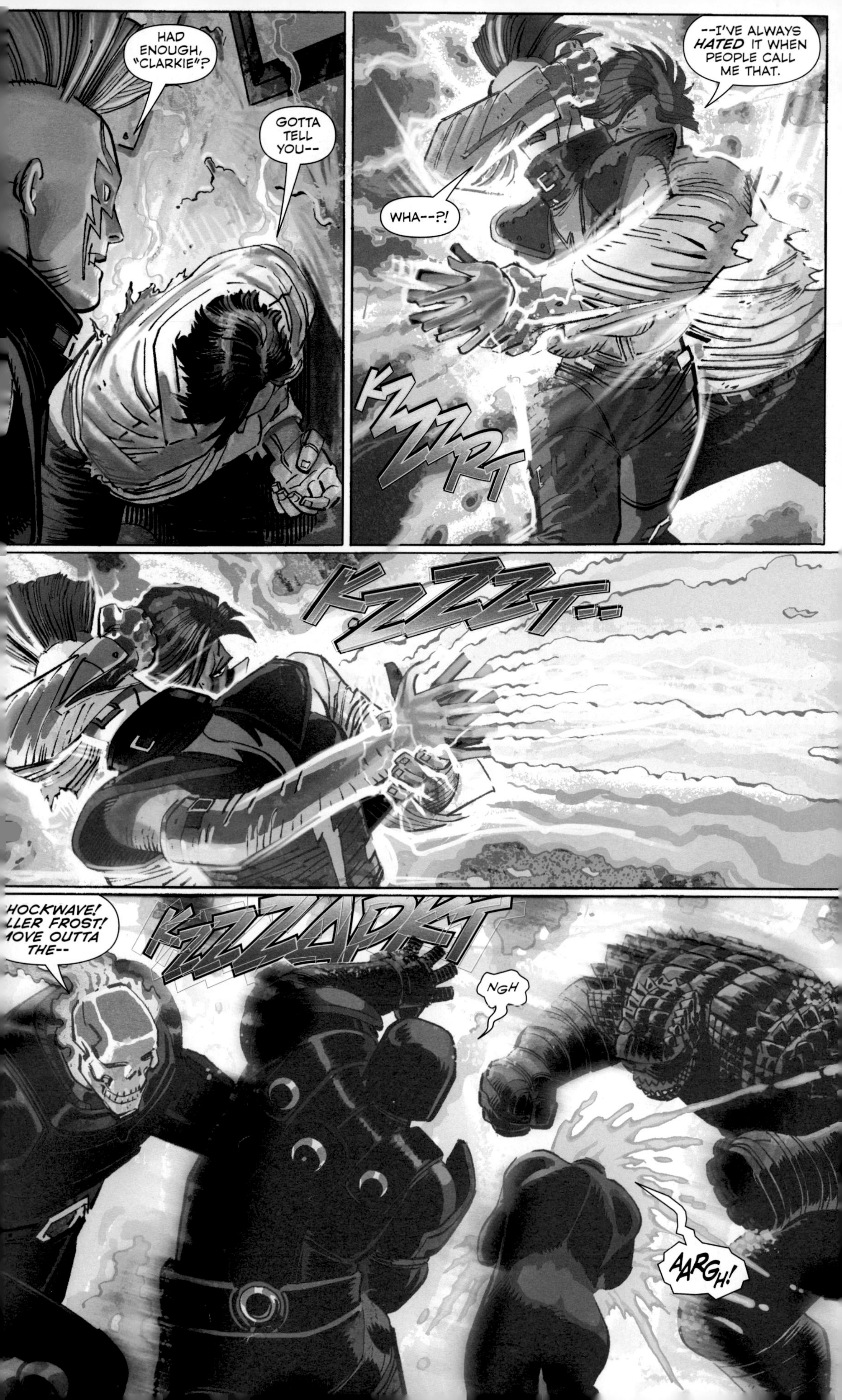
HAD ENOUGH, "CLARKIE"?
GOTTA TELL YOU--
WHA--?!
--I'VE ALWAYS *HATED* IT WHEN PEOPLE CALL ME THAT.
KZZZRT
KZZZT--
HOCKWAVE! LLER FROST! MOVE OUTTA THE--
KZZZAPKT
NGH
AARGH!

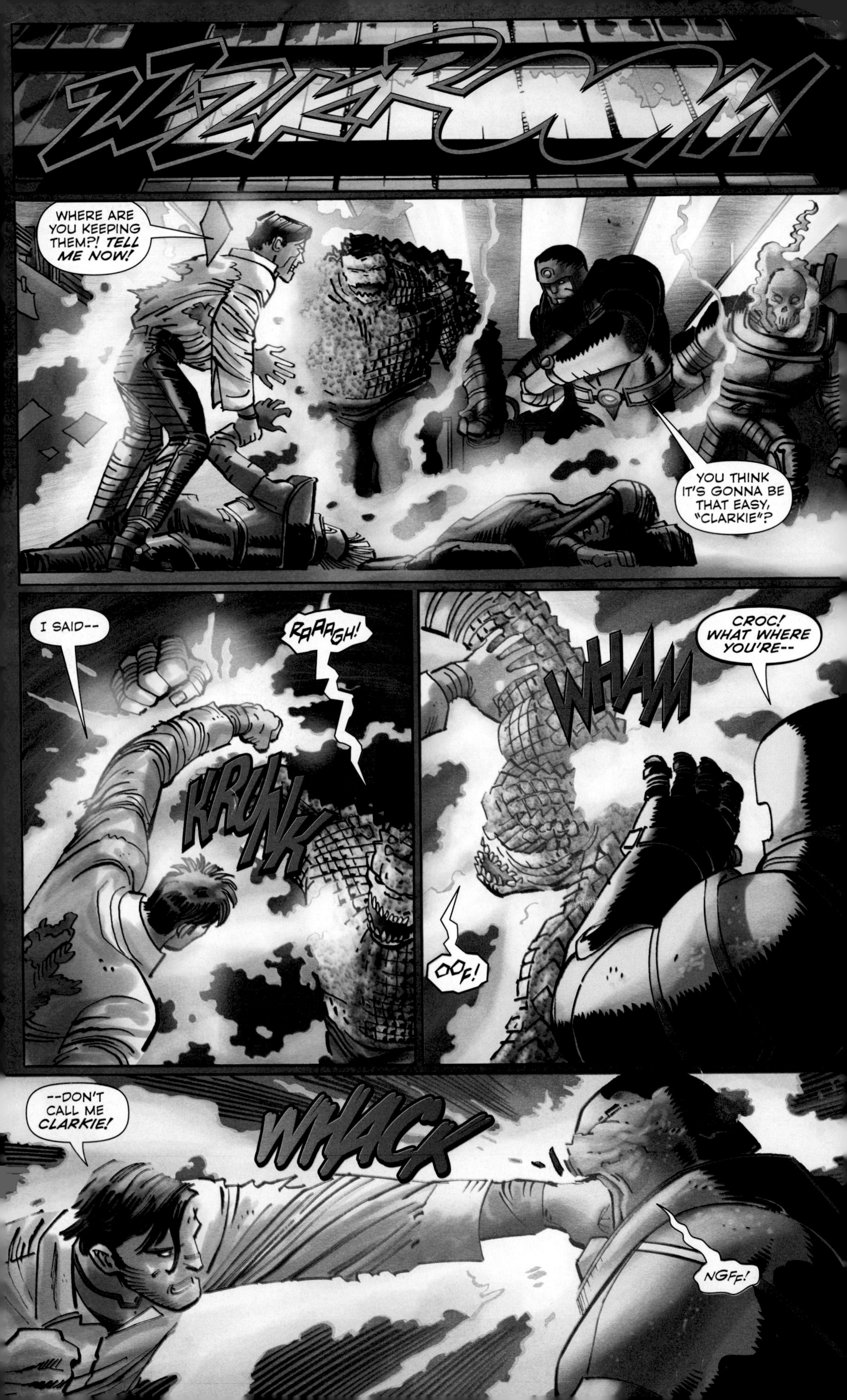
ZZZAROOM
WHERE ARE YOU KEEPING THEM?! TELL ME NOW!
YOU THINK IT'S GONNA BE THAT EASY, "CLARKIE"?
I SAID--
RAAAGH!
KRUNK
CROC! WHAT WHERE YOU'RE--
WHAM
OOF!
--DON'T CALL ME CLARKIE!
WHACK
NGFF!

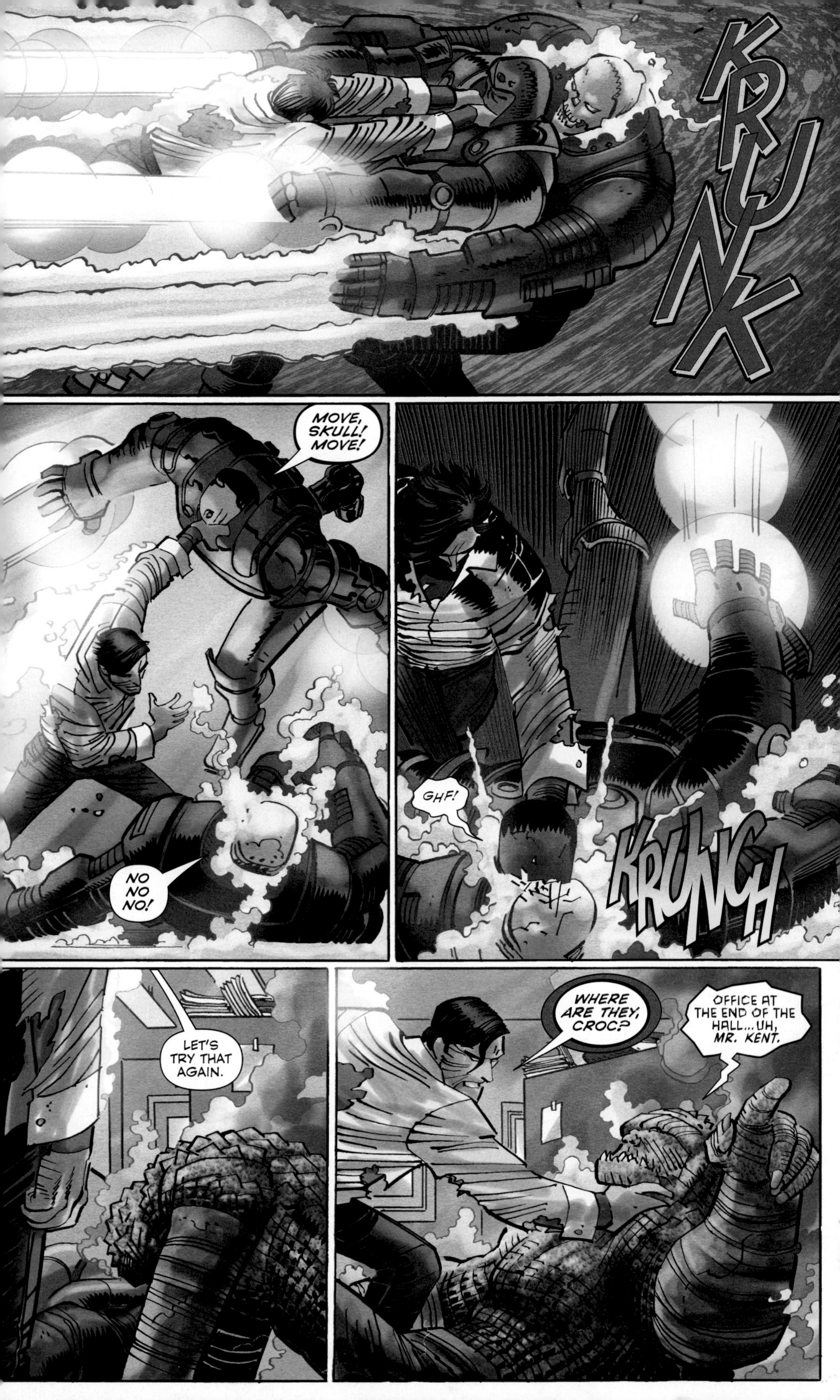
KRUNK
MOVE, SKULL! MOVE!
NO NO NO!
GHF!
KRUNCH
LET'S TRY THAT AGAIN.
WHERE ARE THEY, CROC?
OFFICE AT THE END OF THE HALL...UH, MR. KENT.

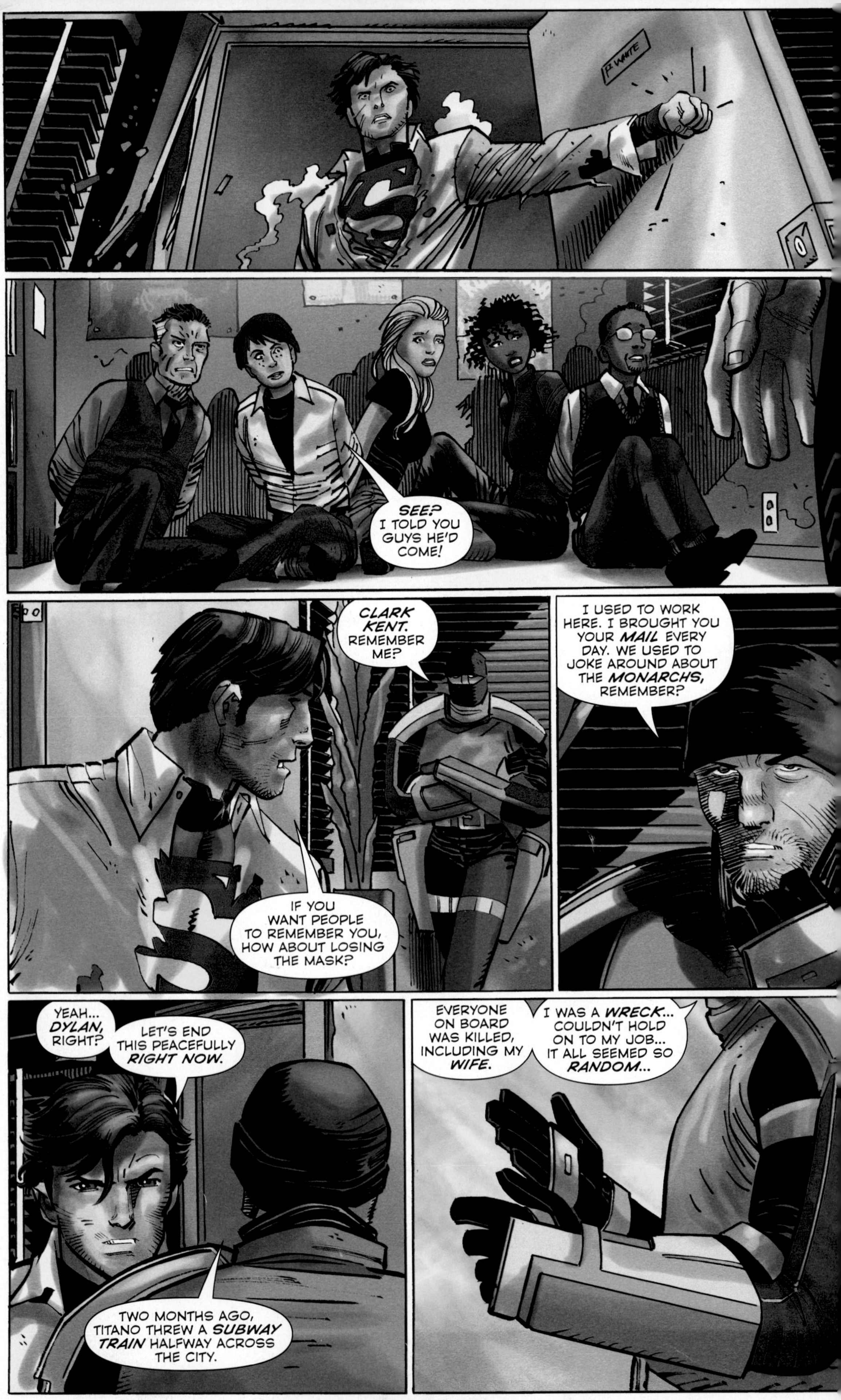
P. WHITE
SEE? I TOLD YOU GUYS HE'D COME!
CLARK KENT. REMEMBER ME?
IF YOU WANT PEOPLE TO REMEMBER YOU, HOW ABOUT LOSING THE MASK?
I USED TO WORK HERE. I BROUGHT YOU YOUR MAIL EVERY DAY. WE USED TO JOKE AROUND ABOUT THE MONARCHS, REMEMBER?
YEAH... DYLAN, RIGHT?
LET'S END THIS PEACEFULLY RIGHT NOW.
TWO MONTHS AGO, TITANO THREW A SUBWAY TRAIN HALFWAY ACROSS THE CITY.
EVERYONE ON BOARD WAS KILLED, INCLUDING MY WIFE.
I WAS A WRECK... COULDN'T HOLD ON TO MY JOB... IT ALL SEEMED SO RANDOM...

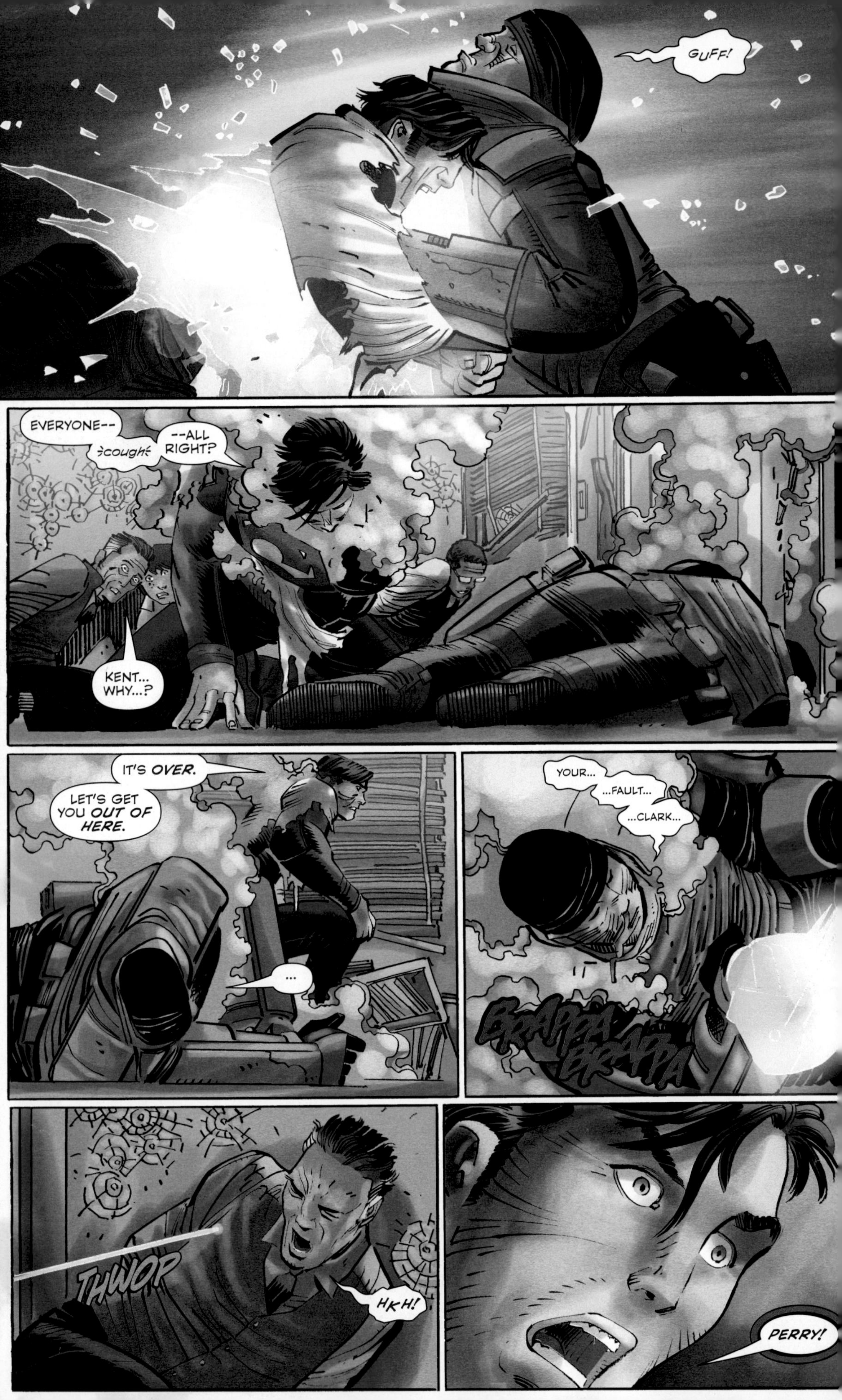
GUFF!
EVERYONE--
*cough*
--ALL RIGHT?
KENT... WHY...?
IT'S OVER.
LET'S GET YOU OUT OF HERE.
...
YOUR...
...FAULT...
...CLARK...
BRAPPA BRAPPA
THWOP
HKH!
PERRY!

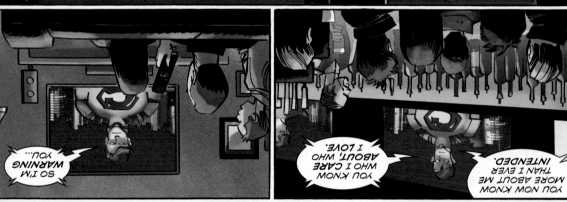

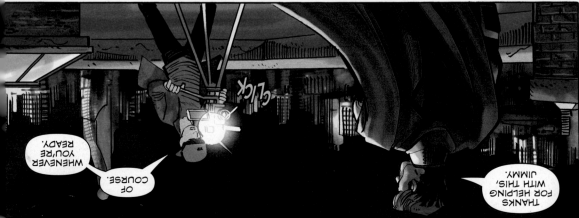

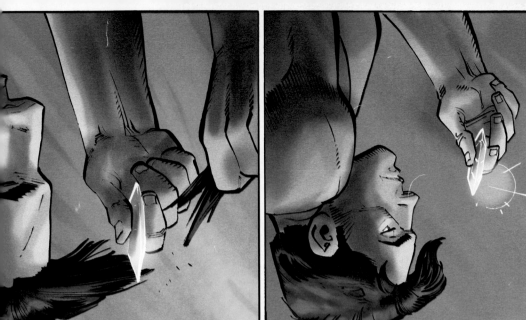

I HAVE CASH.

SORRY, BIG FELLA. YER CARD AIN'T GOIN' THROUGH.

GET✦WAY MOTEL

VACANCY

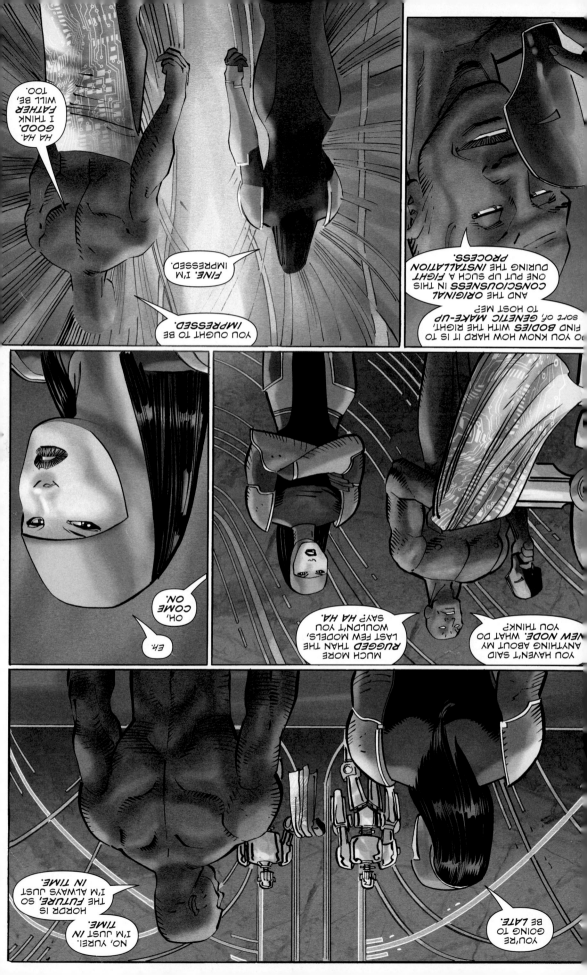

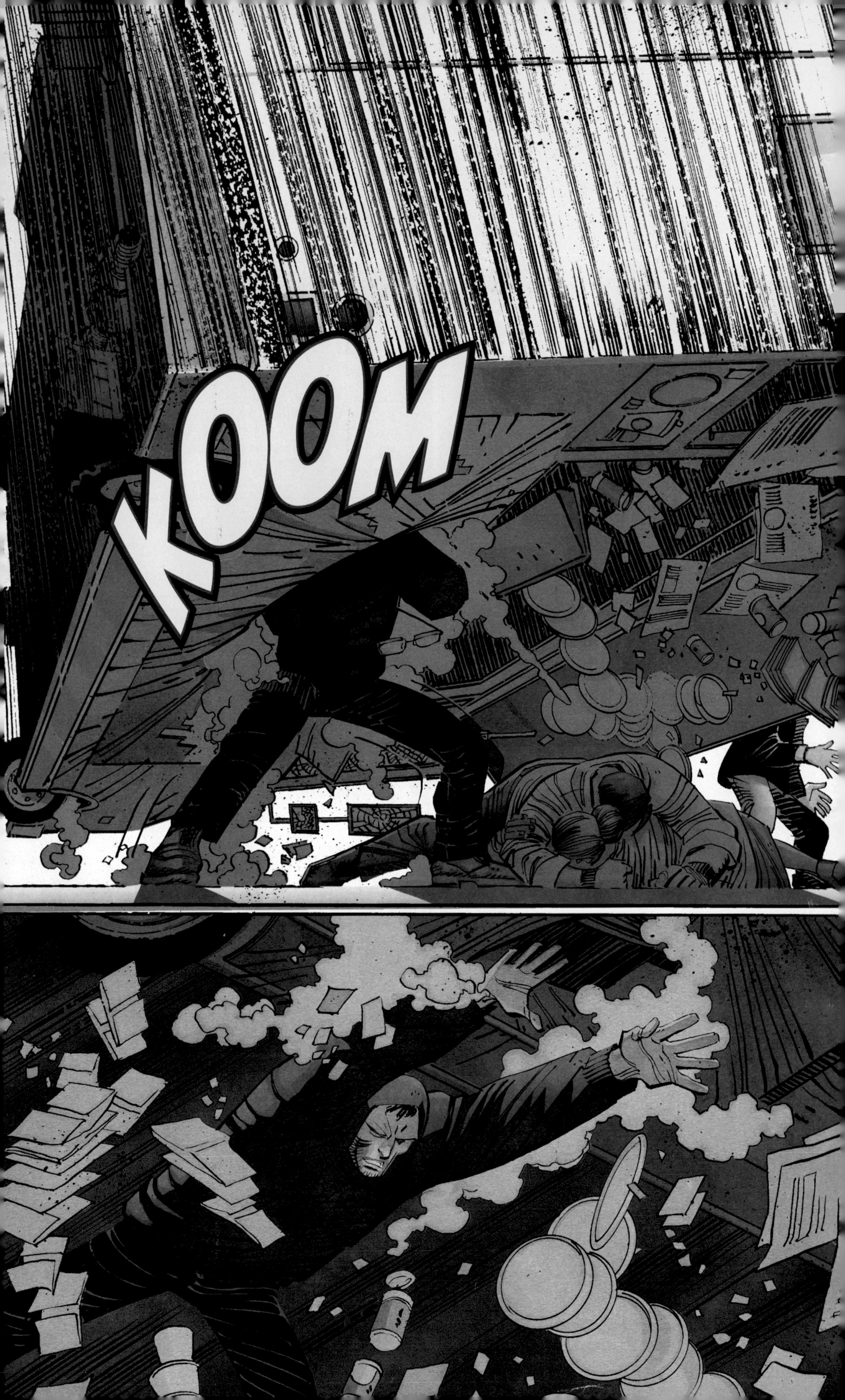
KOOM

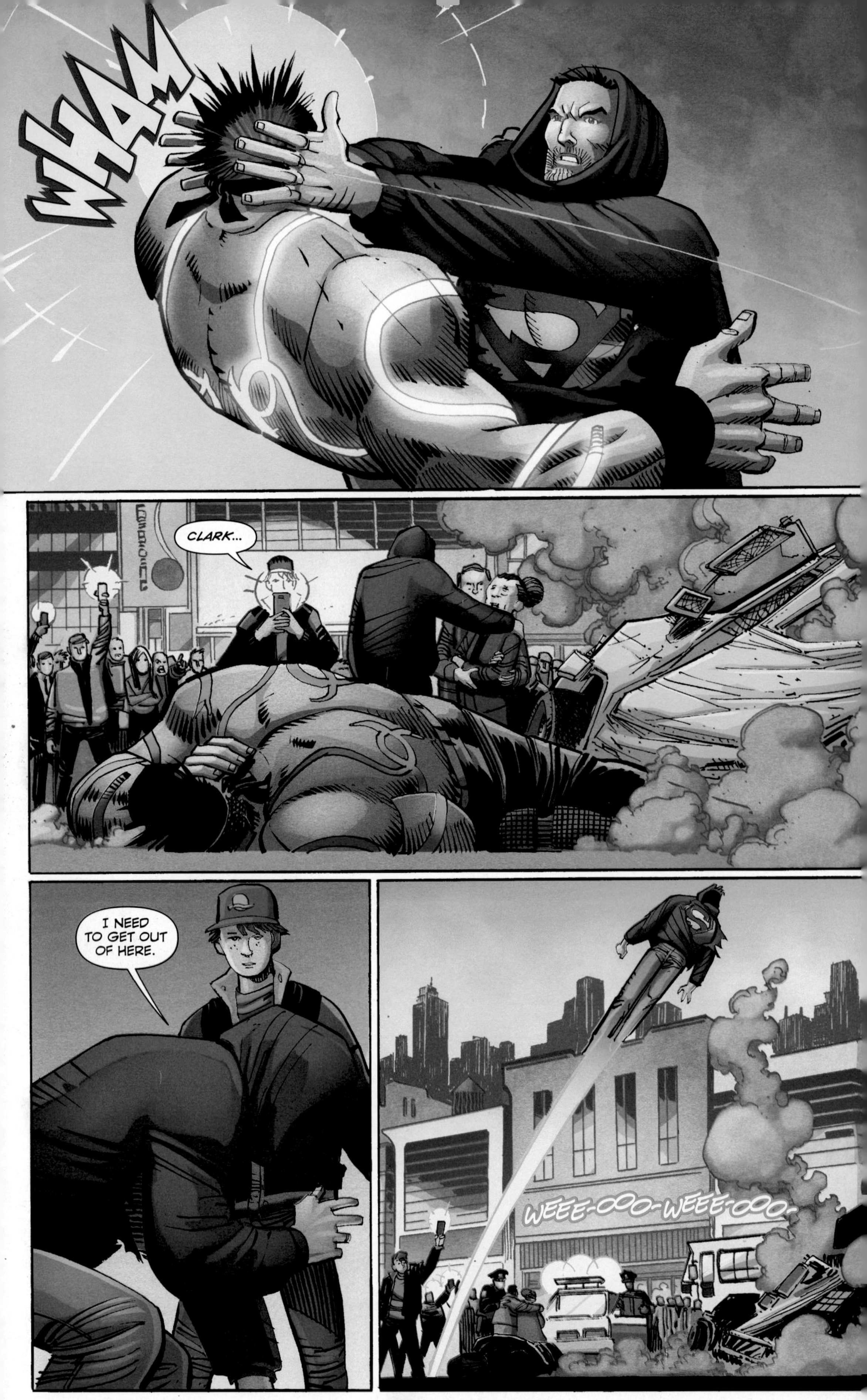
WHAM
CLARK...
I NEED TO GET OUT OF HERE.
WEEE-OOO-WEEE-OOO-

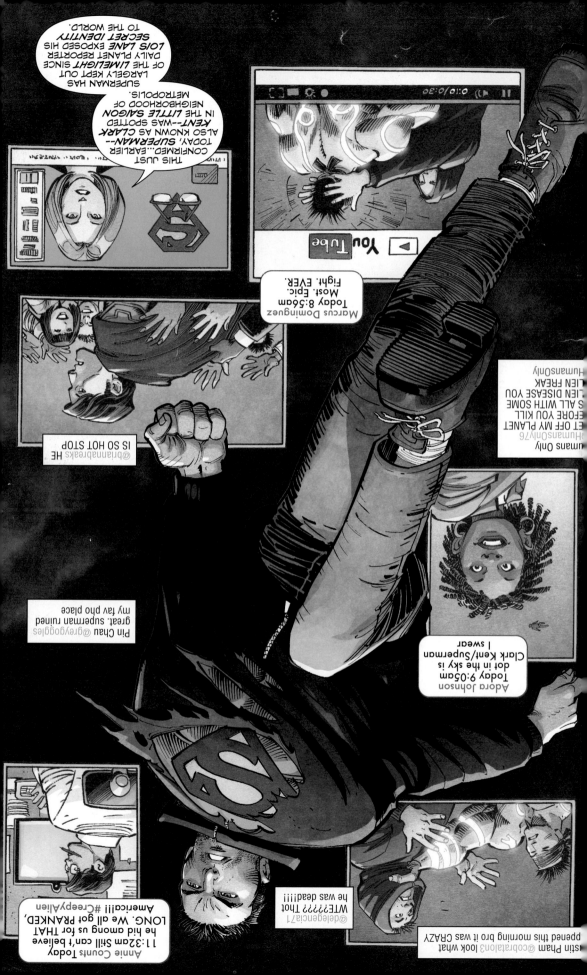

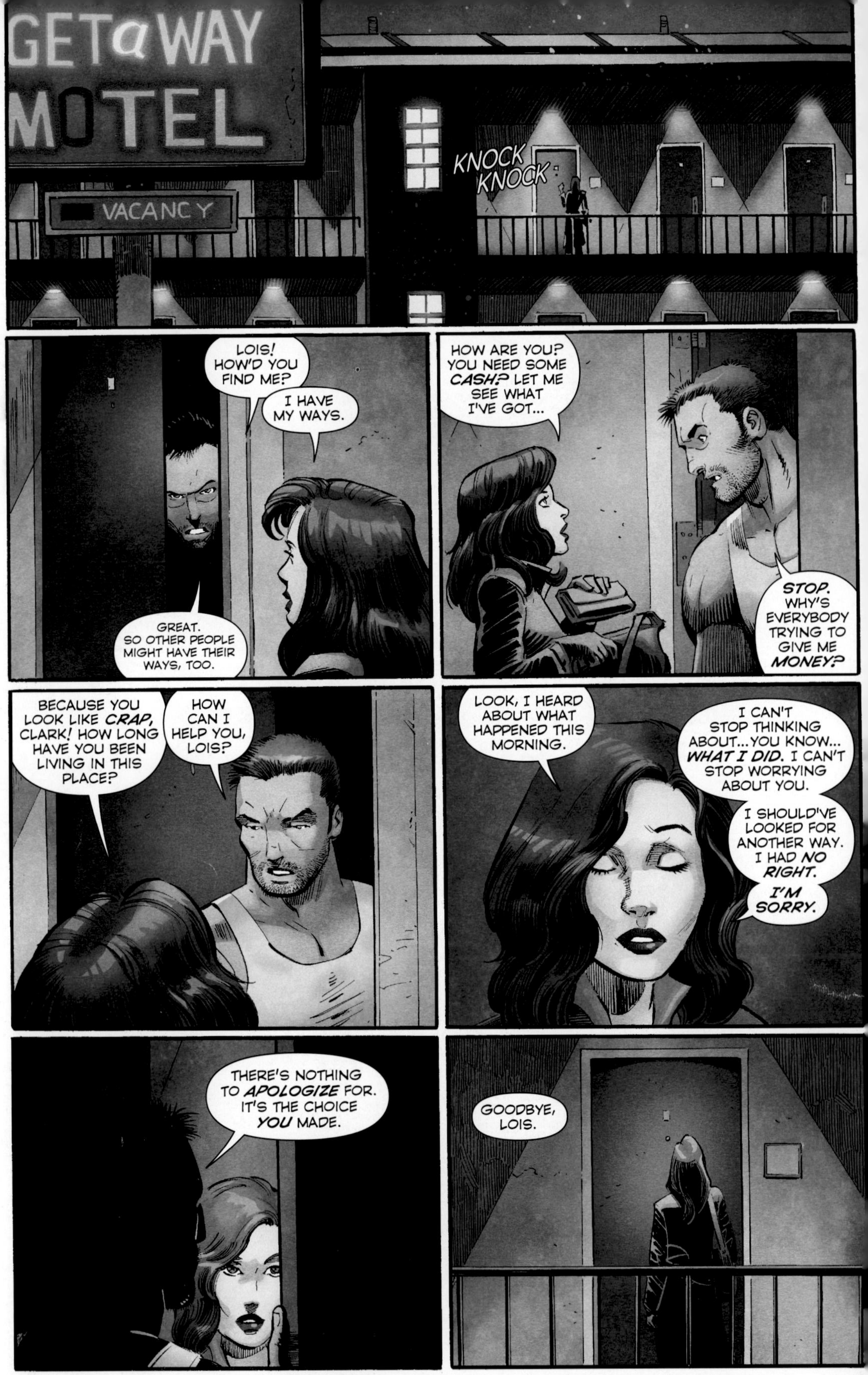
GETaWAY MOTEL
VACANCY
KNOCK KNOCK
LOIS! HOW'D YOU FIND ME?
I HAVE MY WAYS.
GREAT. SO OTHER PEOPLE MIGHT HAVE THEIR WAYS, TOO.
HOW ARE YOU? YOU NEED SOME CASH? LET ME SEE WHAT I'VE GOT...
STOP. WHY'S EVERYBODY TRYING TO GIVE ME MONEY?
HOW CAN I HELP YOU, LOIS?
BECAUSE YOU LOOK LIKE CRAP, CLARK! HOW LONG HAVE YOU BEEN LIVING IN THIS PLACE?
LOOK, I HEARD ABOUT WHAT HAPPENED THIS MORNING.
I CAN'T STOP THINKING ABOUT...YOU KNOW... WHAT I DID. I CAN'T STOP WORRYING ABOUT YOU.
I SHOULD'VE LOOKED FOR ANOTHER WAY. I HAD NO RIGHT.
I'M SORRY.
THERE'S NOTHING TO APOLOGIZE FOR. IT'S THE CHOICE YOU MADE.
GOODBYE, LOIS.

# EXPOSED

GENE LUEN YANG script · JOHN ROMITA, JR. pencils · KLAUS JANSON with SCOTT HANNA inks · HI-FI colors

TRAVIS LANHAM: letterer RICKEY PURDIN: associate editor EDDIE BERGANZA: group editor

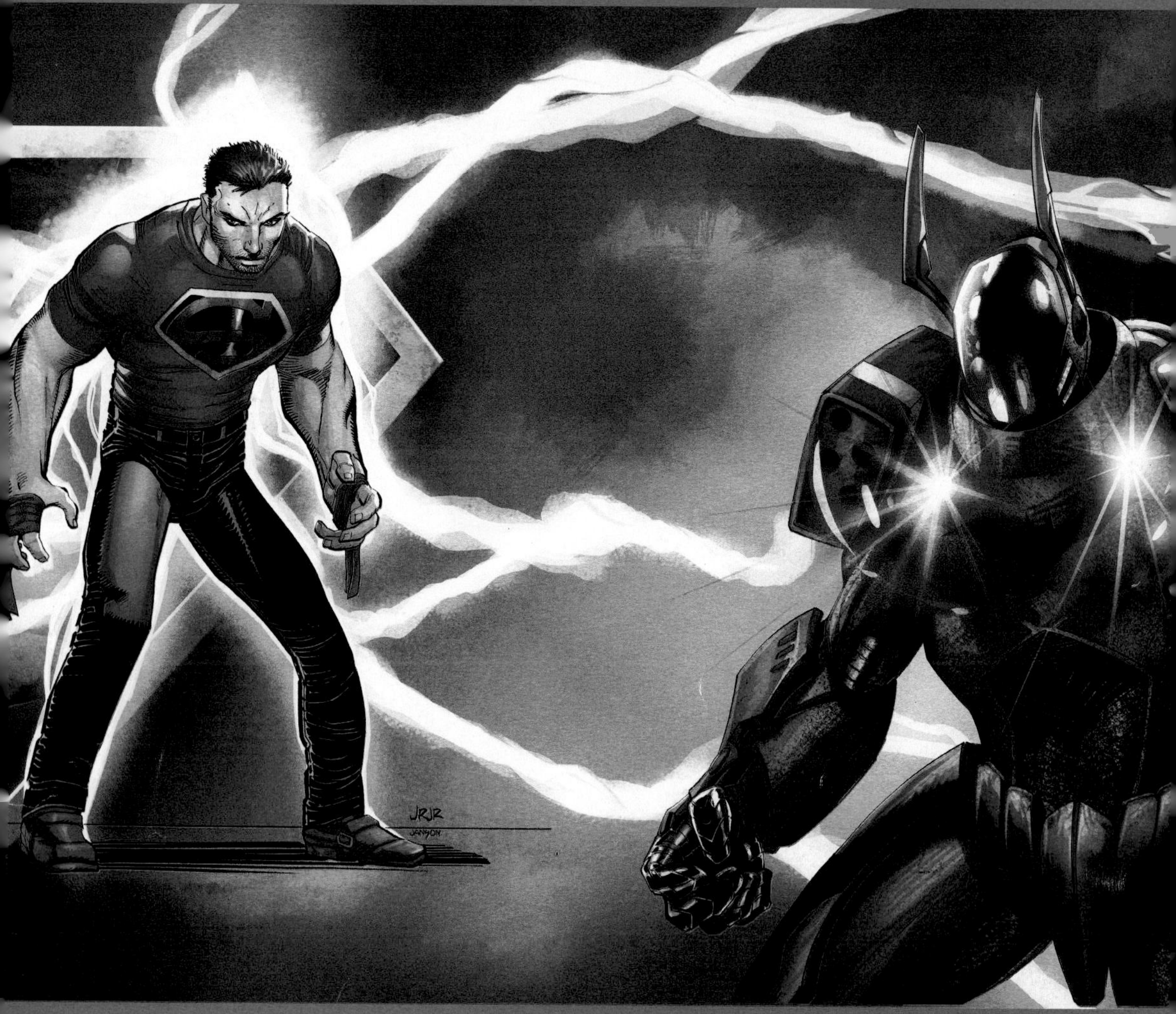
JRJR
JANSON

Second cover for issue #40 by **JOHN ROMITA JR., KLAUS JANSON** and **DEAN WHITE.**

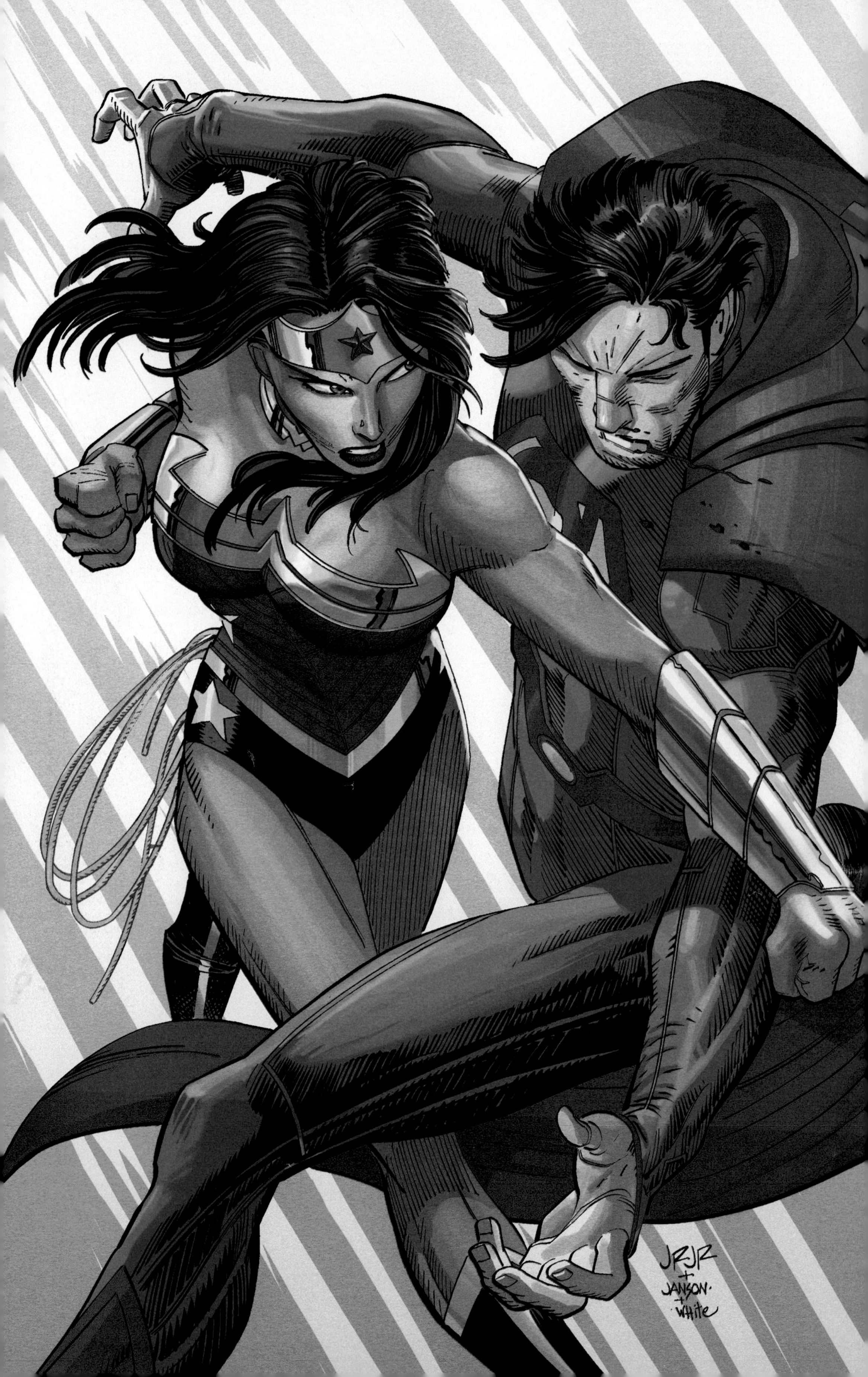
JRJR
+
JANSON.
+
White

# START AT THE BEGINNING!

# SUPERMAN: ACTION COMICS VOLUME 1: SUPERMAN AND THE MEN OF STEEL

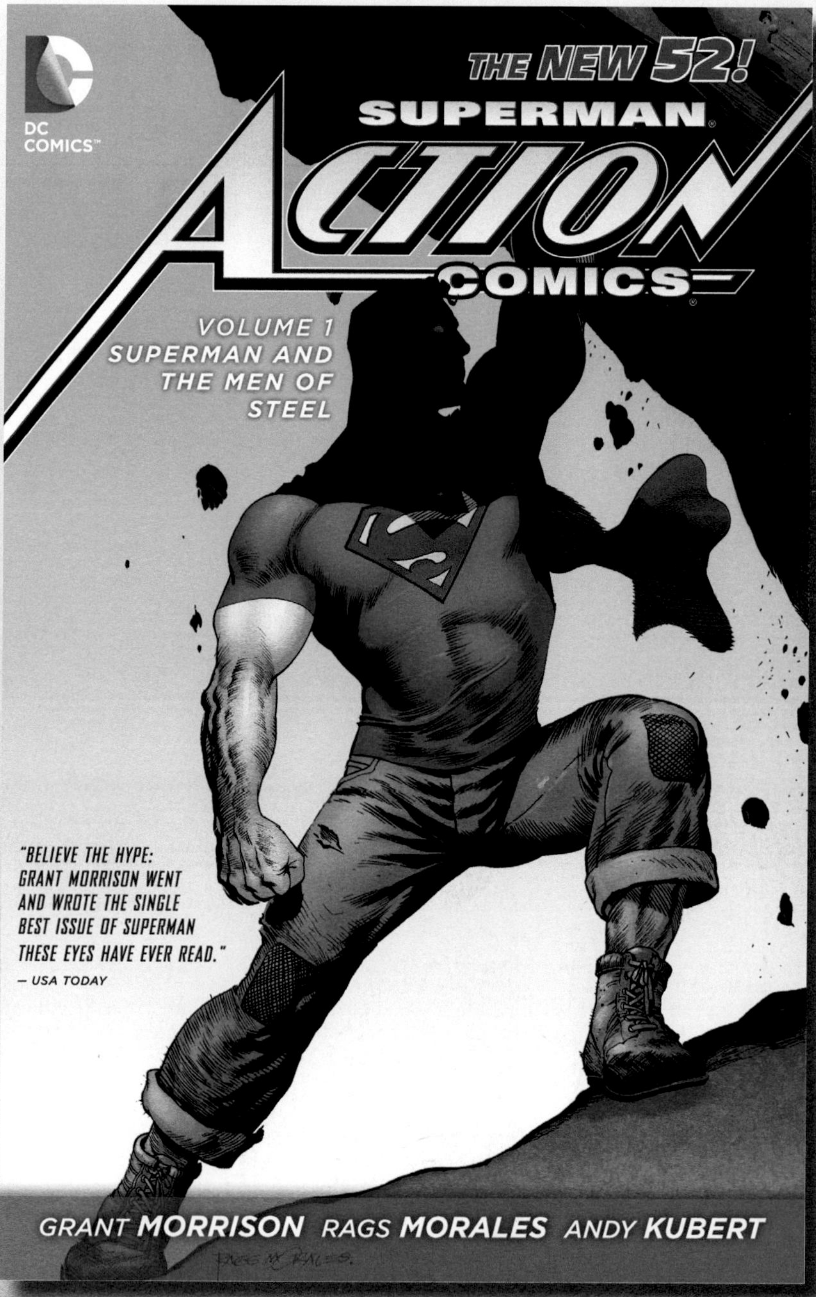

**SUPERMAN VOLUME 1: WHAT PRICE TOMORROW?**

**SUPERGIRL VOLUME 1: THE LAST DAUGHTER OF KRYPTON**

**SUPERBOY VOLUME 1: INCUBATION**

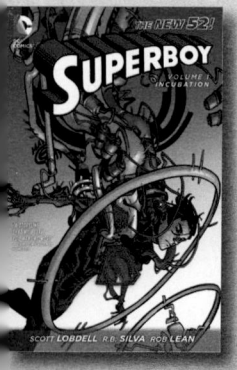

THE NEW 52!

SUPERMAN

*Action* COMICS

VOLUME 1
SUPERMAN AND THE MEN OF STEEL

"BELIEVE THE HYPE: GRANT MORRISON WENT AND WROTE THE SINGLE BEST ISSUE OF SUPERMAN THESE EYES HAVE EVER READ."
— USA TODAY

GRANT **MORRISON** RAGS **MORALES** ANDY **KUBERT**